12 ^{50}
AVIATION

SEPTEMBER CHAMPIONS

THE STORY OF AMERICA'S AIR RACING PIONEERS

SEPTEMBER CHAMPIONS

THE STORY OF AMERICA'S AIR RACING PIONEERS

ROBERT HULL

Stackpole Books

THE SEPTEMBER CHAMPIONS
Copyright © 1979 by
Robert Hull

Published by
STACKPOLE BOOKS
Cameron and Kelker Streets
P.O. Box 1831
Harrisburg, Pa. 17105

Published simultaneously in Don Mills, Ontario, Canada
by Thomas Nelson & Sons, Ltd.

Library of Congress Cataloging in Publication Data

Hull, Robert, 1931–
    September champions.

    Bibliography: p.
    Includes index.
        1. Airplanes racing—United States—History—
Addresses, essays, lectures. I. Title.
GV759.H8   1979   797.5′2′0973   79-15507
ISBN 0-8117-1519-1
ISBN 0-8117-2069-9 pbk.

Printed in the U.S.A.

For Dr. Ruth Davies, Ohio Wesleyan
University professor of English and
humanities, who proposed to the
wise ignorants of her creative writing
classes, "Write me a letter in twenty
years. Tell me what you are doing.
Your answer will be your final grade
in this class."

For Mary and Jimmy Haizlip, race plane
news-makers of their era and my dear
friends now. Their love affair with
each other, with flying, and with life
burns on at blue heat.

And for Lucy Foster of Coshocton, Ohio,
who cares about everybody.

Contents

Those were the days when we flew
for sport, for the thrill of being the
kingpins of speed, to win a medal
or a trophy, for the greater glory of the
industry, when you staked your nerve and
your life against the other fellow
for the sheer hell of the competition.

Paul Gallico

Foreword

It has become popular today for writers to characterize the 1930s as a time of hopelessness and despair. The Great Depression did, indeed, take its toll, but all was not doom and gloom, particularly for a young man with his head in the clouds. Aviation was just coming of age and the heroes of the day were pilots, the men and women who spanned the oceans and flashed around pylons at ever-increasing speeds.

These daring aviators repeatedly put their lives on the line to push back the frontiers of aviation technology and, of course, for a chance at fame and fortune. As in all endeavors, a few made it to the top of the heap and, tragically, others paid the ultimate price for the life they had chosen to lead. Whatever their fate, their fleeting hours upon the public stage were followed breathlessly by the popular press.

This great outpouring of publicity had a number of effects that went far beyond the spectacle and sparkle of individual events. Perhaps most significant was the fact that it inspired in a generation of young people a desire to enter aviation, and in the late thirties and forties when the government opened civilian pilot training programs in colleges and universities, tens of thousands enrolled and won their wings. In December of 1941 when Pearl Harbor plunged the United States into the European and Asian wars that had been raging for years, a reservoir of pilots was ready for military service, largely to serve as desperately needed instructors to train the waves of pilots who would go on to help end World War II in 1945. How much longer that war might have dragged on at how much greater cost in lives without the head start provided by the air-minded youngsters of the thirties will forever be open to speculation.

Author Bob Hull takes us back to the glory days, to the central arena of aviation derring-do of the thirties, the Cleveland Air Races. Here, the fastest airplanes in the world were strained to, and often beyond, their limits by the Doolittles, Turners, Neumanns, Wittmans, Thadens, Cochrans, Fullers, Klings, and many, many others.

It is the story of a more individualistic era. It is the story of genuine heroes, and for many of us it is the story of our treasured youth.

Paul H. Poberezny
President, Experimental Aircraft Association, Inc.

There is no excuse for an airplane,

unless it will go fast.

Roscoe Turner

Preface

I have done the simplest of things. I have gone to the pioneer racing pilots, the mechanics, reporters, historians, and eyewitnesses to important events and said, "Tell me the way it was. Tell it as you remember it."

The question, of course, was full of snares. In many cases the journey back covered half a century. Many of the spokesmen, both pilots and spectators, disagreed about history and about themselves. They disagreed just as stubbornly in the thirties and forties when the whole wonderful adventure took place.

This is a book about men and women who were incredibly daring and brave and who at the time struck a lot of us as half crazy. Oh, there's some talk in it about engines, revolutions per minute, tail flutter, and more technical things than I can ever hope to comprehend, but I'm not a technician; I'm a writer. So I've allowed those who flew and who knew about critical design factors, comparative aerodynamic qualities, and such to simply get their licks in, knowing that no two pilots ever agree on anything, point for point, anyway.

Without the aid and friendship of the pioneer racing pilots, as well as the willing explanations and views of several who polish the pylons today, this book would not have been possible. In many cases they sat and reminisced about a day long past for the first time in twenty or thirty years. For them, the trip back was an adventure, too.

I'm saddened that some of the most colorful pilots, mechanics, builders, and designers who helped so much have died even before this book—so much a memorial to them—was published: Colonel Roscoe Turner, Don Young, Ed Granville, Marion Baker, Mrs. Benny "Mike" Howard, "Tiny" Flynn. Their spirits are everywhere in its pages.

The most painful part of my adventure was selecting from the long exclusive interviews the material to include in a single book. It is my earnest hope to follow shortly with a second volume of aerobatic and air racing stories, also narrated by those who lived them.

I changed the name of one air race pilot who was killed at the request of his brother. All the rest runs as close to truth as I could get it.

I hope this book is *fun* to read. If I've been successful only to that degree, the entire mad cross-country adventure to locate and interview these men and women will surely have been worth it. I hope the reader will feel close to these very special characters who starred so sensationally in the often frightening early capers of aerobatic and racing airplanes.

Long after this book is published, the experience of traveling across country, of meeting the great Jimmy Doolittle, Roscoe Turner, Harold Neumann, and so many others, and sitting with them on porch steps, in offices, dens, and living rooms sipping beer and bourbon, will be a treasured memory.

Acknowledgments

The following, who helped me so much, have my deepest thanks for their unstinting assistance and for that chill of excitement they still feel about airplanes.

The Pilots:

Marion Baker, Port Clinton, Ohio (deceased)

Dick Becker, Willoughby Hills, Ohio

Cook Cleland, Pensacola, Florida

General Jimmy Doolittle, Los Angeles, California

Roger Don Rae, Lakeland, Florida

Jimmy and Mary Haizlip, Pacific Palisades, California

Gordon Israel, Pacific Palisades, California

Nick Jones, Charleston, South Carolina

Colonel Joseph C. Mackey, Fort Lauderdale, Florida

Connie Marsh, Washington, D.C.

Mike Murphy, Findlay, Ohio

Harold Neumann, Kansas City, Kansas

Betty Skelton, Winterhaven, Florida

Colonel Roscoe Turner, Indianapolis, Indiana (deceased)

Steve J. Wittman, Oshkosh, Wisconsin

Walter Barker, Lakewood, Ohio, former prop-starter and stake-down man at the early races.

Mrs. Helen Barr, Leesburg, Florida, sister of the 1931 Thompson Trophy winner, Lowell Bayles.

Henry Barr, Berea, Ohio, former president of the Berea City Council.

Glen Bayles, retired chief pilot for Southern Airways and brother of the 1931 Thompson Trophy winner, Lowell Bayles.

Don Berliner, Alexandria, Virginia, free-lance science and aviation writer; judge at aerobatic competitions.

William N. Bogas, Cleveland, Ohio, Deputy Airports Commissioner, Burke Lakefront Airport.

Jim Borton, retired owner of General Airmotive Inc., and former manager of the Thompson Aeronautical Corporation hangar at Cleveland Airport, for his commentaries on air race years.

Sid Bradd, Solon, Ohio, president of the Cleveland Chapter of the American Aviation Historical Society.

Fred Briles, friend and former business partner of the late Lowell Bayles, racing pilot, who was killed in 1931 while attempting a speed dash record in his Gee Bee airplane in Detroit.

Dudley Brumbach and Bud Yassanye, former photographers for the *Cleveland Plain Dealer,* for their National Air Race pictures and for their recollections of legendary days at Cleveland Airport.

Mrs. Doug Davis, East Point, Georgia.

Richard De Garmo, Cleveland, Ohio, former pylon judge in the 1930s.

Bud Duresky, Berea, Ohio, witness to the 1949 Bill Odom air crash.

Andrew Elko, Cleveland, Ohio.

"Tiny" Flynn, The Pratt & Whitney Company, for his analysis of the Gee Bee years (deceased).

Dorothy Fordyce, Maryville, Tennessee, for her permission to review portions of the unpublished manuscript, *Flight,* the autobiography of Harold E. Neumann, written and compiled by her late husband, Charles A. Fordyce of Kansas City, Kansas, in conjunction with Mr. Neumann.

Tom Foxworth, currently a 747 pilot with Pan American Airlines, chairman of the Airline Pilots Assn. Air Worthiness and Performance Committee, a writer of numerous technical papers and author of *The Speed Seekers,* for his commentary on 1920 versus 1930 racing planes and pilots.

Ben Franklin, director of the National Air Races following World War II.

Mel French, former mechanic and associate to aviatrix Laura Ingalls.

Dr. Samuel Gerber, Cuyahoga County coroner, Cleveland, Ohio for providing coroner's reports of fatal National Air Race crashes.

Ken Gooding, curator, Frederick C. Crawford Auto and Air Museum, Cleveland, Ohio, for his patience and assistance with extensive research, and for his permission to rephotograph and publish air racing photography in the museum collection.

Ed Granville, Manchester, Connecticut, one of the famous five Granville brothers, creators of the Gee Bee racing planes (deceased).

Talbot Harding, retired former reporter for the *Cleveland Plain Dealer,* now in Cleveland Heights, Ohio.

James Hartshorne, retired aviation editor, the *Cleveland Plain Dealer,* now living in Columbus, Ohio.

Cliff W. Henderson, Palm Desert, California, original general manager and creative genius behind the Cleveland National Air Races organization (1929–1939.)

Fred Hotson, Toronto, Canada, member of the Northeast Aero Historians, for his background on Canadian contributions to air racing.

Mrs. Ben O. "Mike" Howard, Los Angeles, California (deceased).

Wayne Ingles, Zanesville, Ohio, who arranged and participated in the important Roscoe Turner interview in 1969. An Ohio historian, he is the author of *Symmes Creek.*

Russ Jack, Port Clinton, Ohio, former aviator and early executive of the Pesco Company and Jack & Heintz Corporation.

Ray Keefe, former chief investigator, Cuyahoga County Coroner's Office, who investigated the Bill Odom race plane crash.

Dr. S. H. Kleiser, Lebanon, Pennsylvania, for his background on aviation's "Doc" Kincade.

Mike Kusenda, Cleveland, Ohio, NASA engineer, for his commentary on racing pilots of the '30s and '40s.

Harvey Lippincott, former Pratt & Whitney representative, currently corporate archivist for United Technologies, for his commentary on the conditioning and loaning of race plane engines.

Charles Mandrake, Painesville, Ohio, former National Air Races historian, author of *The Gee Bee Story,* for his revealing recollections of the Granville brothers and Roscoe Turner.

Howell "Pete" Miller, great airplane designer for Granville Bros. Aircraft in the 1930s; particularly well known for his contribution to the Gee Bee airplanes and as the creator of Frank Hawks' dream ship, *Time Flies,* and of Jacqueline Cochran's *Q.E.D.* Miller is considered by NASA engineers as one of the finest aircraft designers of all time. He lives in Manchester, Connecticut.

Zack Mosley, Stuart, Florida, creator of comics hero "Smilin' Jack."

Lois Naumes and William Naumes, sister and brother-in-law of the late Lowell Bayles, Leesburg, Florida.

Ray Novak, Berea, Ohio, witness to the 1949 Bill Odom air crash.

E. T. Packard, president of Cleveland Model & Supply Company, who, more than any other, pioneered the hobby of detailed model-making made so popular by worldwide focus on the National Air Races in the 1930s.

Joseph O. Peterka, Strongsville, Ohio, for his memorabilia of National Air Race days.

Rudy Profant, historian of the early air races and late owner of the accomplished Keith Rider racing plane the *Marcoux-Bromberg,* made famous by racing pilot Earl Ortman.

George Harry Rhodes, Aviation Training Seminars, Inc., Cleveland, Ohio, for his encouragement.

G. Edward Rice, vice-president, marketing, DeVore Aviation Corporation, Roslyn Heights, New York, for his insight on racing pilots Earl Ortman and Harry Crosby.

Anne Saunders, sister of "Pete" Miller, Bay Village, Ohio.

Robert H. Stepanek, vice-president for history and information, Bradley Air Museum, East Hartford, Connecticut.

Bill Sweet, original director of National Air Shows, Inc., Columbus, Ohio. Author of *They Call Me Mr. Airshow.*

Chuck Tracy, aviation editor of the *Cleveland Press.*

Al Vopel, Cleveland, Ohio, for his observations of early racing days.

Major Truman C. "Pappy" Weaver, past general manager and operations officer of the Professional Race Pilots Association and director of many current air races throughout the country, New Baden, Illinois.

Charles Willard, close friend of the Wright brothers and famous early airplane pioneer, Los Angeles, California (deceased).

Don A. Young friend, associate, and mechanic to the late Colonel Roscoe Turner, Chula Vista, California, (deceased).

The
Beginnings

At Kittyhawk in 1903, an unbelievable event was about to take place for two brothers who certainly were not thinking of the bicycle business that they had left unattended in Dayton, Ohio.

Propellers whirling, their aeroplane started off down the 150-foot slope, quickly outdistancing the one called Orville who was running alongside holding onto one wing to balance it.

In the space of only forty feet the plane was airborne, but almost as soon as the skeletal craft took off, it started and twisted to earth only one hundred feet from the starting point. The pilot, Wilbur, was shaken up and it took a couple of days to repair the ship on the windy dunes. They didn't count it as a flight.

On the morning of December 17, 1903, the most fateful day in the history of aviation, the cold winds of Kittyhawk, North Carolina, were blowing twenty-seven miles per hour but the Wright brothers decided to chance it. About a half-dozen local people were present. The takeoff was to be from the flat instead of the hill.

Orville lay on his stomach on the plane, working the stick. He gave a signal to begin rolling. The fragile craft sped into the wind. Someone took a picture as it was two feet off the ground.

In the years after Kittyhawk, racing, wars, and commercial development accelerated air progress beyond any dream the Wright brothers could have had at the beginning.

Six years after the Wrights' maiden flight, there were enough fliable airplanes in the world to stage the first air race. Of some eighty known aviators, half were American, the rest English, French, and Italian. Most were at Rheims during that wet, windy period from August 22 to September 3, 1909, to compete for $37,000 and the exquisite silver Gordon Bennett trophy, a beautiful model of the Wright biplane mounted by a nude goddess, a trophy symbolic of everything thrilling to the male imagination. Little-known American Glenn Curtiss astonished the crowd by flying at forty-seven miles per hour to win the Gordon Bennett Trophy Race.

The great Rheims race was hardly the only

feature of the first international air show. An imposing list of early twentieth century birdmen took part in numerous other events. Present were such men as Henry Farman, already a famous flier and plane-maker, and Helene Dutrieu of Paris, billed as "the original sweetheart of the skies." Earlier at Versailles, Helene, a brunette and shapely darling, following the lead of a sheep, a rooster, and a duck, became the first woman ever to ascend in a balloon or anything else, raising waves of delicious consternation and scandal.

Henry Farman won $10,000 for flying 111.88 miles in 3¼ hours, thrilling the crowd by landing in darkness guided by searchlights. Hubert Latham won the aerial Grand Prix by traveling 70 kilometers through dismal heavy air in 1 hour, 1 minute, and 51²/₅ seconds.

At the end of ten days of air races, France had much to talk about. One aviator had scared the daylights out of a herd of photographers by bussing the grandstands. Curtiss and Farman had almost collided in mid-air, and Louis Bleriot, idol of France, had barely escaped death when his ship crashed and burned on the last day of the contests.

It was not until 1920 that racing crossed to American shores. Even by the middle '20s, flying was still a circus stunt to the United States general public. Hundreds of young war fliers were back barnstorming. A hop in the sky, even if you were scared, impressed your girl or the folks back home. For a while the industry mistakenly thought this was a workable base for a commercial future. The industry shrank in every direction. European governments were subsidizing their aviation, realizing that a sound industry was the basis of defense. In America there was no subsidizing. Furthermore, the government procured only a few planes. Hundreds of war planes dumped on the market clogged new billings.

To survive, the industry pulled in its horns. Brave young pilots, to keep flying alive, put on weird and mind-boggling entertainments in the clouds. A young man named Roscoe Turner who once had taken apart a phonograph to get materials for a miniature flying machine (it didn't work) billed himself an act titled Falling a Mile in Flames. He was typical of the showmanship, flying ability, and heaping measures of bravado of a small number of daring buddies. Too much credit can never be paid them. Few, if any, received any more encouragement than Roscoe received from his Scotch-Irish farming father back in Corinth, Mississippi: "You won't be worth shooting if you fool around with things that burn gasoline and make popping noises!"

They wouldn't allow discouragement to paralyze their imagination and flare for aerial show business. To keep flying on page 1, or at least on page 6, some even had pink teas in the air, ran flying cigar stores, transported pianos, and flew movie stars aboard alimony specials.

By 1926, though the pilots were still close to starving, aviation was beginning to chalk up some advances. Aircraft continued to improve. Medium and large transports had full and semi-cantilever wings, shock absorbers, and wheel brakes. Most had radio receivers. Amphibians promised new aircraft uses. The lighting of airways was beginning to permit safer night flying. People discovered that airmail saved a lot of time and burned very few letters.

Former parachutist and racing pilot Roger Don

Contented boy in 1927 demonstrates his simple but fliable model airplane, product of a young and flourishing industry. National air racing put model-making on the map. (Cleveland Model & Supply Co.)

The Carnegie-West Branch Library Model Club was one of many groups established to encourage model-flying at Cleveland Airport. E.T. Packard (third from right,) then twenty years old, soon established Cleveland as the model-producing empire of the nation. (Cleveland Model & Supply Co.)

Rae of Lakeland, Florida recalled that aviation was given its first big boost when manufacturers such as Waco and Ford pushed for bigger engines to replace the old and tired OX-5.

"Any airplane larger than the Travel Air," Rae recalled, "had to have a more powerful engine. Otherwise, we had to strap on about fifteen OX-5 engines to make her go anywhere."

For *The Great Waldo Pepper*, Hollywood filmmakers put Hisso engines on the planes before they did the wing-walking shots. That was not only historically accurate, but also historically necessary. The Hisso engine was built during World War I and had double the horsepower in the same weight as the OX-5. An OX-5 would just fly the airplane, nothing more.

"It couldn't handle any kind of added drag, like a human body," Rae said. "But those Hissos, with 150 and 180 ponies—twice the horsepower—could take on a great deal."

The first air meet in America was held November 25, 1920, at Mitchell Field, Long Island. A valuable trophy was presented by sponsor Joseph Pulitzer to Captain C. C. Moseley of the Army Air Service for flying his specially built Verville-Packard 600-horsepower racer to victory in a closed-course meet, a distance of 116 miles around a 29-mile course at an average 154.54 miles per hour.

Though it certainly wasn't known at the time, a competition between America and Britain begun three years later might well have changed the course of world history. General Jimmy Doolittle, behind his desk at the Mutual of Omaha Insurance Company in Los Angeles, explained: "In 1923, Dave Wittenhouse of the Navy won the Schneider Trophy Race. In 1924, the British plane was dropped while being lifted on the boat to bring it over here, so there were no 1924 Schneider Cup races. In 1925 I won the Schneider Trophy.

"Had we been poor sports in 1924 and merely flown the course—that's all we had to do to claim the prize for the Americans—we would have won the Schneider Trophy permanently with a third win in '25, and the Schneider Trophy Race would have gone out of existence. Instead, British went on to win it three times, also. They won it with the forerunners of the Spitfire and the Hurricane, the two airplanes that won the Battle of Britain.

"I think we have to admit that the Schneider Trophy Race had a profound effect on the development of high-speed fighters, and consequently on the outcome of the Battle of Britain and World War II."

Not long afterward, the National Aeronautic Association combined the scattered races and meets then in existence into a single event called National Air Races. In that year, the annual air classic was held at Model Flying Field in Philadelphia. For the first time, crowds in a grandstand heard music broadcast from a Sikorsky plane flying over the field. The use of air-cooled motors in modern pursuit ships marked the return of this type of engine to wide use, eliminating the worry of overheating radiators, leaking fluid, and broken hoses. Although the Pulitzer trophy of the twenties was no longer competed for, the free-for-all pursuit race was a worthy successor. A Navy man, Lieutenant G. T. Cuddihy, won this pylon challenge flying a Packard-Boeing pursuit plane, averaging 180 miles per hour.

Fashions of a bygone day are reflected in this 1929 crowd at the National Air Races in Cleveland. "To please the stands," stunt and racing pilot Joe Mackey quipped, "you tried hard to appear as if you were about to kill yourself, though you were quite sure that could not possibly happen to you." (Ohio Bell Telephone Co.)

Transcontinental and sectional air derbies were inaugurated at these races and they attained such popularity that they were repeated annually thereafter. In 1927 the featured derby from Roosevelt Field, New York, to Spokane was captured by C. W. "Speed" Holman, who spanned the continent in his Laird plane in 19 hours, 42 minutes, 47 seconds.

From 1928 on, the National Air Races were big time show business, and an education to boot. They seemed to suddenly introduce commercial aviation at a point of development that surprised Americans. Prize money totaling more than $125,000 spurred contestants to demonstrate their utmost abilities.

The '28 big show was held at Mines Field, Los Angeles. Nine September days of packed events held over 300,000 people breathless. The Army and Navy sent their best ships and most competent pilots. The Navy's *Three Sea Hawks* and the Army's *Three Muskateers* flew in marvelous eschelon and "V" formations. Colonel Charles Lindbergh put on an unusual exhibition flight as did the nation's darling, Amelia Earhart, in her *Moth, Dill Pickle* and *Baby Bullet* planes.

The year '29 was even better—in Cleveland, Ohio, soon to become the home of the NAR. Fred Crawford, later president of the city's Thompson Products Company and the Air Races as well, referred to Cleveland as The Best Location For Sensation. The press proved to be as factual as it

The horizon over a portion of Cleveland Airport shortly after WW II. In the long, flat building, big enough to house fifty football fields, Fisher Aircraft's 20,000 workers made parts for the B-25 superfortress. Somehow, airport authorities maintained routine air traffic, even during the most hectic of races. (Dudley Brumbach and Bud Yassanye collection)

Curtiss Falcon airplanes lined up on Cleveland Airport's north field awaiting their turn to dazzle Cleveland audiences. Though the program was resplendent with military flourish, all eyes were on a Georgia civilian named Davis, whose backyard airplane, the Travel Air Mystery Ship, *outflew the best the military could offer. (Frederick C. Crawford Auto and Aviation Museum)*

was fanciful with its own slogan: Cleveland: Air Laboratory of the World.

Located some dozen miles to the southwest of the Public Square, Cleveland Airport was carved from a pleasant patchwork of peaceful family farms, where city folks (long before radio) drove on Sundays to pick and buy from the roadside stands plying Rhode Island green apples, tangy pears, and dripping fresh tomatoes, a quarter a basket.

In the thirties and postwar forties Cleveland's surrounding communities—Berea, Strongsville, Middleburg Heights, Olmsted Falls, North Olmsted, Fairview, Rocky River, and Westlake, little more than fruitstands, a trolley track, old shingled city halls, sprawled cottages, and plowed farmland—would be spoken of in Minnesota, Tampa, Paris, and Frankfurt, simply because they were in the line of flight of the closed-circuit race planes. Lake Erie, a few miles to the north of the airport, and the lovely Rock River Valley of the city's Metropolitan Park system which bordered its runways, were household words for many years when worldwide radio commentaries reported the air action lap by lap.

The community of Berea, Ohio, is still talked about today. It was there in the September of '49 that Thompson Trophy race pilot Bill Odom crashed his refurbished P-51 plane into a home on West Street. This crash and other changes ended the great American air races as they once were known.

But for ten years in Cleveland, what a show it was.

There were races of every kind, categories usually defined according to the displacement in cubic inches of the race plane engine. The idea was to give almost everybody with an airplane a chance to fly and win a prize. Since the whole purpose behind the races was to popularize aviation, pains were taken to attract women flyers, sportsmen, the part-time pilot who ran a bank or a gas station—simply to show that the thrill and convenience of the airplane could be mastered by the ordinary citizen, not just the professional airman or the wartime ace.

Nearly everything with wings was flown. The military, firmly entrenched in the air race spectacle from the earliest American air meets, even brought military bombers to race.

The Shell Speed Dash, sponsored by the Shell Oil Company, clocked the speeding race planes over a measured straight course. It proved an excellent contest for honoring the fastest planes, whereas closed-course pylon victories frequently went to planes whose pilots could skillfully maneuver and master air tactics.

The Cleveland Pneumatic Aerol Trophy Race for women pilots had a $3,750 first prize. In dead stick landing contests, both men and women landed their aircraft without the benefit of power. There were National Guard races and parachute jumping contests. There were clowns, bands, and a glimpse of the first autogiros ever made.

In 1929 in Cleveland, military "superiority" was challenged to the point of embarrassment as civilian planes and pilots earned the spotlight. Doug Davis, a handsome airline pilot from Atlanta, Georgia, easily vanquished both the Army and the Navy in the sensational free-for-all race for any plane of unlimited power. He flew his special low-wing Travel-Air at an average speed of nearly 195 miles per hour. Reporters from several cities wrote that Davis with his stunt team and aerobat Freddy Lund with his Waco team surpassed in daring and grace the best of the Army and Navy.

The Thompson Trophy race was the grand finale

of each year's National Air Races. Featuring eight to ten planes on the starting line, it was the big one, the Indianapolis 500 of the Sky. Its purpose was to honor the fastest airplane that could be built. There were almost no restrictions. Any power of engine could be used, any number of engines, any number of pilots, any weight.

It was the most feared of all races and the most exciting, for those who took part were the fastest men on earth. Length of the race and total distance varied over the twenty years it was flown, from 100 miles to 300 miles. Shape of the course also changed. Most familiar was the three-pylon triangular shape which was predominant in the '30s, but which ultimately evolved into the quadrangle enclosure by 1948 and a nearly circular seven-pylon course by 1949.

Such changes were made to minimize the horrendous g-loads, crushing physical pressure, on the pilot making quick, sharp turns in faster and faster airplanes, as well as to minimize the gargantuan physical abuse to the airplanes and the airplane engines, which always constituted a risk to the spectators below. A calamitous crash into the main grandstands was prophesied each year for as long

Probably the best-liked pilot in air racing history, Doug Davis is shown with the famous "$50 tin cup" put up by Charles E. Thompson of the Thompson Products Company for the first unlimited speed event in 1929. Much the opposite of Roscoe Turner, Davis emulated the common man and dressed conservatively, even wearing a necktie when racing. (Frederick C. Crawford Auto and Aviation Museum)

Doug Davis's 1929 winner of the Thompson Unlimited Free-for-All Race was this very swift Travel Air Mystery Ship, red and black with light green and white pencil stripes. Doug's top speed exceeded 208 miles per hour. (Jim Borton collection)

as the races were flown.

It never happened. On the contrary, as early as 1935 it was said of the Thompson Trophy race and its purpose:

"This laboratory of greater air speed is the dynamometer room of the engine builder and the wind tunnel of the plane designer. The ideal proving ground for their combined creative effort is the closed-course free-for-all speed contest for it provides the supreme test of sustained speed and stamina under conditions that demand absolute control on maneuverability.

"The freak 'bullet plane,' all motor and no wings, built for a brief spectacular dash, has no place in the closed-course circuit. To test practical maneuverability, there is no substitute for the bank, the turn at the pylon, the straightaway sprint, the limited take-off and landing restrictions of the high speed closed course. Such demanding tests have already produced barrel fuselages and more efficient streamlining, an improved cowling, cockpit ventilation, prop spinners, the retractable landing gear, and countless engine refinements now standard in commercial and military aircraft. It is a matter of record that these innovations were first demonstrated by powerful single motor planes built for the strains of closed-course speed competition."

Jimmy Doolittle won the inaugural Bendix Transcontinental Speed Classic in 1931, a race in which pilots took off separately and raced the clock across the continent. Doolittle averaged 233 miles per hour on his record run from Los Angeles to Cleveland and continued on to New York to set a new transcontinental record of 11 hours, 15 minutes.

The following year, his young Shell Oil Company associate, Jimmy Haizlip, poured on the coal in the same contest to win flying twenty-two miles per hour faster than had Doolittle.

Drawing card of the 1929 National Air Races (along with Jimmy Doolittle and Al Williams) was Colonel Charles Lindbergh. (Frederick C. Crawford Auto and Aviation Museum)

Aside from the derby races sanctioned by the National Air Races for both men and women, there also were similar contests in the late '20s and early '30s, usually sponsored by engine manufacturers such as the Ford Motor Company and flown independently of the big September attraction in Cleveland.

In the earlier years, some contests took place between a chain of cities with not only overnight stops for the racers, but also restaurant lunch stops. These were not only contests of speed, but also of precise navigation through fog, rain, and high mountain country.

In a real sense, these were not races in the popular sense of the word, but were an exhausting exercise in determining where you were and where you were going. They were totally grueling. Frequently flown above the clouds, they certainly were not a spectator sport.

Such were the Ford Tours of 1928, '29, and '30.

One of the best of its participating pilots was the late Johnny Livingston, one of the most well-liked, most skillful racing pilots of all time. He discussed those days with his friend Major Truman C. Weaver, who manages many current air races.

"When someone mentions air racing to me, my thoughts don't focus on the Thompson or the Bendix classics. I think immediately of the hellish Ford Tours of 1928, '29 and '30. Take, for example, the '28 transcontinental hop from New York to Los Angeles—2,500 miles with fifteen control points. You couldn't just get up there and go.

"The '29 Ford Tour was the same thing only it was 5,000 miles, and control points were every 200 miles on the average. The '29 tour took us up through northeast Canada, across to Portland, Maine, down the coast to Jacksonville, Florida, back up and out to Wichita, Kansas. As I say, every

200 miles of the 5,000 was a control point which you had to hit right on the button.

"The 1930 tour was similar. It was another 5,000 miles—through the northwest to Alaska, back down and over the mountains into Denver, east then to Wichita, some jogging around, and finally back to Detroit again. To me, those were races.

"In 1930 they rewrote the formula so that theoretically, at least, nothing could win but a trimotor. See, they only counted the horsepower of the two outboards. They might have 220s in the outboard and a 450 in the nose and not be charged for the nose. But there were two Fords in that race and I beat out one of the Fords.

"Good speed took navigation between the trees and under the telephone wires. The only navigating

John Livingston beside his Monocoupe racer. (Rudy Profant collection)

instruments we had were our first turn bank indicators.

"The race was traumatic compared to the later Bendix. In those the pilot took off from California and had a tail wind no matter where he flew. He chose whether to make ten stops or none at all. Not so, the Ford Tours!

"In 1928 our only chart was this old 'Rand McNally railroad map. Of course there weren't any concrete highways in those days, except maybe a few, going through Canada. The only maps Canada offered were huge posters each representing a county fifteen miles across. They had lots of detail but were too damn big to unfold in the cockpit. One fellow, flying one hundred miles per hour, was so tangled up in maps that he lost his cool and threw all of his maps out of the cockpit. He couldn't make any sense out of them and just figured he'd try to follow somebody else. The slow airplanes would take off first and then the faster ones would all pass,

so he had a pretty good chance of keeping somebody else in sight. That was navigation.

"They sent us off in zero visibility in New York. We couldn't see the end of the field. They just said, 'Well, you can get on top of it in a little ways and it's clear to Pittsburgh.' We climbed with the new turn indicators we didn't know how to use. We sat in the clear at 3,500 feet all the way to Pittsburgh.

"Practically everybody ran out of gasoline from New York to Pittsburgh in '28. Charley Myers's taperwing ran out of gas. He was fortunate to find open field. He bent his axle, but he got down. He went to a farm for a couple gallons of gas and directions and flew back into the race. Speed Holman landed in the mountains and cracked up. The only two boys who didn't have to get gas were the two Cessnas. They flew until they found a hole, landed, and learned where they were.

"I set down once on route. I dove toward a hazy ribbon of concrete. Right after my landing spot the

Johnny Livingston (center) is presented a check from the editor of the Indianapolis Star *for winning the Baby Ruth Trophy Race. At right is M. E. Stauffer, personal representative of the Curtiss Candy Company. (Jim Borton collection)*

Along with furnishing balsa wood, rubberband, and blueprint, each Cleveland model kit taught "how an airplane works, how it is put together, what makes it fly, why it has to be the way it is." (Cleveland Model and Supply Co.)

road rose over a mountain. I climbed right back on top of the clouds.

"At 3,500 feet altitude there was no landmark to check my position. In my schooldays, I had read about "Smoky Pittsburgh." The clouds looked a little smoky to the right so I said, 'Well, that must be smoky Pittsburgh.

"Moments later I settled the ship down. I was practically on a city street and was reading a sign that said Pittsburgh Drug Company. I climbed again in a hell of a hurry and flew west until I hit the river. Now the airport was south of Pittsburgh. The gas gauge was on zero but I wanted to be sure it was the correct river. I headed up the river to the fork of the two rivers just above Pittsburgh. I turned right around and sank to a foot or two over the water.

"On the way back, I flew under the bridges whenever possible. I flew under some of them and over others, hoping to God I didn't slam into one broadside.

"Finally the fog lifted enough that I could look at my compass. It said I was going *northeast,* instead of south. The river had turned slightly to the northeast. Well, I was sick. A little further, the river turned south.

"As I circled the airport a little later, I saw four or five bridges crossing the river. I figured if I went down to those bridges, the airport would be over the high bank. When I had passed all the bridges, I pulled up but didn't see the airport right away. I sat down on a long, narrow strip of pasture, cracked up, ran through a fence, then was up again, intending to make a right turn, come back, and land.

"But just as I started to come around, there ahead of me was that blessed white circle of the airport. I had missed the airport by only an eighth of a mile. The airport was inland instead of on the bank.

"As soon as I spotted the circle I flew it down.

"There was some awful luck connected with that landing. However, I was already on the starting line before anybody else showed. I knew I had a half hour on the two Cessnas.

"I'd never do it again."

Such a breathtaking time in which to live and take part!

Kids on front porches all over America were carving solid model and rubber-powered flying models of new hero racing planes: the Laird *Solution* and *Super-Solution,* the Travel-Air *Mystery Ship, Ike, Mike, Pete,* the *Mister Mulligan, Chief Oshkosh, Bonzo,* and the *Laird-Turner* racer, the Schoenfeldt *Firecracker,* the *Goon,* and the unbelievable, ill-fated Gee Bee.

With the hero airplanes came the heroes. New names in America's vocabulary of gladiators were Lowell Bayles, Benny Howard, Steve Wittman, Major Jimmy Doolittle, Mary Haizlip and Jimmy Haizlip, Florence Klingensmith, Michel Detroyat, Earl Ortman, Tony LeVier, on and on.

Far back in the memories of many are the hoarse cries of the gimmick hucksters: "Get your sunglasses here, folks. Save your eyes for a quarter. Airplanes. Gliders here. Take home a souvenir. Official lineups and scorecards. You can't see the race without one, folks. Gas balloons! Here you are, sir. How about a souvenir pennant for your auto? Carry a solid bronze coin with you—going at one small quarter each. Two? Thanks, mister."

Pennants and horns, flags, whistles, coins, pins, toy airplanes of a hundred designs, Graf zeppelins, gliders, and balloons were mementos of a day to remember.

A typical National Air Races crowd basks in the September sun at Cleveland Hopkins Airport in the 1940s. (Dudley Brumbach, Cleveland Plain Dealer)

2

Fred Crawford

I Don't Want Just a Nude Woman Waving a Flag

Early in the search for sponsors, the air race committee called on Fred Crawford, Thompson Products vice-president, who already had a reputation as a whipper-snapper with plenty of imagination and moxie. "What immediately caught my eye," Crawford recalled years later, "was the free-for-all speed race. I thought speed was the truly interesting thing and I quickly said, 'We'll take that one.' We put up a $5,000 prize and a tin cup that cost fifty bucks. The races were new, and they were feeling their way, but that interested me in the air races."

Thompson Products president Charles Thompson was immediately interested in the promotion and suggested a Thompson Trophy for the second year of competition.

Soon afterward, Crawford told an architect friend of his firm's intentions and of his hope to throw open a competition among sculptors for an appropriate design for a magnificent prize. Mr. Crawford characteristically cut to the heart of the matter: "Now I don't want just a nude woman waving a

flag. Every trophy you see these days is of a nude woman sitting up there with her ass in the wind. I don't want any of that."

"Why not something allegorical?" suggested Walter Sinz, popular Cleveland sculptor known for his lovely churches. "The bottom of the trophy could show ocean waves. The body would be rocks or a sort of a cliff. On top, the sun would be shining. There would be birds on the corners and above that, an airplane."

"Something about the thought caught my imagination," Crawford recalled. "Walter Sinz proceeded with the idea and designed the winning sculpture. Orville Wright and the secretary of war helped us determine the winner."

Thompson was a very likely sponsor of an air race, for its specialty was valves for autos and airplanes. Though the company swelled the prize money from year to year, Fred Crawford, who moved to the helm of Thompson Products at Charles Thompson's death, never doubted the value of the publicity. Neither did other big busi-

29

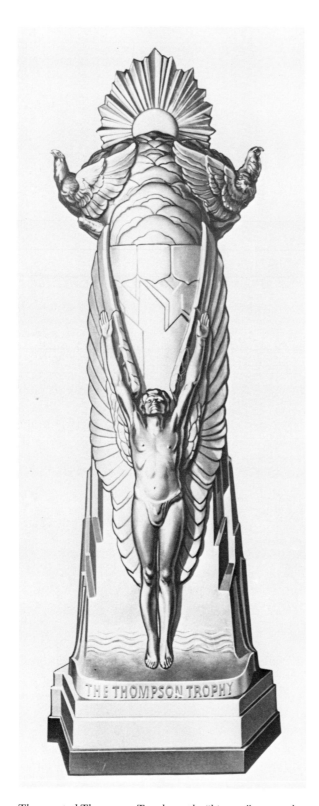

ness sponsors: Greve, Bendix, Sohio, Tinnerman, Halle, and Goodyear. It was money in the bank for them all.

"Thompson Products was then a modest company," Crawford admitted, "and we became known more for the Thompson Trophy race than for anything we did on the assembly line. It was a great piece of publicity because of the interest then in speed. The newspapers of the world reported the Thompson Race, and the radio devoted a full hour to that spectacle.

"Many countries of Europe at that time never heard of Thompson Products," he said. "However, in traveling abroad, I would discover myself casually mentioning Turner or Neumann or Doolittle and the current year's Thompson Trophy speed records. 'Oh, *that's* the company you work for,' they'd shout, and their faces would light up."

Fred Crawford not only went on to become president of the National Air Races, but he also quickly picked a young fellow with the reputation as the best salesman and showman in the business to be the event's general manager—Cliff Henderson. Crawford and Henderson were personally responsible for the races' association with Cleveland in an age when every major city yearned to host the speeding airplanes.

For the pilots, finances were still shaky. In his executive office at Thompson (presently TRW INC), Mr. Crawford recalled a typical adventure of the most colorful of the aviators.

"Roscoe Turner had borrowed his wife's savings account, mortgaged the home, and put everything he had into a little Wedell-Williams racer. Pratt & Whitney had loaned him an engine. At ten o'clock in the morning, the process server arrived at the airport to seize Turner's airplane for debt. He entered the hangar and asked, 'Where's Turner?'

"A smart mechanic, sizing up the situation instantly, said, 'Oh, you want Roscoe? Well, then you better stick close to his plane right over there. (He points to the wrong airplane.) Go sit in that and you'll catch Turner, all right. He's flying the next race.'

"Then he ran out and tipped off Roscoe. The boys

The coveted Thompson Trophy—the "big one"—was the most sought-after trophy in aviation in the 1930s and '40s. The Thompson race was for racing planes with unlimited horsepower engines. (Frederick C. Crawford Auto and Aviation Museum)

The Vincent Bendix Trophy was given annually by the Bendix Corporation to the winner of a free-for-all speed dash starting in the Los Angeles area and finishing at Cleveland, Ohio. (Dudley Brumbach and Bud Yassanye collection)

Charles "Speed" Holman was recipient of the first Thompson Trophy in 1930, averaging almost 202 miles per hour in the hundred-mile race over a five-mile course. Harassed by engine fumes, he repeatedly stuck his head out of the cockpit to keep from passing out. Matty Laird, who built the plane, called it the Laird Solution—the "solution" to the Travel Air Mystery Plane. After the embarrassment the military suffered at the hands of civilian Doug Davis in 1929, its 1930 offering was Captain Arthur Page, a Marine flying a cleaned-up Curtiss biplane minus its lower wing. Leading on the seventeenth lap, Page was overcome by monoxide fumes. Sixty thousand fans saw Page lose total control and smash into the ground at 280 miles per hour. (Rudy Profant collection)

"Speed" Holman's 1930 Thompson Trophy-winning plane was said to have been built in less than a month and was completed not a moment too soon. A last minute replacement pilot, Holman test-hopped the airplane for ten minutes, made minor changes on the rigging, tuned the engine, and landed at the Air Races just as competing planes were lining up. Holman and crew quickly pulled the plane on line, and had time to paint only a crude numeral on her side before the starter flag. (Cleveland Chapter, American Aviation Historical Society)

serviced his real plane out on the air field, out of sight. He won the race and had the money to pay off his debts. *That's* how we financed aviation in the thirties."

To what degree the National Air Races contributed to eventual Allied superiority in the air and ultimate victory in World War II may still be disputed by some, but among persons close to those September assaults on the pylons, there is scant argument.

"I sat in the stands the one year with General Arnold," recalled Fred Crawford, "and looked at Roscoe Turner's 1,000-horsepower radial motor. Keeping right up with him in the air was a little bitty plane with a 400-horsepower engine.

"General Arnold said, 'Crawford, look at that, 400 horsepower versus 1,000 horsepower and they're

flying at the same speed. There's a hell of a lot we don't know yet.' "

Crawford said, "Of course the big radial had terrible frontal resistance. This problem led to the interest in the water-cooled motor, which found its way into the F-51 fighter."

Turner always held the power most important, and all other aerodynamic factors second. For him, it usually worked. With the big, air-cooled, radial engines he used (so-called for their circular shape), double rows of cylinders could be added, but their failing was obvious. The more power one added, the larger they became, and the more wind resistance they created, right up front where it caused the most damage. The radials were often called "waffle irons."

In 1936, the Frenchman Detroyat became the

first foreign entry in the Thompson speed race and easily won the prize with his sleek and streamlined in-line engine, whose cylinders were arranged in parallel rows.

Some fledgling engineers put all their stock in mid-wing racers. To others, mid-wing was slower than low-wing. Others, of course, championed the high-wing.

Then there was the big engine theory versus the light ship. Steve Wittman from Oshkosh, Wisconsin, did anything to save a pound. Race competitor Roger Don Rae said Witt went crazy figuring ways to make things smaller. If he could make a thing smaller, he could make it lighter. Light! He wanted to take off every possible bit of weight.

"Art Chester and Witt would be close at the start

The biggest selling job in Cleveland's history—the National Air Races—was the task of well-liked Cliff Henderson (wearing white suit), air races general manager, and his business manager brother, Phil. Asked by General "Hap" Arnold in 1939, "My God, Cliff, how many people are involved in this thing?" Henderson replied, "Well, if you include the start of the Bendix out on the coast along with the Powder Puff Derby, the Goodyear and Thompson races, the ushers and nurses, program sellers, cashiers, and ticket-takers, it involves over 7,000 people."

In 1930, flat broke for the dozenth time, Roscoe Turner talked oil man Earl Gilmore into buying the Lockheed air express, Black Hornet for $15,000 in order to break a few speed records. Ever conscious of the power of showmanship, Turner acquired a lion cub, naming him Gilmore. The furry mascot, fitted with his own parachute, flew with Roscoe everywhere, including most transcontinental Bendix races. (Frederick C. Crawford Auto and Aviation Museum)

of any race. Witt usually got the jump on the takeoff because he was so light, but he never had the power. He could never work his engine over and get the power that Art Chester could, but they were inevitably neck and neck. They were two great rivals and it was a toss-up as to which would do the better.

"The engine was so important. Old Harold Neumann of Geneseo, Kansas, used to tell of leading the pack with his 550-cubic inch Menasco six-cylinder. Somebody was gaining on him and Harold was holding his own. Just barely in front.

He prayed that the guy behind him would have to throttle back a little bit because *his* engine was just about to blow up. Temperature off the gauge. Oil pressure starting to wobble. He told himself, 'Wish that guy would slow down a bit so I could slow down!'

"I would have liked to have seen a race between all these great guys without any engine problem. We didn't have a fuel mixture that would hold down both the knock and heat. It was usually the heat problem that drove a guy to throttling down his engine. If he pushed it longer than he should have, if he should have hauled it back about a half a lap ago but didn't, he could throw a piston. Anything could happen.

"Of course," sighed Rae, "it was another ballgame after World War II. They had exotic instruments to determine the exact peak combustion, just like Indianapolis. They mixed peroxide and nitroglycerin in their fuel. Today, they know exactly what they're doing.

"In the old days, Old Doc Kincade watched the exhaust and put in another drop or two of Ethyl or something. The lack of good instruments to help them determine the right fuel mixture to prevent detonation was just pitiful. Even if you had the right mix, you had to throttle back or burn the engine.

"The cowlings they have now! The way they can cool with air!

"Thompson winner Rudy Kling had his own notion of engine heat. He had a six-cylinder Folkerts and what he asked for was 'a real good half-worn engine. I want a good one but I want it about half worn out! I don't care if it uses oil. I just want a good loose engine that won't give me a lot of heat.'"

A man who could write tomes about engine headaches and frustrations of the 1930s and be-

yond is Harvey Lippincott, corporate archivist for the United Technologies Corporation at Hartford, Connecticut. With Pratt & Whitney in the glory days, Harvey talked nostalgically of loaning the big engines.

"Most of the racing pilots truly were flying on a shoestring—when they could *find* a shoestring. In a number of cases, we would simply loan the engines on consignment. In a few cases where there were a few more bucks available, engines were rented, so much an hour. And for Howard Hughes we figured we could sell him an engine, but he never paid for it. Down at the Smithsonian his racer is hung from the ceiling, but we're seriously thinking of going down there and claiming our engine.

"Almost without exception they were stock engines that had been doctored up or tinkered with to get a little extra power. The compression ratio might have been changed to a higher ratio by some new pistons. The supercharger might have run a little faster with higher gears, but it was still the same basic supercharger. The carburetor setting often was altered. Most importantly, special fuels were used.

"Of course in the early days the good fuels we have today did not exist. The Ethyl man would pour

Steve Wittman (in his tiny race plane Bonzo) *is revered even by modern race pilots as the genius of them all. A master innovator and an unrelenting competitor, he is still racing at age 75. The names* Buster *and* Bonzo *were also the names of two dogs who were constantly kicked around in a 1930s comic strip. The significance was never very clear. (Frederick C. Crawford Auto and Aviation Museum)*

In 1937 the great Thompson went to newcomer Rudy Kling of Lemont, Illinois, shown here with his wife and Thompson Products' Fred Crawford. The trophy, showing Icarus of Greek legend before the heat of the sun melted his wings of feathers and tar, was sadly prophetic of Kling's approaching fate. Just a few months later in the first lap of a race in Miami, Rudy Kling crashed and was killed. (Jim Borton collection)

a few drops from his bottle into the gas we had and that suddenly made it a high octane fuel. Generally speaking, the pilot simply pushed hell out of the engine. They usually overboosted them but we all recognized that the engines had a short life.

"Normally, takeoff power on a Pratt & Whitney engine was limited to five minutes. Well, the boys might use it for an hour. By the end of the race, the engine was ready for an overhaul. This explains why a great many engine and piston failures occurred. Engines were simply pushed beyond maximum limits.

"Famous racing pilots used to say, 'Now this year I want to get another 100 horsepower or 200 horsepower out of the engine. Will it take it?'

"On the test stand we ran the engine as he requested. We might tell him to change his carburetor a little bit or do a few things to it, but that it would work for only maybe two hours. So they took the two hours and away they went. Basically the engines were not really specially designed engines. Maybe one exception was the Packard X engine that Packard developed for Al Williams's Mercury racer group.

"The major reason why engine companies didn't design special engines for racing planes was, of course, the cost. They cost a terrible sum of money and most of the flyers couldn't afford steak twice in a week as it was. They tinkered with the engines they had and princed them up to get that little more power."

Laughed pilot Joe Mackey, "I called Pratt & Whitney on the phone to find out the proper valve clearance. I talked to about ninety-five people and finally reached some guy with a little authority. I said, 'What the hell should the valve clearance be on the intake and exhaust valves of this Wedell-Williams airplane?'

"He said, 'Hell, we don't know. What do you use?'

"That is pretty expressive of the great and wonderful technology of that day. Nevertheless, the 420 horsepower engine in our airplane was putting out 1,000. Pratt & Whitney must have learned *something* from designing it.

Cleveland Model President Ed Packard today, posing with a 1937-built model of the Martin China Clipper. *Tape measure in hand, Packard crawled over and under all the race planes to guarantee precision models. Although the company no longer manufactures kits, it sells full-scale plans of the oldest and newest planes ever built. Packard and sixteen volunteers including a foundry president, a government inspector, and a college professor design the old beauties in their spare time just to keep the hobby and the firm alive. (Cleveland Model & Supply Co.)*

Gee Bee Super Sportster Model Z, black and lemon, powered by a Pratt & Whitney Wasp Jr. engine. Lowell Bayles made arrangements to fly this stubby Gee Bee against a 1931 Thompson field dominated by Jimmy Doolittle in his Laird Super Solution. Doolittle's engine went sour and Bayles easily swept the victory, averaging more than 236 miles per hour. (Cleveland Model & Supply Co.)

A model of the Jimmy Wedell Number 44, in which Jimmy set a new world speed record of over 305 miles per hour with a specially mounted large Wasp engine. Aircraft engineers had looked forward to the 1933 battle of the pylons as the supreme practical test of the claims of two schools of designers, one sponsoring the extremely stubby Gee Bee, the other, the slimmer, more streamlined Wedell-Williams. Ironically, both Gee Bees were damaged en route to the West Coast and the Bendix contest. It was the beginning of the end for the Granville brothers. (Cleveland Model & Supply Co.)

Aircraft designer Robert Hall, who deserves primary credit for Lowell Bayles's Thompson Trophy winner Gee Bee City of Springfield, later broke off from the tempermental Granvilles and began designing for himself. His Springfield Bulldog, which some critics call the most unusual pretty airplane ever created for air racing, was engineered to beat the Gee Bee. It was hopelessly unsuccessful. One of the unsubstantiated legends of early years is that pilot Hall was so furious and frustrated over his airplane's failure that he literally took an axe to it. (Cleveland Model & Supply Co.)

"Today they sit down with a piece of paper, fourteen computers, and twenty-eight other aids and something comes out the end to tell them what to do. They don't have to fly the wings off an airplane to predict what will work. In those days, who the hell knew what the wing curve was going to do? You built them, you flew them, and you found out, frequently at the cost of the airplane, a year's time, and the life of the pilot.

"In the '30s particularly, the pilot didn't trust the engineer, nor the engineer the pilot. Each was sure he was the only one who knew anything. The pilot landed, stomped over to the engineer, and said, 'Doggone it, *this* is still happening.'

"The engineer shoved his kisser against the pilot's and snapped, 'It *can't* be happening. This here paper says it can't be happening.'

"Something of value came out the middle of those scraps, and neither pilot nor engineer could have accomplished anything without the other."

The late Ed Granville of Granville Brothers' Gee Bee fame had to agree. "The only real way you can test an engine is to fly it," Ed mused. "There are things you can't duplicate too well on the stand. Also, an engine changes when mounted. There are differences in vibration, in mounting characteristics, in cooling.

"People ask whether the Thompson Trophy race was sufficiently controlled for engine experimentation. It was very short, but there was no doubt that the engine was under extreme pressures, temperatures, and stresses.

"Anytime you stretch the state of the art, whether with automobiles, airplanes, engines, you begin to learn."

Air crashes, however, were anyone's guess.

"A crash could be caused by a mechanical failure," Joe Mackey comments. "Something fell off or fell apart. A cable broke or any one of a thousand things. You never knew for sure what had happened. Today, with all the sophisticated equipment, the voice recorders and all this junk, you may be able to find the cause, but you couldn't then.

"Whenever something drastic happened to a buddy in the air, we sat and tried to agree that it was something that couldn't possibly happen to us."

3

The
Race Horse Start
and
Other Crimes

Joe Mackey

Joe Mackey was typical of the scores of pilots who came from nowhere to fly the Thompson—and often returned there.

"I was born in Columbus, Ohio," recalled Mackey, "where the big attraction to the kids on my street was Norton Field, a small grass landing strip for military airplanes. Every two or three weeks a military airplane would come through. I camped out there every weekend just to see one occasionally. Inevitably, I went to Cleveland where some said you had hopes of seeing a real airplane every couple of days.

"In Cleveland as a gangly youth I went to work for Stuart Aircraft which had the first wooden hangar on a grass field (now Cleveland Hopkins International Airport). I got a job for two dollars a week and the privilege of sleeping behind the boiler and a half-hour's flying instruction. I didn't get a half-hour a week of instruction but I got something. When I had accumulated eight or nine hours and had soloed, the company passed me off as an instructor.

"There weren't any flying licenses in those days," Mackey smiled. "One day Bill Robinson of the Department of Commerce came out to declare, 'All you guys got to have licenses.' We ran him the hell off the airport. The only unfortunate part was that he came back the next day with the sheriff and started to make it stick.

"By this time I was in what was then an honorable profession, flying whiskey across Lake Erie, and I probably had a couple thousand hours experience, but only twenty-five or thirty in my logbook.

"I obtained a license, nevertheless, following three weeks of 'official' instruction. In the eyes of the Commerce Department, I was at last legitimate."

Of all the thrills and chills of the Thompson speed race, nothing was quite as stomach-wrenching as its famous race horse start. Lined up across the airfield, wingtip to wingtip, awaiting the drop of the starting flag, "it was a toss-up," recalled Mackey, "whether everybody was going to get to that first pylon alive. In the first place the airplanes

"Gas tanks were a hell of a problem," said Cook Cleland in 1946. "They burned 350 gallons per hour in the race and I couldn't use external tanks as the Navy did. Luckily, my Corsair had some leaky long-unusued wing tanks, but to change the plumbing we badly needed slushing compound. Long distance phone calls—$150 worth—finally located some in California. The regular airlines refused to ship the highly explosive compound, but the Flying Tiger line flew it in for $125." (Frederick C. Crawford Auto and Aviation Museum)

This photo was taken moments after the sizzling racehorse start of a postwar Thompson race. In 1947, the length of the previous year's course was cut in half, from thirty to fifteen miles, to offer the fans twice as many passes in front of the grandstands (and twice the agony in pylon turns.) As one wag put it, "The great Thompson was like a play, one actor walking across the stage and in five minutes walking back." But with a shortened course, the 1947 races concluded in the bloodiest, crash-filled three days in racing history. (Dudley Brumbach and Bud Yassanye collection)

of the '30s were not highly controllable on the ground and were apt to slide again and again into each other's lanes. Once you got them airborne, they flew well, at least mine did. You couldn't ask for a better flying airplane, except for a few problems. For instance, the oil temperature would hit the pin even before the Wedell got off the ground. I put a piece of tape over the gauge. I didn't want to look at it anymore."

Racing pilot Don Rae echoed Mackey's dismal memory of the horse start. "It was bedlam, pure and simple," he laughed. "I saw any number of fellas simply chop their engines to keep from colliding. You could never be sure whether guys were pressing you deliberately or avoiding an uncontrollable ship next to them. The next moment one could be half-way into your fuselage. So many unknown factors went into a race. The biggest strain of all was simply sitting out on the line waiting for the damn thing to start. You had to have the guts and determination to go through with it."

"To tell the honest truth, we were apprehensive as all hell," agreed pilot Dick Becker, Thompson Trophy race flyer of the postwar era. "I don't mean fear. If I had been afraid, I would have shut the engine off and got the hell out. If I'm really afraid of something, I won't do it. That is the way I make up my mind. No, at the time there was more determination than fear.

"Nevertheless, you were so darned apprehensive. The first race I took off, in '47, I swore to Christ that all those guys were converging long before they got off the ground. The rules were to maintain a straight track while on the ground to give everyone a fair deal. Officials supposedly would watch you take off to see that you could firmly control your machine. But, man, these boys were heading for that first pylon long before their tires left the runway. In '48 I didn't want a repeat of the revolving door atmosphere of the year before. I immediately went for altitude and let them all gang in down there, planning to dive back into the mass when it got straightened out a little after the first pylon.

"I had a real bagful just getting that damn machine off the ground and keeping in a straight line. It was a holy terror. We had cut down the rudder and tail wheel on my Corsair F-2G airplane.

I couldn't see over the nose of this machine. I had to scan out from the sides. It was a horrible brute."

Mike Murphy laughed out loud at Becker's statements, but couldn't challenge a one of them. Seated in his easy chair in his Findlay, Ohio, home on a fall afternoon in 1975, the man who was starter for the Cleveland National Air Races lived the scary scene all over again.

"The race started at four o'clock. We tried to be right on the second because we were set up with the radio network. So the airplanes were pulled out early and put on the line. Now they all took off on grass in the early days and there were lime lines laid down on the grass to keep the planes nice and straight. A half-hour ahead of time the pilots would all come to the center and I briefed them for the second or third time on the wind conditions. They then returned to their airplanes and warmed up for ten to fifteen minutes.

"When we were ready to go, I looked back and cleared the field behind me, checked for a clear sky, checked my watch. Then I pointed to every man for a nod. If a pilot shook his head no, I held it for a few seconds until he said he was ready. When they were all ready, I held up the white flag for ten seconds, counting off the seconds.

"During those ten seconds I knew all that horsepower was there. I placed myself in the middle of the airplanes and far enough in front. They could all see me and I could look into their eyes. The minute I whipped that flag down, I ran the fifty feet and ducked between two airplanes before they were out of position. As they passed, stones, rocks, and cinders struck me like shotgun pellets.

"I turned immediately to watch the airplanes because it was still my job to note any infraction of the rules. Some crossed over. Some went this way, others that way. Some pulled off too soon and had to settle back. Everything happened. My stomach ached from the noise and vibration, especially with the war plane racers in the '40s.

"Now," sighed Murphy, "your racing today? Frankly I don't know why they're doing it anymore. It's so expensive. Before an engine cost a hundred dollars, an airplane, a thousand. Now you pay fifty thousand dollars for an airplane and ten thousand for an engine. You win three thousand if you're lucky. You see, in the early days Rudy Kling, Roger

One of the first posters advertising the Cleveland National Air Races in 1929, the first year Cleveland hosted the event. Only biplanes are shown, and a live person, flag in hand, is at the top of the pylon. (Frederick C. Crawford Auto and Aviation Museum)

Rae, Harold Neumann, Steve Wittman, Art Chester, I could name many of them, all engineered and built their airplanes. They built them, worked on them, flew them. Today, pilots have money. They simply buy them and fly them.

"Did I *enjoy* being an air race official? I learned early in the game that if you can handle pilots, they respect you. They're disciplined. If they don't respect you, they're a bunch of bastards.

"Once in Detroit after '49, Continental Motors sponsored the small planes that Goodyear had sponsored earlier. There has always been a little friction between eastern race pilots and western race pilots. Bob Downey was a western pilot, Bill Brennand an eastern pilot. In this one race they did every dangerous thing in the book. They actually tried to crack each other up. It was like two guys hitting each other with their bare fists, only they were using airplanes. At the end of the race I disqualified both of them. They both could just as well have stayed home in bed.

"I also grounded a man in Florida one time. His name was Moriarty. A good Irishman. I found him in a bar having a drink. I had to tell him he wasn't flying in any race. Then I bought him three more drinks."

Pylon judge Dick DeGarmo had the best seat in the house to watch the racing. "Some people look at me two or three times when I mention that I stood near the top of a pylon as powerful racing planes dived and banked around me in the Thompson Trophy race. Though I was still a ragtail kid, I was a bona fide pylon judge.

"I just wanted to be around the air races. I started working in the hangars—dusting and sweeping—when I was twelve. My dad had sold wire to the hangar people and that helped me get in.

"One man stood on the ground and sighted up through a series of rings to make sure no pilot cut inside. A second man stood outboard of the pylon to watch for interference between planes. The third guy was stationed on top of the pylon, ready to wave the infraction flag.

Standing on or near any pylon during the heat of an air race might easily prove unhealthy and unholy. Most pilots try to leave very little sky between their wingtip and the pylon bunting. (Bill Sweet collection)

Thirty-foot Goodyear Trophy race pylons are towed by tractor to their positions at the Cleveland Airport in 1947. At treetop altitude and in heavy air traffic, the diminutive towers were hard to spot. The waving flags helped. (Frederick C. Crawford Auto and Aviation Museum)

"In those earliest days, the pylons were topped by a four by four platform with a little railing. Some of the pylons were constructed of wood and some of pipe. None of them had steps. To get to the top, one had to crawl through that mess of framework. They weren't very high, three stories, perhaps.

"Two rings were located in the center of the structure I tended. One ring was about three inches in diameter and the other one, about eighteen inches higher, was perhaps a foot in diameter. The judge stared up through these rings at the central core of the pylon. If he detected any part of an airplane go by, that was an infraction. He signaled me and I waved a flag from the top of the pylon. The only way the pilot knew whether he had cut the pylon was by immediately looking back to see if the infraction flag was flying. The steep turn was the most dangerous point in the race; the planes were jammed and trying all kinds of maneuvering tricks. It was a bad, bad place to be looking around.

"Could we have been anxious, blinked an eye, or anticipated an infraction? It was just calling balls and strikes. Admittedly, the stakes were damn high to be making mistakes. Still, you gained a few and missed a few.

"There were not many violations. I can remember calling three pilots back, two in one race, one in another. They had to recircle the pylon. There were no complaints because they had to be darn close in order for there to even be a question about an infraction, and we were in a far better position to tell than they. After all, we had only one thing on our minds.

"This judging arrangement wasn't carried on too long, three or four years, because it was preposterously dangerous. Obviously the planes were cutting the pylon and diving to shave as closely as possible without cutting. I could have been wiped out in a shot, along with my buddies. So many near misses occurred.

"I stood there on that pylon and until they dipped their wings to go around that structure I honestly believed that I would soon be wearing that wing around my toenails. I felt their backwash in my face. It took a few seasons of this for the risk to sink into my brain. After that, the management, too, realized that they were truly inviting human tragedy and out-of-sight insurance premiums.

"Then, instead of a flesh and blood man at the top of the pylon, they employed a mechanical device. If a plane cut in, the judge below would simply pull a lever. A flag popped up at the top of the tower to signal the pilot. No pilot was going to wipe out his landing gear on a guy's nose.

"I don't think my mother ever knew I was on the pylons. I must have told her I was dusting airplanes. In a crazy way, it was almost the truth."

"Of course," grinned Steve Wittman, the elder statesman of all U.S. racing pilots, who flew and won tough air contests even in his seventies, "we were extremely tense because the least little error lost the race. Some of the later races were long. The last 375-cubic inch race was a hundred miles on a five-mile course. That really gives it to you. The course was triangular. High g-loads. The air that day was rougher than a cob, and rough air, by itself, gives you a high g-load.

"Keep in mind," smiled Wittman, "that as you sit here, that's one g-load. Two g-loads doubles your weight. When you start multiplying by five, if you weigh 200 pounds, you're sitting there with a thousand pound load. About the most a person can stand in a sitting position is only from two and a half to three g's. Then he passes out. He can increase that for a short period but not for any length of time. On a triangular course, one bank comes quickly after another. I constantly pulled it until the horizon went gray. Then I had to ease off a little bit or it got dark in a hurry.

"In racing we also had to play with the structure of the aircraft. Sure, they razzed me for years but I worked very hard trying to build extremely light so that I could arrive first at that first pylon and eliminate most of the hazard. That's been my philosophy for most of my racing life. Another advantage of being out front is undisturbed air. I could pick the course, that is until they started passing me and generally screwing things up.

"One time, to curb the effect of the g-forces, someone hatched the idea of taping the pilots. They never did it again. Had they used an elastic tape it might not have been so bad. But they used a *solid tape,* and oh God, we just couldn't do anything. The entire abdomen was absolutely taped tight. We just wouldn't hold for it.

"I think the same guy who came up with the tape

idea marked the pylons with huge balloons. Half the balloons then proceeded to blow down or get punctured or some damn thing, and both the time trials and the race starting time were delayed. Balloons were always a bad idea because balloons sway. Anchoring them with cables would still be dangerous, and would prevent the close race I insist on flying.

"Now and then too many planes showed up to race. Somebody had gotten sore and decided to race even if he hadn't qualified. He brought his plane on line at the last moment and the officials forgot to count noses in the confusion. Too many airplanes on a course can be real bad. The first turn, in particular, can be hysterical.

"I recall a particular race using the five-mile course at Cleveland. We took off with nine or ten airplanes. Real wild. I was in my *Chief Oshkosh*, a light airplane, and I didn't get way ahead of them that time. There were quite a few around me. When you're going down the lines, you try to figure where everyone's going to be. You try to fix yourself a slot

somewhere. This time I was squarely in the middle, some under me, some over me. Suddenly I was in the turn. It was dark as hell. I looked up and Lee Miles's wheels were right on my canopy, and there was nowhere to go because I knew some guy was right under me."

"It was not at all like the Reno races today," added Roger Don Rae, "where if you are going to pass somebody, you can easily get him on the radio and say, 'I'm right behind you. I'm going to take you on the next pylon.' The fellow ain't about to look back as in open cockpit days. These guys are going so damn fast that they have to keep their eye on that pylon. These guys blink and they're past it. So it's very likely that they do talk with each other.

"We just had to look.

"There were many things to remember in the closed-circuit race. As soon as you turn your forty-five degrees or ninety degrees, is your next pylon in line? Are you sure? If not, steal a few seconds and see what your head temperature looks like. Watch those birds ahead of you, then turn the corner and

Taking a fast turn around the pylon are these three post-WW II racers. Wheels on the plane at left appear jammed and have not retracted completely. (Bill Sweet collection)

be gone. Try to figure out, in a fraction of a second, how far you are behind, what place you are in, what lap you are on. If you have the headwind, you might want to get a little lower or else stay at pylon height going downwind.

"It flashes through your mind that the guywires on a certain pylon are way out here and maybe on the other ones are little closer in. You don't want to unhook one of those. You try to remember where the rough spot with the turbulence was and try to avoid it.

"Your attention shoots back to the temperature. Let's see, last time around she went up a few degrees. Is it holding now? You watch your time. How's your fuel holding out? You look for oil leaks. A little oil's on the windshield. Where is that coming from? What are you going to do?"

Postwar race pilot Dick Becker viewed the Thompson Trophy skirmish as rougher physically and mentally than brief combat clashes. "In a combat situation, self-preservation dictated everything you did, but in the Thompson you were after a bit of cold cash. In the Thompson you were inclined to discount self-preservation in preference to financial rewards.

"The other difference was that in aerial combat we wanted to be aggressive, not defensive, because they taught that a couple of feet of altitude made us the aggressor. If we lost that advantage we were instantly second best and going to get our behinds shot off. That second-best posture was caused by self-preservation taking over for a few seconds, but it actually was fatal and had no place in air combat.

"Of course, Cook Cleland used to say air combat and the Thompson were about the same odds—twelve planes in the race and one guy gets killed. He also said it was just like a fast pass on a combat mission; we were pulling six and a half to seven g's on a turn and we did twenty-one laps times four pylons, so we were doing eighty-four turns. He pulled vapor trails every time and if he didn't, he figured he was slacking off. When he raced the Thompson in '47, they had to lift him out. He had bent his back double. They shut the cameras down after that.

"Did we fly as low in our high-power jobs as Turner and Ortman did in the '30's? We weren't right over the treetops. The faster you go, the more you need altitude so that you can see farther ahead.

You have to predetermine what the hell you're going to do. You don't just fly along jumping over treetops and when you arrive at some pylon, start your turn.

"Hell, a different set of circumstances was involved in the postwar Thompson. The last prop races in Cleveland were being won in excess of 400 miles per hour. Although the measured and timed course was 15 miles, we flew more like 20 miles each lap.

"We knew damn well the Corsairs were running in the neighborhood of 450 to 460 miles per hour. As speed increased, ground turbulence tore the hell out of us. We were thrown around in that stupid airplane. When that air became rock hard, we were abused beyond words.

"The noise didn't bother us. It was just a big roaring whine. I'm sure the absence of any noise would have bothered us a hell of a lot more. The louder that engine roared, the surer we were that things were going right.

"Incidentally, the one rule of the Thompson race was that there were no rules. There were no horsepower limitations, no limitations of any sort. If you brought over something you thought could qualify, you got in there, paid your qualification fee, and you were in. The supposed purpose of the pilots meeting the morning of the race was to review what was legal in the race; to brief us on any problems and their solutions; and to prescribe the proper reactions under certain conditions. But little Shorty Fulton, the chief starter, would inevitably stand up there and say, 'Now damn you guys, you obey and you mind and you tend to all the rules.' But then he'd add, 'Don't forget, however, that we've got a crowd of people who paid good money to watch you buggers, and you give them a good show!' It was an open invitation to go out and bend the rules at will.

"Although it was not even spoken of or indicated as a rule, it was just presumed that no women were allowed in the Thompson race for unlimited power airplanes. Under that sort of duress, no woman to my mind could handle the panic situation. I'm talking about moments such as that bloodsucker takeoff on the home pylon. During the race one pilot could easily clobber so many people that he caused a catastrophe without half trying. How it avoided becoming a total catastrophe, I'll never know.

"Little Betty Skelton, the girl aerobatic flier, ran up to each airplane prior to the start and cautioned each one of us to be careful and be a good sport about everything. She was a pretty little thing, a very popular, nice girl. Still is. And an all-around good sport. I think everybody respected Betty strictly on the magic she could perform with her Pitts-Special airplane in aerobatic flying. So one might have said, 'Well, if anybody should race in the Thompson, it should be Betty Skelton.' Again I say no. Betty Skelton, in her repertoire or whatever the hell she did, had it all to herself. She was totally in control. Any panic situation, by virtue of her incredible training and practice, would not be at all like finding herself in an airplane sandwich at 450 miles per hour at the home pylon.

"Physically, they couldn't horse it. Sure, there was a mental strain, but even more physical. We were totally exhausted from the heat alone. The cabin temperature was tremendous. We came out soaking, wringing wet.

"We put on our g-suits and put this g-load on ourselves sixty times. The suit grabbed in the belly, thighs, and calves. It stopped us from blacking out, but the physical damage was still taking place. I'd hate to see any girl I cared for in that kind of picture. She just couldn't last it."

Becker sighed and half smiled.

"Once I got a call from the fellow who still has my old airplane.

" 'Dick,' he said, 'since the Reno races are starting up, how about putting 74 back in flying condition? You fly it and we'll both go out there.'

"I said, 'Hell, Walter, first off I'm too damn old. I'm 53 years old. I don't want any part of it any more. And there's nothing to go out there for.'

"I participated so briefly in the Thompson. How I wish I had been a part of it years earlier when pilots actually built their own creations. Now there was an accomplishment. Those boys did it all, but to say you've gone out and done what Cleland or somebody else had done—put in a successful bid and bought a military surplus thing that the poor taxpayers spent this million and a half bucks for, and to boast you've won a race with it—that's no real accomplishment.

"I idolize the hell out of the guys of the thirties. I would have liked to have been one of them."

Even the most daring and dashing of those pioneers, Colonel Roscoe Turner, got scared to hell fever in the heat of the race. Roscoe re-created the life of "the most dangerous profession in the world" in an article "Air Racing Was Like This."

"TEN . . . NINE . . . EIGHT . . . SEVEN . . . seconds, the clock on the dash panel says, ticking them off. And you sit there in the cramped cockpit and sweat. Waiting for the starter to drop the flag.

"The tiny racing plane trembles. The propeller clatters. The skin throbs.

"You're in number two position, next to the orange job with the taper wing, second from the end of the line. There are nine others. Wing-tip to wing-tip. All raring to go. Stinging, snorting little hornets. And you've got to fly each one of them besides your own. Because you never know what the other guy is going to do.

"This is the Thompson Trophy race. The big one. The National Air Races. The one that really counts. Aviation's Kentucky Derby. You've got to win. Everything you own is wrapped up in this trim and powerful little racer. Everything. Even your spare watch is in hock.

"For 365 days, since the race last year, you've been getting the ship ready. Wings clipped to cut through the air faster. Engine souped up to get more power. One thousand, two hundred h.p. in your lap and a feather in your tail. That's what it amounts to. Enough to make any aeronautical engineer beat himself to death with his slide rule.

"For what? For fame and glory and headlines and the prize money. So you can pay off your debts and come back next year.

"Check your instruments. Fuel gauge. Pressure gauge. Oil temperature. Tachometer. Cylinder head temperatures. Glance at the chronometer. The clock has stopped. No, it's still running.

"SIX . . . FIVE . . . FOUR . . . Why is a second a year? Tick, tick, tick, it sounds like the bong of Big Ben in your ears. Tension, nerves, fear. It drowns out the roar of the crowd.

"The grandstand: a kaleidoscope of colors. It'll be a blurred ribbon the next time you see it flash by. See that black and yellow job down the line? Keep your eyes on him. He's the guy to beat. Get out in front of him and try to stay there. Number eight, that's him. *Number 8 . . . Number 8 . . .* Beat him . . . Beat him . . . The engine sings it. A battle cry.

Remember what your mechanic said—'They're ganging up on you. Look out! They're going to try to box you in—just like they do in a horse race!'

"THREE . . . TWO . . . *One* second now to go!

"Why won't your feet be still? They're jumping up and down on the rudder pedals. Dammit! You can't stop them. And your hands? Sticky, trembling on the stick and throttle. Shaking like you've got the DT's. Goggles streaming with perspiration. Your clothes are soaked. They're soggy. Itchy. Hell fever, that's what you've got. *Scared-to-hell* fever. You always catch it right about now—with one second to go. It'll go away. As soon as . . . There's the flag!

"Slap the throttle. *Werrummm!* The ship leaps forward. Your feet stop jumping. Hands? Cold and steady. Now, crouched in the cockpit, this is your world. Nothing else matters. It's up to you.

"Faster, faster, shooting across the field. Pull back on the stick. Not too fast. Easy does it. You're free. The ship leaps forward again like a shot from a gun. No more ground drag. Too much speed. You'll rip the wings off it you don't slow down the propeller.

"Where are the others? Count 'em . . . *one* . . . *two* . . . *three* . . . They're all up. Don't get too close. One error and it's curtains for both of you. You're no longer human. You're a machine. Every move is timed to the split second . . . There's the red roof. Pylon coming up. Left rudder. Left stick. Wing up. Wing down. You're around. The straightaway. More throttle. The wind whistles in your ears.

"Brown roof. Big tree. Another turn. Here come the others. Who's that on the left wing? He's cutting in too close. You'll get his prop wash on the next turn . . . Here it comes, boy . . . Hang on!

"Too sharp. Take 'em wider next time. Don't try to cut so short. Let the other guy kill himself. You're doing all right. There's the grandstand again. Swoosh!

"Pull off a strip of tape from the dashboard. That's how you count the laps. Thirty laps. Thirty pieces of tape. Twenty-nine now. . . Check it the next time you go by the crowd. The guy with the big numeral card. It should read 28.

"Where is Number 8? You can't see him. Red roof again . . . Turn . . . Straightaway . . . Throttle . . . Brown roof . . . Big tree . . . Pylon . . . The grandstand. Okay, it says 28.

"There he is! Just ahead. You're gaining on him. Faster, faster . . . Pour it on. Pray this thing will hold together . . . Red roof coming up . . . Try to cut it real short this time . . . Take the chance . . . Maybe you can get him on the turn . . . now . . . Wing down deep . . . Snap back . . . Jerk . . . Shake, tremble, roar! . . . But you made it. There's nobody in front of you.

"Instruments? Oil pressure . . . Supercharger . . . Gas . . . Speed . . . Okay . . . If they only stay like that. Remember what happened last year—when the supercharger blew. It was only doing 2,000 rpm then . . . Now it's doing 3,000. You improved it. But *that much?*

"Pylon. Grandstand. Tape. Round and round going nowhere. Brown roof. Red roof. Big tree. Straightaway. Pylon. Zoom, zoom, zoom. Wing up. Wing down. Level off. More pylons. More trees, more roofs. It's hot. Like an oven. Is something on fire? Glance around? No, don't, you mustn't. At this speed you can't take your eyes off what's coming up ahead . . . Grandstand. Tape. There's one piece left. One more lap.

"You're still out in front. If you could only look back and catch that number card for a recheck. It was so blurred. Maybe you missed a pylon. Maybe they'll disqualify you. No, not that, please. And let 'er hang together another two minutes.

"It's over. You won!

"You're shaking again. You can hardly control the ship after she's on the ground. Your heart beats louder than the engine. Uniform soaked, sopping wet. Hands tremble. Knees buckle as you climb out to meet the reporters and photographers with a big forced smile . . . Headache. Muscle ache. Exhaustion. Oh, for a great big soft bed.

"Air racing is like that. It's the toughest test of all on men and machines. I know. For ten years I was pushing pylons in the Thompson. For ten years I was chasing records across the country in the big Bendix Transcontinental. Three times winner of the Thompson, many times loser. But it gets in your blood, and it stays.

"It's the most dangerous profession in the world."

4

HOTEL CARTER

ALLEN JAMES LOWE
MANAGING DIRECTOR

Cleveland's

AVIATION HOTEL

Send the Kid out for Hamburgers

As bell captain of Cleveland's Hotel Carter, Andrew Elko was an honorary member of the racing fraternity.

"The night before the big Thompson race in the '30's, the pilots came into the hotel lobby in groups of two or three, occasionally a loner. They were wide awake, drinking, the whole 'Auld Lang Syne' routine. Someone always sent me or some other bellhop down to the corner for hamburgers.

"The lobby was a massive hall with marble floor, beamed ceilings, and pillars. They talked of past races, near misses, how they beat other guys, and little tricks of the trade. The charwomen rolled up the furniture and moved these guys around from one spot to another. All of us who served as help—the hotel clerks, the house detective, the elevator man at that late hour, and myself—were not only intrigued but hypnotized by these men and the hairy tales they told.

"The rest of the world had gone to bed.

"Among the divans and the large comfortable chairs was my bell captain stand, directly in the middle of the action. So between telephone calls and messages, I became engulfed in these guys reliving their lives. I was on the fringe of all these tales, but never intruding. I was neither needed nor wanted at the moment, but there I was, anyway, an honorary member of the racing fraternity.

"We ranked them as good people—down to earth, friendly. Nothing snobbish. No arrogance. Very enjoyable.

"Their drinking appeared to be an eleventh hour attempt to uncover new courage. They were basically brave and heroic men, but they certainly knew the next day could be their last. How many would spin out? Who could say if those high compression engines would erupt or blow out or some other damn thing?

"Every year these pilots gave us all free passes. They were grand and personable. Yet I had to wonder how they could even see the instruments in their cockpits the next day. It was obvious some of their erratic turns and maneuvers were not calculated. They were pure and simple mistakes due to poor judgment accompanying a hangover, anxiety, or lack of sleep.

"About two or three in the morning before the Thompson race, several of the race pilots still sat there. In the door came Jerry Goodman, chief electrician at the Palace Theater. Jerry used to set all the stage props for the vaudeville acts and was a pal to the fliers.

"Though not raucous, ordinarily, at times the pilots would laugh uproariously, and some of them would square off in a wrestling match right there on the lobby floor.

"Sure, the race pilots made a little noise. They brought a few complaints from other guests, but not as many as the baseball teams or the Washington Redskins or the big bands that played the Palace Theater.

"A nice quiet guy was 'Wrong Way' Doug Corrigan. He had a permit to fly to California, but took off and flew to Paris, instead. When they tried to arrest him, he simply said, 'I just went the wrong way.' Doug was inevitably seen in a brown leather jacket, like he was born in it, to which he often added a pretty white scarf. He was amazing. He could

Miss Amelia Earhart relaxes on a touring car runningboard with American and foreign pilots in 1931. (Jim Borton collection)

navigate the Atlantic Ocean perfectly but had trouble locating California.

"Arlene Davis, the aviatrix, dropped into the old Carter. So did Jackie Cochran. There was a comraderie among these competitors. Sex didn't play a role. The men didn't imply, 'Get the hell off, buzz out of here. You're just women amongst men.'

"There was comraderie and an exchange of experiences, thrills, and trade secrets. On the other hand, the Thompson Trophy race was a very serious thing and represented big money to all of these guys who didn't have two quarters apiece. So they

may well have respected and admired one another, but when the juice began to flow, they might well make an immodest boast just to draw out important information.

"The reputed feuding fliers, Roscoe Turner and Earl Ortman, often were in the lobby together, with an air of respectful competition. Certainly no real animosity showed through. On the other hand, there was no phony Jack Benny—Fred Allen baloney in their personal feelings. Maybe they hated each other's guts, but I'm positive that neither underrated the hazardoud potential of the

In addition to speed and navigational skills proved throughout the National Air Races, Jackie Cochran had an imaginative and commercial head on her shoulders. On the first day of the races, in 1949, she sponsored a demonstration of aerial spraying techniques over the crowd of more than 75,000. Instead of the usual insecticide, the plane let loose with Shining Hour perfume. (Jim Borton collection)

Jackie Cochran in the cockpit of her P-51 race plane immediately after placing third in the 1948 Bendix transcontinental race, behind Paul Mantz and Linton Carney. A decade earlier, she had placed first, and in 1946, second. In '48, Jackie also flew 447 miles per hour over a 2,000-kilometer closed course to establish a new world's record. (Frederick C. Crawford Auto and Aviation Museum)

other. Both knew very well that 'today it's me, but tomorrow, by the turn of fate, it so easily could be you.'

"Despite the showbiz flare of Turner, I saw Colonel Turner as a gentle, almost timid man. I think that cornered with a physically aggressive counterpart, he would have backed down. I believe he was shy to the point of pain and worked horrendously hard to cover it up.

"Part of the coverup was the waxed mustache. It had more than a show business function; it helped create a character he wasn't. He used to send me

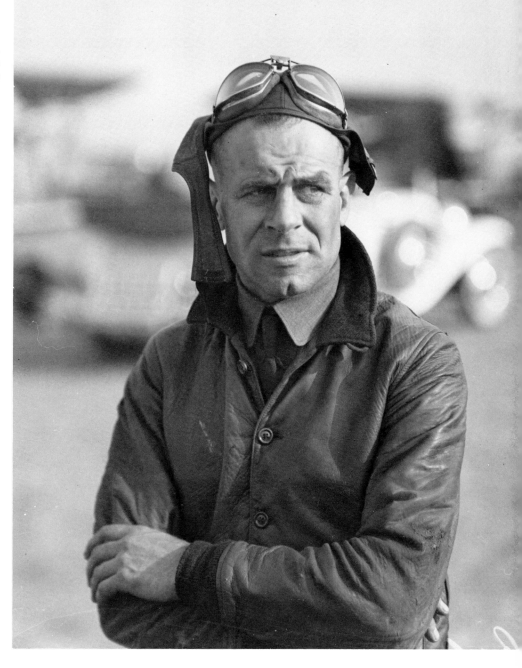

Jimmy Doolittle "was never, ever loud, flamboyant, or show-off. He even drank with a purpose." (Rudy Profant collection)

down to the Carter Pharmacy for a little tin of mustache wax. His lion mascot stayed right in his room. Well, that wasn't too surprising. Gene Autry's horse was stabled in the lobby next to the elevator. The management built a little stable there. Every day they put two or three bales of fresh straw in there to keep the Board of Health from screaming.

"It's been forty-plus years but I can still see Jimmy Doolittle seated slumped in the hotel lobby in a wingback chair. A naturally quiet guy. Had more hair then, of course. He was quite a drinker prior to the races and in service. It seemed only to

sharpen him. He was never, ever loud, flamboyant, or show-off.

"He was authoritative. He was competent, so I'm hardly surprised he went as high as he did. A precise man, he was known as a guy who inevitably calculated his risk. He even drank with a purpose. The gears were turning and we respected him. He rarely engaged in idle chitchat, yet he liked a good joke, a good story, a well-told dirty yarn. He had an honest laugh and was marvelous company, yet was always willing to be in the background.

"His authority was evident without a word. You

Factory publicity picture of Jimmy Doolittle in 1929 standing in front of the Curtiss Hawk he demonstrated in Holland and Germany. The same year, putting on an aerobatic demonstration at Cleveland, he lost the wing of his military Curtiss airplane as he attempted to recover from an outside figure-six maneuver. Jimmy fought off the weight of centrifugal force and bailed out. In filing the required report, the typically concise Doolittle wrote, "Wing broke." (Jim Borton collection)

The commotion out at Cleveland Airport in 1931 was the flurry of well-wishers around young Jimmy Doolittle who just won the Bendix transcontinental race from Los Angeles to Cleveland with a time of 9 hours, 10 minutes, 21 seconds. (Jim Borton collection)

Doolittle flew the still talked about Gee Bee Super Sportster, red and white Model R-1, to a runaway victory in the 1932 Thompson Trophy race. (Cleveland Chapter, American Aviation Historical Society)

might easily kid Jimmy Doolittle because you knew he enjoyed it, but you never put him down.

"Understand that I associated with these men over the years because they provided a source of income. Their dimes and their quarters were a livelihood. Beyond that, they were simply people.

"The fliers were as human as you or me. They talked to us kids. Sometimes they even had small banquets, real banquets. They got all us guys and elevator girls off duty and we all sat and ate and drank and heard all of the stories of the uncertainties and glories of show business.

"People asked me which celebrities were differ-

ent in real life than they were in public. One who was entirely consistent was Tallulah Bankhead. She was raucous, coarse, vulgar, obscene, loveable. She was Tallulah, off stage and on. Regular customers usually asked for the same hotel people to assist them, and also for the same room or suite each time they came to Cleveland.

"'Have Andy help me, please,' she'd call down to the desk.

"First thing she'd do was walk into the other room, leave the door open, disrobe completely, put on a silk robe, come out with it completely unbuttoned, her breasts fully exposed, her privates in full view. No, she was neither vulgar nor obscene by her personal definition. She was simply Tallulah. I have never forgotten her nor that cigarette hanging from her lips, a triple Bacardi in her hand. She could not have been nicer or more friendly to me. Loveable, really. There was no intent to shock me or to embarrass me. She never made an improper pass.

"The Three Clowns were another story. They were regulars on the Palace billing, and at the hotel (just as in their movies) you never knew who was chasing whom up and down the halls at all hours. Once, one of them sent me down to the pharmacy for a box of condoms. He had picked up some chicks backstage at the Palace. Girls hung around that stagedoor all the time, waiting for anything in pants and the Clowns lassoed the lot of them.

"Next morning in a crowded elevator filled with families, several young women, and school girls, this same big bald comedian who had sent me on the errand piped up, 'Hey, son, you know those rubbers you brought me last night?'

"I looked at him in dismay and disbelief. 'Yes sir.'

"'They're no damned good. I used them for chewing gum.'

"That in a crowded elevator! He did that deliberately to set off all those people. Then, to make matters worse, he nudged me and laughed in that special way of his—yuk, yuk, yuk—that you've seen a couple million times in the movies.

"Aviators, Broadway performers playing the Hanna, and screen stars and big band people playing the Palace would ask, 'Andy, where's the nearest cathouse?' They told me that if they went to a commercial lay joint, they wouldn't get into trouble. If they picked up somebody, they might easily be set up; charged with rape; be photographed, sued, or blackmailed. They were there for a week's run. What the heck were they going to do?

"We didn't have any television.

"The girls would give us their cards: 'Our going rate is this. You come up and visit us.'

"It was an education if you could keep your perspective. After a short apprenticeship with the hotel business, a number of bellhops bootlegged or pimped. To my credit, I didn't. I was brought up differently. I'm neither a prude nor particularly moral, but I couldn't see pushing either booze or broads.

"Still I've never forgotten two attractive young things. They had an apartment at Eighty-third and Euclid. 'Come on up, Andy. Have dinner with us and you can sample the merchandise and we'll talk business. We'll make it worth your while.'

"Did any of the racing pilots disappoint or disillusion me? No. Of course, there was hero worship in my veins. I was a boy and these were adventurous, exciting men. But had one of these guys been a bully, a fighter, a cheapskate, then despite the hero worship, despite the stars in my eyes, I would have said, 'I do not like this man.'

"The pilots loved good food late at night, especially western sandwiches. Sometimes raw steak. As our kitchen was closed at that hour, I had to borrow a car or take a taxi to the all-night diner on Fourteenth Street or go to one of the Greek joints around the corner. Sometimes at two o'clock in the morning one of them would have to go to a cathouse. 'C'mon, Andy, take me down to the nearest place where I won't get knocked in the head.'

"The pilots, trying to relax, may have taken a couple of movie actresses to their rooms. They were very real, very human beings. They were not base. They were not animals. You could not say, 'These are simply a lousy, drunken, fornicating bunch of creeps.'

"All this in the wee hours of the dawn before the big race. All the loudmouths, all the hypocrites, all the promoters and the con men were gone. All that was left were the room clerks, the charwomen, and the performers—whether race pilots, comedians, singers, dancers, actors, or actressess—sitting, laughing, talking, Indian wrestling or just coming from work.

"I'm sure these men couldn't sleep. They came down to the lobby in bedroom slippers with open-neck shirts. Maybe they asked for warm milk because booze couldn't get them drunk. They'd be drinking, talking, go up, come back down. They just couldn't sleep.

"The Carter Hotel was home in the City of Cleveland. They had done everything they could to and for their race planes. They had eaten supper, either in our dining room or somewhere else. They had read the paper. Some of them played cards, some listened to the radio. The later the hour grew,

Florence Lowe Barnes, more popularly known as Pancho Barnes, added to the robustness and color of the National Air Races. Hardly a neophyte with a hot airplane, she had incredible physical strength, and claimed to have been a Missouri mule-skinner and to have shipped in the merchant marine for two years as a male. She was possibly best known for her Happy Bottom Riding Club in the California desert, a retreat for some of the biggest names in aviation, politics, entertainment and the military. Pancho imported lovely women from Hollywood to raise the spirits of her male guests. She also was a serious hog farmer and had a contract to collect garbage and trash at nearby Edwards Air Force Base. (Jim Borton collection)

the more friendly, the more intimate they became.

"Everyone who sat there, eyes closed, not joking anymore, might have held back the dawn, had he the power.

"Yet they all had courage.

"Anyone who rolled up to the starting line of the Thompson Trophy race, the most gruelling air battle in peacetime history, had courage.

"There were no cowboys in that one."

5

Doug Davis

If Only Doug Can Get through Monday

Though former Waco Airplane dealer, lay churchman, and first Eastern Airlines captain Doug Davis, Sr. died forty-seven years ago flying the Thompson Trophy race, the romance between the dashing Doug and the young Glenna Mae Davis of Atlanta has never been more alive in his widow's eyes.

"Our son, Doug Jr., was a portrait painter. He was killed in the Air France tragedy that took so many Atlanta lives. The art association was taking off from France one Sunday morning after a study tour. He died the same age as his race pilot father, thirty-three years of age.

"My son painted a portrait from a newspaper clipping made when his father was flying open cockpit airplanes. There are lines around the eyes as if he were squinting into the weather and the sun, but it also has that pleasant expression, the partial smile I never saw him without. Always a most friendly look. Everybody's friend. I think Doug Jr. captured his personality so well in that portrait.

It's my favorite. He was six when his father was killed.

"So many people thought I had asked Doug not to race. I hadn't, certainly not in so many words, not that I didn't have uncomfortable feelings about it. I prayed so much about it.

"Of all his activities in aviation, I was truly concerned with only one flight, the Thompson the year before he was killed. That one year I went with him to Cleveland. That year he let someone else take over. He said, 'I brought you here to have a good time and you won't enjoy it if I'm in it.'

"The next year he said, 'Well, now, I know you're going to be busy getting Doug Jr. ready for school, the first grade and all.' Of course, thirty minutes in a department store and he would have been ready for school.

"But I took up his lead. I said, 'Oh, yes, I'm going to be very busy getting him ready for school.'

"I didn't go to Cleveland that year because I knew he would be thinking about me and his flying. He hardly needed to divide his attention.

"I was fourteen, a freshman at Barnesville High School, the day I met Doug. He spent numerous hours working his way through school, yet managed his studies, was president of the class, captain of the football team, fastest man on the track team. I recognized very early that he put his heart into everything he did.

"In the early years, persons all about the area had assumed Doug would be a minister. He was clerk of the church while in his late teens. The Sunday evening before the fatal race, they were baptizing some three hundred children from our State of Georgia Baptist Orphanage. I have a wonderful mental picture of him standing down by the pool drying those children's faces when they came up out of the water. He just loved them and they loved him back.

"He never mentioned whether it was difficult for him to decide against the ministry. I suppose from that first day he flew, he knew that that was it. Airplanes *had* to be his first love.

"It was most uncommon for seniors to know freshmen as well as Doug knew me. Being against all the rules is what made it so interesting. Those senior girls gave me a hard time, I can tell you, because they'd had him for four years. Some of the competition was pretty keen. I was young enough and probably not too interested—probably that's what made *me* interesting. I hadn't grown up and he had, and it made a difference.

"He and his entire senior class went into Atlanta to enlist when World War I was announced. He was the only one to pass their thorough physical. To his great disappointment, Doug wasn't sent to Europe but was kept as an instructor here, being deemed a natural pilot.

"He did enlist his senior year and left before the year was over.

"Barnstorming had not yet begun. I don't know how many planes they had, but it must have been a very small beginning for the military. Doug took to it so easily. He came home in a war surplus Jenny with *Glenna Mae* painted in boxcar size letters all down the side. First thing we did was to loop the loop over Barnesville High School, then land and say hello to the principal, faculty, and all the old students.

"There was a time right after Doug's service years and before our marriage when he didn't get to Atlanta very often. He made a point of getting there at least once a month, even though sometimes he had to come from Detroit. He would not let me know he was coming. If he had the opportunity to come, he'd come. I was one of those people who, if I already had a date, wouldn't break it. Like I said, he was nearly five years older than I. It took awhile to catch up with him. I was not going to sit home and wait on the chance he might come.

"Although we were engaged, it was understood I could have other friends. I made it very plain that if I wanted to go out to dinner or to a movie with somebody, I could. So little hardheaded me would say, 'No, you didn't tell me you were coming. Now, if you're still here tomorrow . . .' and he'd get so mad at me that we'd have a big fight and I'd give him his ring back.

"About the third time my ring returned to its original owner to the accompaniment of tears and anger, Doug was scheduled to do a publicity stunt in a matter of hours. A man by the name of Curly Burns was directing the photographing of Doug picking up a man from a racing railroad train. It had never been done before.

"The camera crew and a crowd of spectators were riding on top of the moving train. Of course they had to coordinate the speed of the airplane with the speed of the train and there was a limit to how slowly Doug could fly. They were supposed to have removed all the wires that crossed the top of the train at all points along the track, but someone slipped up. The rope that hung down from the plane for the young man to grab hold of suddenly wrapped itself around one of those wires.

"When that happened, the plane normally would have been pulled into the train, but Doug applied all the strength he possessed to holding the plane on course. Part of his wing tore to bits like shattering glass and he managed to get loose and fly to the nearest emergency field. He had ruined his airplane. I saw the movies of it later. People on top of the train tried to cover themselves as best they could from the fragments and debris from Doug's wing. Under those conditions, the plane normally would have crashed into all of those people.

"The project's director, Curly Burns, went

Photo shows Doug Davis of Atlanta, Georgia, on his return home from the National Air Races at Cleveland, where he established a world's record in 1929 for commercial planes by reaching a speed of 194.69 miles per hour, beating the fastest planes of the Army and Navy. (Jim Borton collection)

straight from there to where I was working. He said, 'It's all your fault; if you hadn't given Doug back his ring, he would have seen that wire. His mind wasn't on it. He was thinking about you.'

"Then finally one day I thought, 'If he doesn't ask me one more time to marry him, I'm going to die.'

"I had finally grown up. Fortunately, he did.

"Doug soon had a contract with the Baby Ruth candy people. In just a little time he had three flying circuses and did aerial advertising. Within a year's time, his little company was the third largest aerial advertising business in the world.

"We were married Christmas Day, 1925, and Doug couldn't fill Baby Ruth candy orders fast enough. Doug himself designed a small parachute that would float a five-cent candybar down gently enough to not hurt a child struck on the head. He threw them out over school playgrounds. The notion of the Baby Ruth people was that the kids who didn't catch the candybars would make a mad rush to buy them. A store that didn't have them would think it had better order them.

"In New York on the Fourth of July of course everybody was at the beaches, and Doug dropped out all of his candy bars in their little parachutes. I wasn't with him in the plane that trip but he came back to the hotel so disturbed. Some persons had been hurt in their exuberance to grab the parachutes and candy. Some had climbed up on the concession stands and had fallen through. Doug just hadn't realized what a mob can do.

"He was disturbed for their welfare. I think the police department made a pretense of looking for him to arrest him, but it wasn't for real. They just told him he had better move his plane and get out of town. One lady broke a leg. He got more publicity than he wanted.

"He had a distinctive style of flying. I can best describe it by recalling a stunting competition where I was so impressed by someone else's incredible stunts. I was surprised when they gave my husband first prize. Frankly, I hadn't felt he deserved first prize. I happened to be standing next to a judge who didn't know who I was and I expressed my surprise at the decision.

"He looked at me so strangely that I guess I was admitting my ignorance. He said, 'Didn't you see the smoothness and perfection of the way Doug flew? That he didn't flop around over the sky? That he didn't jerk his airplane? It was superb coordination.' He set me straight. Gradually I learned to distinguish flying. Doug was one with his airplane, moving perfectly together through the clouds.

"After World War I, our friends had built this plane and were trying to get it on the market. Aviation was a mighty small group back in those days. Everybody who flew knew everybody else who flew. Doug, as usual, wanted to help these people and so he became a Waco dealer.

"I went with him to Troy, Ohio, to pick up the fourth Waco ever built. We were heading across the mountains of Kentucky and the engine of this little airplane simply stopped without warning. The prop was still and everything was so quiet. Doug carried on a conversation with me all the way down to keep me from getting scared. Well, I hadn't known enough to be afraid. I thought he was putting it down that way on purpose. He would dive the plane to gain a little flying speed. He would go as far as he could, lose that, would dive again and go a little further, and after we glided engineless across a wide river, Doug cleared a fence on the far shore by inches and set her down. He had flown that little airplane dead-stick across an entire river and had landed it safely, talking and laughing every moment to buoy my composure.

"We arrived once in Atlantic City in complete blackness only to find no lights at all on the pier. I had assumed that anyplace as big as Atlantic City would have someplace to land, but there was none. I didn't begin to truly worry until Doug had circled for the fifth time. I was doing my best to help look for a landing place.

"He brought the airplane down in a playground right behind the Atlantic City recreational area. It was completely encircled by a stone wall. The next morning when we went to take off, there was a tall, exceedingly handsome man waiting by the plane and wanting very aggressively to purchase it. Doug told him he would return to Troy and deliver him another one.

"The man said, 'But I don't want another one. I want this one.'

"Doug tried to convince him that he hadn't done something special to the airplane. Nevertheless, the man refused to believe that any other airplane could have landed in that tiny schoolyard. He said again and again, 'You've done something to this airplane and I want this one.'

"Finally, Doug gave in, and then came the matter of price. In the end, I found them flipping a coin to settle the two hundred dollars that separated them.

"We then had to get on the train and get another airplane.

"We never learned whether the man took off from that tiny playground and lived to tell the story.

"Ultimately Doug decided that I'd rather stay at home and not travel so he opened the first hangar on Candler Field and offered Atlanta's first air school and charter service. Later he kept it but didn't participate nearly as much. He sold out to the company that became Eastern Airlines and became Eastern's first captain. Eastern was the first scheduled airline. Delta followed shortly when it was clear Eastern was making a go of it. Doug was a buddy of the boys who started Delta. I remember their coming over to the house to talk of the possibility of a second airline.

"My husband had a very different style than a showman like Roscoe Turner. Roscoe was so colorful: bright blue jacket, fancy scarf around his neck. When Doug stepped out of an airplane, he usually had on a business suit and tie, and he took off the helmet and put on a hat. In other words, he looked like any other very ordinary business person. That's what he wanted people to think. He wanted them to accept aviation as a common, ordinary, average means of transportation, rather than merely a stunt machine for heroic persons. He felt that his female students should not wear men's pants and boots, but should fly in the type of dress they wore grocery shopping.

"Doug was an extraordinarily farseeing person. He said that the railroads were going to make Atlanta. It's a crossroads of transportation today. He said aviation was also going to make this a big city if the persons in charge just grew smart enough to see it as a continuation of transportation. Today, Atlanta has one of the busiest airports in the world, and Doug saw that coming forty-five years ago.

"Doug was the Eastern pilot on the first scheduled trip from Atlanta to New York. All of the governors and mayors from here to Washington and back were aboard that plane. It was a huge

aircraft for its day. They came in to land and blew a tire. Not a person aboard that plane knew. Doug landed on one wheel. He nearly broke both arms holding the plane erect and straight, and nobody knew about it.

"Forty years later, the Eastern Airlines people called me. They were going to host this very nice big luncheon downtown to celebrate the company's fortieth birthday. They said, 'Do you remember anything special about that first flight?'

"I said, 'I do, but I'm not sure that you'll want to print it.'

"I told them what it was and they said, 'No, ma'am, we're not going to mention that.'

"Doug always did his own repairs. He was the only man I ever knew who could work on an airplane and not get his hands dirty. He kept himself physically fit at all times. He inevitably had a freshly showered look.

"Doug's racing helped him finance work on a device to throw sound away from the ground. Today, the sound of modern airplanes is thunderous, but even back then the sound of airplanes was a nuisance. People who are unfortunate enough to live in the takeoff and landing patterns of airports literally have to stop their conversations every few minutes.

"Approaching Atlanta, Doug used to fly over our yard. We lived near the airport. He would circle and get my attention so that I would know to drive over and pick him up.

"One day someone else brought him home. 'You didn't wave to me this afternoon,' he said.

" 'I didn't hear you.'

" 'Well, you were right there in the yard and I circled you several times.'

" 'But I didn't hear you! I couldn't wave at you if I couldn't hear you.'

"He said, 'You said exactly what I hoped you would say. I was testing an instrument which I think is going to revolutionize living near airports. This thing will throw the sound up instead of down on the ground.'

"That was just a couple of weeks before he left for the races in Cleveland. To this day I do not know what the device was or what happened to it.

"Doug was always thinking ahead. He was the first person who ever put a cowling on a plane

"Breakfast in New York, Lunch in Atlanta." Doug Davis *left New York at fifteen minutes to seven on November 7, 1929, lost thirty minutes refuelling en route, and reached Candler Field in Atlanta at fifteen minutes to twelve, setting a record of 175 miles per hour. (Jim Borton Collection)*

engine and pants on wheels. He came home and told me, 'The most steamlined thing in our universe is a raindrop; it is the most resistant to wind. Therefore, the more I shape my cowling and wheels like a raindrop, the better the wind will slide off them.'

"At the races I noticed the deep affection. the pilots had for one another. They enjoyed getting together. It was just one huge family. When the German aviator Ernst Udet visited not long before the war, the Americans and the German walked across the airport with their arms about each other. Brothers. Comrades. So beautiful to see. It impressed me more than anything else.

"Once Doug won a transcontinental race, and the young man who came in second said that Doug had spent all evening before helping him. Tired as he was, Doug did that. He had nothing but trouble going out there with his plane. He spent most of his time working on it. Still his competitor said, 'Doug spent the entire night before the race working out *my maps*. He gave me so many tips. Otherwise, I simply wouldn't have made it.'

"I wanted whatever made Doug happy. He *was* happy. He was doing exactly what he wanted to do. Knowing that, I was able to relax, more or less, and go about daily things. Yes, he knew so much more about what he was doing than I would ever know. I had complete confidence in him. Most of all, he was a Christian and he was doing the thing he loved most. I don't think anybody can ever tell anyone else what to do with his life.

"I never went to many of the races; it was, after all, a man's world. Why should I spoil the fun? Doug never said he didn't want me to go, but of course he didn't have to. He said, 'You're just going to be so busy' and I said, 'Oh, yes, I am.'

"Nevertheless I think his conscience still hurt him that he wasn't taking me that last year, so he gave me a trip to New Orleans. One of the tour guides met the plane. I had to be shown the town—the works. And of course Eastern Airlines had a suite of rooms for the pilots at the end of the line. It was just a fun weekend. But all of it was building up to not taking me to Cleveland. I saw through it, of course, but never let him know. Doug had a horror of my being present should he crash in full view of the stands.

"He won practically everything that week, but I couldn't be happy or excited. My thought was, 'If Doug can just get through Monday . . .' I seemed to know of the tragedy even before the radio announcer said everything.

"Not being of a technical mind, I didn't try to figure out the truth of what caused his plane to crash. I always thought that it was too much pressure on the wings. We know that he was flying close to the pylons and that there was terrific strain (knowing how he flew, how he and his airplane were one). It looked like he wrapped those wings around the pylon.

"In the '34 Thompson race, the judges shortened the course against Doug's admonitions. They shortened it so people could see more of the race from the grandstand. He warned them it would put far too much strain on both the planes and pilots. His last words to them were, 'Someone will get killed this afternoon.'

"So Doug flew that race realizing there was a very great possibility of death, particularly the way he flew. He always flew tight. He put his heart into everything he did.

"Once I went with him to the Chicago World's Fair. We had two babies at home but my mother was there and had a good girl to help. Doug insisted I needed a vacation. He said, 'I'm not telling anybody we're coming so that we won't be entertained. We'll just have a good time.'

"But when we landed, a number of other airplanes were having a little air race he hadn't known about. The pilots, who recognized him instantly, all said, 'Doug, come get in this and win yourself some money. Pay all your expenses.' He said no, his plane hadn't been worked on. Then they said, 'But it'll make the race look more important if you're in there with us. People will enjoy it more if there are more airplanes.'

"Their final volley was, 'Come on. You can at least make your expenses even if you come in third, even fourth.'

"Well, he was dying to get in it. He asked me what I thought. I told him to do what he wished. So he was in there like a little boy. They clocked him and he was the fifth slowest airplane in the race, but he won first prize. His airplane was slow, but he and the airplane were one, cutting those pylons. He

Doug Davis lands as winner of the 1934 Bendix. Doug addressed 150,000 Cleveland air race fans following his California to Cleveland win, confessing his trials en route and promising never to fly the race again. (Jim Borton collection)

Like a swarm of white ants, scavenger fans swarm to the scene of Doug Davis's fatal crash. Fans used handkerchiefs to soak up souvenirs of the pilot's blood. (Jim Borton collection)

just gradually passed everybody in turn. So even if you said, 'Just win third prize, Doug,' he was going to put everything he had into it."

Jimmy Haizlip, winner of the 1932 Bendix Trophy Race, believes that there was not a bit of pilot error involved in the Davis crash.

"I saw Doug Davis go in at Cleveland in 1934. Until the other Wedell-Williams plane came around, I thought it was Roscoe Turner. In the haze of that far west pylon—looking toward the evening glare—I saw the actual movement of the airplane. Doug was flying Jim Wedell's Number 44, and our Number 92 was the youngest sister of the 44.

"Jim Wedell had fixed ideas about things, and one of them had to do with the tail structure. The tail of the original 44 was the best-rigged that he'd ever done. He was strictly an eyeball engineer. He did it all with one eye; the other he had lost in a motorcycle accident as a youngster. He rebuilt his Number 44 the summer of '32. He used a chrome moly tubing on the entire fuselage except the tail group. Of course he was an expert welder, never needing bolts or nuts. Instead of putting fittings and turnbuckles on this steamlined tie-rod, he bent the streamlined tie-rod and welded it right to the spar of the stabilizer. Everybody who looked at that place said that it was bad. He had taken the strength out when he welded it. Instead of having six thousand pounds of tensile strength at that spot, he had perhaps half that. So here was this empenage of mild steel welded to the longerons of chrome moly.

"In my mind, that was the weak part of the airplane. I can say this so strongly because a similar thing happened to me that same year in the Wedell-Williams Number 92. I almost missed a pylon in a smaller race at Cleveland because of the smoke and haze. The windshield became smudged. I lurched so fast at the pylon that I actually went into an accelerated stall. I can still feel the shiver through the entire airplane!

"Inside the pylon, I lurched sharply, then lurched again, and just caught it. I was stalled and going in—a little higher than the pylon because I stayed close to it—but I was able to just catch it with full power and keep going. There was no use telling anybody about it. I won the race. Near as I can tell, Davis was about to miss that pylon also. He likewise lurched his aircraft, and never stopped. His tail came off.

"To give an idea of what the wrenching will do, during the wartime I was down at Orlando in the service. One of my old friends in charge of the depot said, 'Come around here, Jim. I'll show you something about these Cessna C-74s.' They had been using the little utility planes to test young military pilots on twin-engine planes. They had been maneuvering, pulling tight turns. He showed me an empenage where they'd stripped off the download and broken one side of the stabilizer. The unbalanced load on the other side just twisted off those four longerons. One part fell one place, the other part another.

"In the same way, I found out what that load will do when flying the Gee Bee. An unbalanced load on the tail will just turn into tons, so I'm sure that the wrench force stripped Doug's tail off. No way to ever prove it.

"After the crash, we ran right from the grandstand and were on top of it. When all was done that could be done, we went from there over to the National Guard hangar where the local chap was quite a host and we had a few libations. The kids were hawking bits of the Davis crash for souvenirs before we left the airport. We were so distressed over Doug that Jim Doolittle, my wife Mary, and I drank three full bottles of pinchbottle scotch at the Lake Shore Hotel. We just couldn't shake the shock, the sorrow of it. We just couldn't stop that night, simply from general distress."

Gordon Israel, National Air Race pilot and a designer for Grumman Aircraft and Benny Howard race planes, summed up the feelings of many when he said: "The Wedell-Williams airplanes? I only know of one structural failure on one of them and that was when Doug Davis was killed. And I'll tell you, mister, that one made a lot of grown men cry."

6

It All Grew from Coo Coo the Bird Girl

Bill Sweet

Bill Sweet's fabulous National Air Shows played backlot bergs and cities alike during the National Air Race years. Several aerobatic fliers flew for both shows. Joe Mackey, Bill's premier stunter, even took a stab at the Thompson and Bendix races. Bill's credo was that nothing was too corny, too farfetched, or too nonsensical to spill into a microphone if it helped the paying customers have fun.

"Running a show I was mighty particular on timing. At two o'clock I want that jumper out of that airplane coming down and he has an American flag hanging down below him. Then I have at least 200 aerial bombs out there that I control electrically. They shoot up in the air. 'The Star Spangled Banner' is playing and the jumper's streaming down. When he gets so close I chew up 180 bombs all at one time.

"Then W-E-L-C-O-M-E all up there on parachutes. That's show business. But always the show had to be sandwiched together with split-second timing. No overlays. No dead spots.

"You still see the ghosts of the great old acts, wingwalking, for example, but they didn't do it then like they do it today. Today they hang onto a heavy bar. You couldn't tear them off there. In the old days they stood right on top of the spar. I used to say if a Jenny was rigged right you could put a sparrow in the middle of the wires and he couldn't fly out.

"We had 200,000 people on board at the Dayton National Air Show in 1938 when Joe Mackey did an outside loop and the cowling flew off his airplane, came back and rapped his skull, nearly removing it. Joe landed that airplane in a semiconscious condition. The deep scar he still wears is where he went out through the front end of his Lockheed. That airplane just went crazy. Joe straightened it up, leveled his approach, and landed it. Spectacular as hell.

"Things happened in those air show years from 1931 to 1972 that you couldn't believe. Eddy Scula, for instance. He fell two thousand feet. His chute failed to open. He lived. Every bone in his body was broken. He tried to stand up and fell over in a ball.

"Harold Krier worked for me in later years—a superior aviator and the finest gentleman I ever met in my life. A Tidybowl Christian, he never talked crude or dirty or goddamned anybody or even messed around with women, which made him an uncomfortably unusual pilot by our high fraternal standards. I went to church with him every Sunday.

"As a kid, I put my little sister Betty up in the cherry tree in our back yard. She sat in a nest wearing plumage on her head, cooing and generally acting nuts. I called her Coo Coo the Bird Girl and charged kids pennies to climb up and take a look at her.

"After that act, my old man beat the hell out of me, mostly because I had cut off all of Betty's hair. Dad never used a paddle on me; that would have been uncouth in his estimation. He used his fist encased in a glove. He took me in the barn and beat me. Mother would call out, 'Stop it, Bill. Stop this minute. You'll kill that boy.'

"My mouth and my teeth are all gone. Lots of beatings. He had a terrific left. It was typical of those days. Your dad was master of the house. He was king. He was king because he went at you— not with his razor strap or other feeble flourishes—but with his two gnarled fists. 'We'll go out in the barn and see who's the best man around here.'

"First thing I knew I felt that left hook connecting with my nose. I was flat on the floor. Now, Dad was a terrific man, I won't deny it. Boy, did he have arms.

"Dad had twenty-four head of whitefaced Hereford and Jersey cows. They all stayed in the woods. A stream flowed under those lovely Columbus woods and it was a good place for them to go in the summertime. We kids would go in there, too, and swim and make a dam. We'd have a swell time. Swim all day. We lay in the old mud and rolled around like hogs.

"Betty and I used to ride out on one of Dad's old

Interviewing a television commercial celebrity, Bill Sweet was a past master at making crowds laugh and enjoy themselves, regardless of what was happening in the air. (Bill Sweet collection)

work horses to gather the little pamphlets the pilots threw out to attract a crowd. (Just start throwing stuff out of an airplane any day and the public will swarm like ants.)

"When I was thirteen or so, two Jennys with Triangle Flying Service painted on their bellies landed in our field and tied up to the cherry tree. As usual, they had starting problems. The pilot gave me five dollars to bring as much motor Ethyl as I could bring home in a bottle. I rode on my bicycle to Doc Watson's Linden Pharmacy, got the liquid gold, and raced home again.

"The pilot measured the drops into the top of the spark plug, then counted down and started his engine. Bam! Bam! Bam! It sounded great. 'Get in the front cockpit,' the pilot yelled, so the first ride I had was an acrobatic ride—looping, spinning, all those things. My pals knew I was a hero. I wasn't a bit sick. Shorty Garing, the pilot, did snap rolls and a slow roll. Dust and dirt from the field flew into my face and water drenched me from the overflow. That sweet old Jenny.

"Then he cracked up that Jenny in the same little field. There was a ditch running through there and he hit it. He sheered a gear off, and Jenny rolled on her belly. Poor lovely Jen.

"One of the best memories of my boyhood was my meeting with the whole country's hero aviator, Frank Hawks, and scrubbing down his Travel Air *Mystery Ship*. I can still smell that old yellow bar soap. First I had to wipe down the whole plane. It had a big Wright engine which was a notorious oil dripper and oil thrower, and I cleaned it all up with gasoline.

"There wasn't much light in that old Curtiss-Wright hangar. I scooted under that airplane's belly and washed her down with octagon soap that had a lot of lye. It burned my hands to pieces. It was a cold night, wet and miserable, the lye soap running down my arms, making a little swamp in my armpits, but I felt tremendous pride when daylight came around. I barely got done in time. I fired up that big Wright engine, sat there in the cockpit, and imagined I was doing three, four hundred miles per hour. I was the great man Captain Frank Hawks flying cross-country. I said to myself, 'I'm over Wichita, Kansas, down there and I'm hellbent for Cleveland to win this race.' On the way, of course, I

established a new world's record for transcontinental flight.

"At sunrise, Frank showed up in a coon skin coat down to his ankles. He handed me thirty dollars. The great Captain Frank Hawks said, 'Willie, here's thirty dollars for a damn good job. I've got the sharpest plane on the line today.'

"It was Joe Mackey who really lured me into the airshow *business*. Joe simply said, 'Bill, there's something about your flair for the dramatic that's good. Better yet, I think it's commercial. I like it and I want you to go out and do air shows.'

"We went to Mount Vernon, Ohio. God, we had a crowd of people at twenty-five cents each. I had a guy who was crippled in his left arm taking in the money hand over fist as fast as he could. We showed to 100,000 people up there at the old Department of Commerce Airport.

"We traveled all over the United States, small towns especially. At first we weren't sponsored by anybody, but eventually we became the Linco Flying Aces, representing the Ohio Oil Company of Findlay, Ohio (now Marathon Oil).

"At first, people would simply hire us to come to their town. Some guy would say, 'Hey, you're the best damn announcer in the country, bud. I want you to announce my air show. How much you want?'

"I said, 'I want as much money as you're paying the top act on the bill. I'm just as much of that show as he is.' I got my money.

"At first I used a long megaphone, and learned to throw my voice, make it really boom. You huff it out, bounce it off buildings. The announcer was kind of owner, manager, everything rolled into one, like the role in *The Great Waldo Pepper*. My most important duty, though, was thinking up new ideas to get the crowd out. That's all I thought about. Get that crowd out! Get that money!

"Then as now, I looked at announcing as the heart of the show. My philosophy was to resist announcing for the pilots. I didn't care about pilots at all, or anybody who flew an airplane. I focused on the guy who had paid his twenty-five cents or his buck and a half to see that show.

"In announcing an air show, I made up most of my material, many times on the spot. Cobra roll was when a pilot climbed and rolled as he went up, then

There was never a connection between girls in snug swimsuits and aviation, but that didn't stop Bill Sweet from having scads of them perched on wings, propellers, and occasionally around the neck of a pilot. (Bill Sweet collection)

Bill Sweet was a frequent guest at the home of Zack Mosley, creator of the comic strip "Smilin' Jack." Many Mosley story lines were based on air race and air show events and newsmakers. (Bill Sweet collection)

capped off, sank, and came down in a fast spin. I called air shows sky tacklers. Everything was sky tackler or regal or Popeye the Circus Man. People used to say, 'You talk like a circus man, Bill Sweet.' I advertised everybody as a champion. Everybody was a captain or a lieutenant. Most of our fliers and jumpers had never been forty miles from home, but everybody had to have a title. Bill Sweet's Flying Circus (later the National Air Show, Inc., America's Prestige Airshow) offered nothing but Transatlantic World Fliers and Licensed Planes, Licensed Pilots. I'd quickly have about twelve Congressional inquiries on my hands if I tried that stunt today. No one's allowed to have fun anymore.

"One of my best pals of the thirties was Zack Mosley, creator of the comic strip, "Smilin' Jack." "Downwind" was in real life a captain with TWA. I was the character known as "Sil Bweet." Mosley picked out characters then in aviation news and built something around them. I'd go to his home in Stuart, Florida. He'd put me in the guest house and fill me up with eggs, bacon, and whiskey—good whiskey, too, no junk whiskey. I said, 'Zack, I brought along all kinds of input this trip.' We sat down with a tape recorder and I gave him new terms, many that I'd made up and used in the show, like flame-talking, which meant a guy who was mad.

"I had a marvelous snoring act. Took to snoring different types of snores. I could hold a crowd for two hours just on snores alone.

"I hardly talked about pilots at all. People weren't interested in that. Today, *you're* not interested in what plane is taking off to fly you somewhere, or who the pilot is or where he was born. Only one man I know had that glamour, Joe Mackey. When I later worked for his airline, passengers would say, 'We want Joe himself to fly us.' If the plane taxied up and someone else just as qualified was behind the stick, people would ask for their money back.

"I never told more about the planes than I had to. I just said 'I don't have to tell you much about *this* airplane—you can see for yourself.' Joe had a way to bring that aircraft straight up, then straight down, smoke just pouring out. Oh, how they ate that up.

"Preparation was never the key to good announcing. Say an airplane flew by. I told them some lie. 'He's doing five hundred miles per hour, folks. It's a spy plane from Germany up there. Flew nonstop.' All kinds of crazy stuff. The crowds just sat there and laughed like fools. I said, 'Give that performer a big hand, folks. Get your hankies out.' They waved their hankies. I said, 'I've never seen so many dirty hankies in all my life.'

"They applauded and said, 'That guy Sweet's always got an answer for you. Gotta remember that one.' Lot of guys today try to pick up the patter but they don't know the timing.

"People ask how I built my showbiz knack. Just a gift, that's all. It all sort of grew from Coo Coo the Bird Girl. Something about me loves things going on. One time I put a haystack on the other side of the hill from the crowd. They didn't know it was there. Long before showtime, I doused the haystack with oil and tar. Then as part of the act, I had a hot airplane go into a power dive. The crowd never saw

A rare view of Bill in the pilot's seat. Though an accomplished aviator, he was far more at home on the ground with a microphone in his hand. (Bill Sweet collection)

Historians of the National Air Races insist that the clown acts were by far the biggest crowd-pleasers though they rarely received the press they deserved. In 1931 Dewey Noyes put an old time pusher airplane through its paces in Cleveland. (Jim Borton collection)

him pull out because the hill obstructed their view. They just heard an explosion and saw a mountain of awful smoke.

"Well, I had confederates on the other side of the hill. As soon as the diving airplane was out of sight of the stands, my boys lit some powder and fired that tar-soaked hay. The illusion was perfect and though the plane simply pulled out of its spin and flew on down the valley, the crowd was certain he went into the ground. They emptied the stands in ten seconds and raced for the other side of the hill, eager to view the terrible remains.

"Not one demanded his money back when he learned it was all a fraud. Many said, 'You sure are a card, Bill Sweet.'

"I did a show in Sheldon, Iowa, when they were naming the local airport Roscoe Turner Field. On our way there, Roscoe and I took off in a Waco cabin plane with a Jacobs engine. We were halfway up there on the other side of Des Moines when the engine went out and Roscoe landed.

"Then we took off down this old dusty road on a swell hot afternoon in the early thirties. We walked up to a farmhouse. This old boy said, 'I'll take you two to town where you can get some transportation. You going to Sheldon, Iowa, to that World's Greatest Air Show?'

"Roscoe, standing there with his uniform on, said, 'Yeah, I'm Roscoe Turner.'

"That old guy turned white as a sheet. That's the way things were in those days. 'Roscoe Turner in my house? Sit down! Get you something to eat. Mother! We got celebrities here!'

"Hollering. We're standing on the back porch, flies all over the place. Lots of flies in those days.

"Meanwhile, the guy who brought us to the farmhouse had a balloon out back which he commenced to inflate with gas. Roscoe and I got in the little wicker basket and the thing went sailing across the fields. I yelled, 'Where the hell we going, Roscoe?'

"He said, 'Only place we can go is where there's another damn free meal or the gas goes bad.'

"Roscoe yelled to me to heave over sandbags. They went flying through orchards. The bags broke up, sand flew all over. Startled chickens soared into the air like exploding shell fragments. I loved the action. It was as though I was bombing something in the war.

"Later, the balloon envelope grew flabby. Roscoe yelled to a guy in a field, 'Hey, you know Clayton Folkerts, the airplane maker? Where's his place?'

"I can still see that fellow cupping his hands, yelling, 'Hey, Clayton Folkerts's right up here to the first road, turn to the left.' We sailed across some miserable field. Damn if he didn't land us almost in Folkerts's back yard.

"Roscoe loved the balloon business. He liked hooking a harness contraption around his arms so that it appeared to an audience that he was hanging on with his teeth. He flapped his arms like a bird. He ascended in balloons a number of times; it was just another way to make a buck.

"But giving airplane rides was still where the money was. We had to put up with all those dramatic farewell scenes. Before leaving this earth in my airplane, people embraced and kissed one another. Some even asked to hold mass right there in front of the wing. I've even seen them baptize a guy before he went up with me, and I couldn't pass up the temptation to make hay with that: 'Now, this chap's going to get baptized, folks. Step right up. No extra cost to watch it all.' People would come around, huddle in close and holler, 'Hallelujah!' and all that jazz. In the hillbilly community, fire and damnation preachers said, 'This man's being saved!' Down in Tennessee, after a ride, passengers got out of the airplane, dropped to their hands and knees, and kissed the ground. But I think they liked the rides.

"When the great and honorable Lieutenant Joseph Mackey performed his skywriting in the Bible Belt, folks really thought it was the Second Coming. I remember one old lady in Kentucky who raised her skirts and ran about, screaming, 'It's the Second Coming of Christ.' They were plenty confused when the sky message read Drink Pepsi-Cola. Nevertheless, they all hid underneath the bushes and houses. I couldn't resist saying, 'He's going to find you all *this* time. Hiding won't do sinners any good.'

"When they found out it was just a little airplane and some smoke, they didn't like me at all. They wanted it to be the Christ. But I can still see those preachers rolling on the ground screaming and yelling 'Repent. Repent now.'

"In Jackson there were cow manure patties all over the ground. Joe flew through these and they would splatter up all over the wings. I shouted, 'Now keep your heads on the inside, folks. You see what goes on around here.' Sometimes it got so thick on the aircraft that Joe stopped everything and said, 'Hey, boss, this is just getting to be too damned much!' I'd get a rag, dip it in the creek, and at least dilute the patties encrusted on the wings and fuselage. They were actually affecting the air flow of the craft and adding little to the general enjoyment of the experience.

"A real money-maker during some of those years was towing advertising banners. I made ten thousand dollars towing a banner that read Fight V.D., Wipe out V.D. Heck of a big campaign here in the state of Ohio. Did the banner-towing convince anybody? Hell, no. They went out and got more of it.

"In the old days, you really did an air show just to entice the public to take airplane rides. Towards that purpose, our show featured a reasonable dosage of sex. We, too, carried a woman out on the wing, just like *Waldo Pepper,* and purposely blew off her clothes. The girl wouldn't be standing up like you see today, she'd be sitting on the top center section of the plane with her legs draped over the leading edge of the wing.

"We called the one girl "Moll Woods"—Jesse Woods's wife. A piece of rawhide (which Moll pulled) loosely held on her clothes. The cord was strung through large eyelets. Next thing you knew, Moll just opened her arms wide (keeping one foot in a sort of stirrup) and the wind would get in there and blow the clothes clean off of her. It all came off. Guys nearly trampled themselves to death trying to catch Moll Woods's panties.

"A parachute jumper had a breakaway act, also, and would float down like an angel without a stitch on. When she yanked on that rip cord, her clothes blew away at the same time. Heck of a crowd as she touched down. No cops—policemen didn't do anything back in those days.

"When she landed she was escorted to a little tent. For an extra quarter you could see the little lady there. Taking her picture cost an extra two bucks.

"Prosperity was where you found it.

"They were hard times. The best place our stunt flier, Mike Murphy, had to sleep was in used cars. He'd go downtown to a used car lot, open a car door, and climb in. What's more, so many of the girls were spoiled in the thirties. Not too many would settle for behind the wooden horse on a merry-go-round or the wing of an airplane. They all thought of themselves as queens and preferred the grand style of a hotel bed, even if it was in the worst room in the joint.

"One time, Joe Mackey and I set up house in a pup tent in Jackson, Ohio. It started to rain and water came up over our arms in the tent and headed up my nose. I woke up and said, 'Hey, Joe, we sure hit the big time. I'm laying in the middle of the ocean.'

"Joe was always one good guy. He got me out of jail in Jackson. I got drunk in those days and I was out directing traffic wearing a flying suit with a big sign on the back: Bill Sweet's Flying Circus. They threw me in jail and through the bars I could see little airplanes going around. I yelled, 'I got to get out of here. Those airplanes are flying out there.'

"Sprung from the lock-up and driven to the show grounds the next morning, I could already hear folks yelling, 'Let me ride with that Red Devil, Joe Mackey.' The men all had tobacco juice cuds in their mouths as big as baseballs. When the men of Jackson, Ohio, threw away their cud, we were a hit for sure. When I saw all those hands smear across those farmers' mouths and juice thrown on the ground, I said, 'We've got them.'

"Joe Mackey was the epitome of the American idol. It is true he never flew without a hangover. He used to vomit in his gloves. He wore white silk gloves—it was one of the blurbs I used: Lieutenant Joseph C. Mackey flying with silk gloved hands. He used to take off those white silk gloves and throw them out of the cockpit, the puke dripping from them. He was sick from the booze.

"The Carter Hotel was racing headquarters in Cleveland. The booze that went through there! One airplane manufacturer sent a case of Four Roses whiskey to my room every morning for the little plugs I'd give him on the p.a. system. I invented little ways of letting him know I needed a refill. I said, 'I've a package here for you.' That meant I was all out of the liquid joy and wouldn't mind a second helping.

"Meanwhile, broads poured in and out of the

Every Bill Sweet show sported a Miss Golden Wings whose function was to pose for the spectators' cameras while standing on an airplane or anywhere else. Her other function was to kiss any male pilot who won anything at all. Melvin Robinson was eventually handed a trophy. (Bill Sweet collection)

Batman Red Grant performs his car to plane pickup trick. Assured show director Bill Sweet, "The stunt was deceptively simple; it was our most dangerous feat. Timing had to be precise, the guy could get the soles dragged right off his shoes, and the plane easily could have suffered excessive drag and crashed, dragging the stunter along the ground." (Bill Sweet collection)

Carter like syrup over pancakes. I've seen the pilots get thoroughly acquainted with them right there in the stairwell. Couldn't wait to get upstairs. A lot of companies picked up the tab, contributing to morale in general.

"One of my saddest memories is about Earl Ortman. He died in my arms in Fort Lauderdale, Florida. I was working for Mackey Airlines, and went into this bar called The Deck right along the inland waterway of Fort Lauderdale. Suddenly I heard a guy in front of the place. He peered in at the doorway as if straining to find someone he knew. He saw me and called, 'Hey, Bill. Bill Sweet. Let me in the door, Bill.'

"I started for the door, but just as I reached for it, he just went down. I grabbed hold and sort of cradled him on the floor.

"Earl said, 'I'm—I'm done in, Bill.' He died right there. He was a tiny guy, but what a hell of a racing pilot. A lady's man? Probably. He was married to a French girl from Quebec, a six million dollar looking gal. His problem was the booze. Too damn bad.

"One thing we were big on was parachute acts, but there were a good many injuries. Opening one of those early chutes was like putting a rope around your neck and running full speed—about nine g's. Jerked them all to pieces. There were injuries, especially to the back. Knocked the vertebrae out. Hitting ground was also dangerous in the early chutes—about equal to a twenty foot free-fall jump. Then, if the wind was blowing twenty miles per hour, you took real physical abuse.

"The movie *Gypsy Moth,* which made Burt Lancaster famous, was about a touring company of parachutists that featured the Bat Cape Act. In real life, that was the act of our own Bat Man, Red Grant. In the movie, the jumper came out of the plane and slammed into the ground. They explained that the cape he had worn had a hypnotic effect on the jumper, a fixation, we called it. The delusion that you had no need to pull the cord was true to life. Red Grant would get fixation and come down straight as an arrow. I was often so sure he was going to crash straight into the ground. His mind told him he didn't have to pull the cord. Every man I ever had who did the Bat Wing always thought he could land without the parachute. Somehow, wearing that floating cape, weird things happened in your mind during your plunge. You were in a different world.

"Then again, they always dreaded the sudden opening, which sometimes nearly tore them out of the chute. It jarred the whole skeletal frame, beat the hell out of them, and sometimes even knocked them senseless. Today, of course, parachutes have been completely redesigned. They've slowed up that opening blast. Touchdown is almost an enjoyable experience.

"Wind currents used to be another problem. One man, an Irishman named Patrick O'Timmons, once opened his parachute and went straight up! O'Timmons hadn't even been drinking, but he had an awful time. My ace, Harold Krier, went up and started circling around. He tried to catch O'Timmons in his prop blast and *blow* him back to the airport.

"We also had Santa Clauses jumping out of our airplanes. One landed inside the Mansfield, Ohio, Reformatory and caused quite a stir. They had many cops on the scene, a pack of cruisers wailing their sirens, spotlights flashing all over the place, Thompson submachine guns at the ready—all because of Santa Claus on the end of a parachute.

"Another of our Santas landed in the Ohio River. That didn't go over at all. Kids on the shore cried, 'Don't drown our Santa Claus.' That was bad for business.

"I used to invent names for our fliers that the newspapers would go for, such as Cannonball Mast from Mansfield, Ohio, who jumped parachute at night holding a flashlight and almost got run over by a train at Athens, Ohio. I had 100,000 people out that night, all screaming 'Open up that parachute, Cannonball.'

"I said, 'He won't be able to hear me but if you all yell loud enough . . .'

"'Open up that chute, Cannonball. Hell, open it up!' Together, we watched his black shadow drop down, down.

"Then I said, 'He's going to get killed, sure as heck.' As I looked to the south of the airport, I could see a fast freight train bearing down as Cannonball drifted casually toward those westbound tracks. It looked for a while like a tie for sure, an obviously fatal situation. But old Cannonball landed smack-dab between the rails and without hesitation threw his body into a somersault, out of danger.

"And if some guy *was* killed? Oh, the crowds didn't care, except that it held up the next act. If he was killed, they ran to the point of impact with their handkerchiefs and sopped up the blood. I saw them do that in the Thompson Trophy race in Cleveland.

"When the trailing edge of a wing came off Doug Davis's plane, I saw him go into the ground. I roared over there with the rescue squad. He was beyond rescue. I saw him lying there and people were yelling, 'Here, take *my* handkerchief. Dip down in that blood.' They sat on the ground and wrote on the handkerchief for posterity whose blood it was and all the statistics.

"At Akron, Rod Jocelyn looped, came around, stalled out, did an inverted spin, brought it out, and went into the ground. There was an explosion. A guy in the crowd says, 'I know where that pilot is, Bill. You're not kidding us this time. He's standing on the other side of that fire there. I saw him jump out before the airplane hit.'

"That airplane hit so hard, it bounced and turned around right there in front of the crowd at Akron-Canton Airport. Did he get out? No, he was killed. It was one time I didn't have a surprise happy ending for the act. Rod's airplane was a Dart with a 220 horsepower Continental engine in it. His gas tank fractured and sprayed flaming fuel all over that field.

"I think our greatest promotion had to be the great grudge race between Harold Distlehorst and the fair and fabulous Lieutenant Joseph Mackey. It was totally staged, of course (though the script was altered at will) but we advertised it as real.

"I made up a story about mysterious people fiddling with Joe Mackey's airplane, and I told the commander of the Ohio National Guard, 'Hey, we need help out here. I think they're spies for Distlehorst.' So they came out, actually set up camp at old Norton Field, even dug in a machine gun placement. It made the front page of practically every newspaper in Ohio. You never saw so many people in all your life as showed up at old Norton Field in Columbus that day. Reporters and cameramen were everywhere snapping away at this great grudge airplane race.

"Mackey pulled a good one that day. He climbed from the front seat to the back seat of his airplane in mid-air to coax a little more speed out of his machine. Mackey owned a little bar and eatery called The Black Cat, so even before the epic was over, I told the crowd, 'You'll all want to relax after all this history making today. You'll all want to buy a beer off of Joe Mackey across the street as soon as this epic spectacle goes into the history books in ten more minutes.'

"It was also Mackey's idea to rig a siren on his airplane, but sometimes it wouldn't turn off. You could sure hear that airplane coming into Jackson, Ohio, right down over the poor farm. We had to drive through the poor farm to get to the airport. Folks there were dead broke. We were dead broke, too—but we had ideas!

"We were in a promotion *all of the time*. Take, for example, the dairy promotion. We had transported a dairy calf aboard our trimotor during the Indiana air tour. Just imagine sixty planes flying together from airport to airport, making three stops a day. We had just one dairy calf aboard our plane and a bunch of dancing girls. Once in the air, the calf got sicker and sicker all over this gorgeous fourteen-passenger airplane, wetting and doing the other and throwing it all over the place. The dancing girls, splattered head to toe with nature's own, swore their aviation days were finished as soon as we either crashed or landed. Oh God, it burned your eyes something terrible, just like acid. I can still hear Joe screaming 'Goddam you, Bill. You and your damn promotions. I'm gonna break your ass.' He did, too.

"Another time, south of Windfall, Indiana, during a great horse promotion, a handsome animal came aboard our plane from the Steel Pier at Atlantic City. In western films they hobble a horse with rope around its front feet and back feet. Well, don't do it in an airplane. A few thousand feet in the air, this critter broke loose and started going round in circles. She kicked her head off and slugged me with two hind hooves to the chest. With a single lurch, she headed straight for the door into three thousand feet of space.

"She kicked all the way down. I saw her land, on her back, feet straight up in the air, in the middle of a cornfield. Before she took to flight, that horse had kicked man-sized holes right through the roof covering of that airplane. We quit the animal transportation business soon after that.

"I've painted old Joe Mackey in bright colors, even if he occasionally called me bad names. Just once was Joe truly scared. It happened at the Blue Grass Airport in Lexington, Kentucky. He was upside down doing a snaproll when all the fabric came off his left upper wing. He landed the airplane and just sat there. He wouldn't even bring her in. I had some other boy fire her up and taxi her in. Mackey walked over and said, 'How'd that look, Bill?'

"I said, 'That looked good, Chief.'

"He said, 'Good enough act to quit on?'

"I said, 'Good enough to quit on.'

" 'Okay,' he said, 'I quit.'

"He left in a cab from the Bluegrass Airport. He did come back after that, however. He got his nerve back and started flying for the Army on regular

Tommy Boyd, like Batman Red Grant, used the bat cape as a specialty act. With his arms outstretched during a fall, the cape would cause him to soar and float, at times creating the delusion that he could land safely without opening his chute. (Bill Sweet collection)

Wing walker Shirley Stafford was killed in Florida when the lower left wing of this airplane snapped off in level flight in a fluke accident during the filming of Bill Sweet's National Air Show for a television special. Said Sweet, "Shirley wore a parachute and normally could have instantly freed herself from her support wires. Perhaps she was in shock. She still stood astride the wing as it struck the earth. Her pilot burned in the crash." (Bill Sweet collection)

When Charlie Hillard first went to work for Bill Sweet's National Air Shows, Sweet described him as "an engineering student at Georgia Tech, a tall, rawboned Texas kid with a squeaky voice." He hired him because he listened, and Hillard soon grew into a smart and flashy sensation. Said Sweet, "Genius aviators who won't listen don't live very long." (Bill Sweet collection)

Harold Krier was a later year pilot hero on the National Air Show payroll. He was less flashy than the dashing Joe Mackey of earlier years, but he could make airplanes do everything but dance. (Bill Sweet collection)

A special heavy tank of light oil was built into Harold Krier's aerobatic airplane for dramatic smoke trails during stunts. (Bill Sweet collection)

active duty. And he flew air shows on Sundays until the eve of World War II.

"I should end on a positive note—the story of the crash into the cathouse. All hands safe and accounted for; one delayed. I'm thinking of the Harold Neumann-Len Povey collision. 'Butterfingers' Roy Hunt rammed them and they both crashed. It occurred over Wilmington, Delaware, all in the spirit of good, clean fun. Povey was flying a Waco taperwing which was struck by Hunt's Great Lakes in a fit of foolishness. Neumann had no chute and Povey did, but Len Povey stuck with his buddy all the way down.

"Povey somehow managed to land at the airport with wide open throttle. The brakes locked and the aircraft slid the entire length of the field and ground looped at the end of the airstrip, knocking off a wing-tip.

"Meanwhile, Hunt's plane, by a stroke of luck, spun into a lodging with young ladies' services. Moments later, 'Butterfingers' landed his parachute fairly close to his plane. Gallantry prevailed and he knocked on the door of the establishment to let them know he was the man who had jumped out of the airplane that had just crashed into their abode.

"I believe the girls administered to him and were of a forgiving nature."

A fan reacts to a Harold Krier stunt at Columbus, Ohio. (Bill Sweet collection)

Mike Murphy

World Premier Acts

Modern glider technology has its roots in the considerable experience and research of Ohioan Mike Murphy. There isn't much he hasn't done, from wing-walking and skywriting to leading the gliders in the invasion of Normandy. In that landing in total darkness, the brakes on his *Fighting Falcon* failed, and his glider coasted into trees within fifteen feet of a German reconnaissance tank column. Murphy survived and was the first D-Day Normandy casualty returned to the United States. He is just as proud of being the first to land a pontoon seaplane on land.

In his salad days as a hungry barnstormer, Murphy employed his share of fraud and good humor to stay in groceries, while his more noble peers dropped out of aviation for lack of imagination or too much principle. Later, in the biggest air spectacle ever staged in Cleveland, he was paid $1,000 a throw to conceive and execute world premier flying acts.

"For many years, aviation was joyrides for passengers, plus a little instructing. On a weekday,

I picked out a town of no more than a thousand or two people. At a thousand feet, I selected a field, one with a gate to the road. Then, in the true American tradition, I did a couple of snap-rolls, loops, and somersaults to attract attention, landed, and started my spiel.

"When I grew more experienced, I would first do some loops, rolls, and wingovers. As they came running over to the field, I looped, stalled, and threw out a dummy from the front seat. A pair of overalls stuffed with straw, it fell with limbs flailing. The crowd rushed out. When they saw it was a dummy, and that I wasn't killed, they were usually just amused—and I sold rides.

"We did every possible trick to draw attention. It was so much per ride; I never passed the hat. If I sold five dollars worth of rides on a weekday, I was doing all right. I carried people for as little as twenty-five cents, but that was part of an advertised deal. In Kokomo, Indiana, the ad read AIRPLANE RIDES 25ᶜ. The price was in huge numerals. In smaller print was 'from 7 to 8 o'clock Sunday morning.' From eight to nine and from nine to ten, the price rose until it reached a dollar. The advertising brought people out anyway. The plane rides were a little short, too.

"Sometimes we even purposely turned one of our planes smack on its nose in a field and plopped ourselves on the ground. People motoring by were shocked. They couldn't resist planting their brakes; jumping out, and racing to see if we both were dead. When they got close, of course they could tell it was simply a ruse. A few voted to hang us on the spot, but most of the time everybody laughed. True, the act lacked dignity, but we usually sold a good many airplane rides.

"I did do one thing that was crooked as hell. I should have been ashamed of myself. I advertised a parachute jump in the newspaper. I set her down early in the afternoon. The parachute jump was advertised for four or five o'clock. I carried a balloon chute because I could pack it myself, and because it was foolproof.

"About three o'clock I paused in my passenger hopping and looked all around. I asked the crowd, 'Has anybody seen my parachute jumper? He certainly should be here by now. Well, I'll go ahead and give more rides. Somebody call out when he arrives, you hear?'

"Well, he never showed up, of course, because

There isn't much Murphy hasn't done, from wing-walking and skywriting to leading the invasion gliders in the invasion of Normandy. In that landing in total darkness, the brakes of his glider, Fighting Falcoln, failed to hold, and the craft coasted into trees within fifteen feet of a German reconnaissance tank column. Murphy survived and was the first D-Day Normandy casualty returned to the U.S. He is just as proud of being the first to land a pontoon seaplane on land. (Mike Murphy collection)

Mike Murphy and friends, including his most prized possession, the Freddy Lund Trophy for Aerobatic Flying (right). Lund still is considered the greatest aerobatic flyer who ever lived. His stunts served as the model for scenes in The Great Waldo Pepper. *(Mike Murphy collection)*

there wasn't any parachute jumper. Always some young man in the crowd—once or twice a girl—cried out, 'Hey, I'd like to try it.' I dumped them out and that was the parachute jump.

"In a scene in the *Great Waldo Pepper* the girl perched far out on the wing, frozen with fear, ultimately falls to her death. The story was fiction, yet it was taken from an incredible true incident that involved Freddy Lund and the Gates Flying Circus.

"At one particular show, a nightclub girl talked Gates of Gates Flying Circus into letting her make a parachute jump. Of course they spread her figure and everything across full-page ads.

"They used balloon chutes in their acts. The parachute container was like a bushel basket made of canvas. The parachute was packed like today, but the end was tied to the bottom of the bag. The whole bag was tied to the airplane. At the end of the parachute was a ring, on which four ropes were tied with a big snap hook. As the girl jumped, she would pull directly on the ring which pulled the chute out of the bag. The chute bag stayed with the airplane.

"Clyde Pangborn was flying her and a second

Aerobatic star Bevo Howard in an inverted maneuver in his Jungmeister airplane was a master of all of the air maneuvers created in the 1930s, plus many of his own. A man who won flying exhibitions all over the world, Bevo was killed in this airplane on October 17, 1971, performing an inverted pickup. The aircraft was rebuilt for display in the Smithsonian Institution. (Bill Sweet collection)

Cockpit of the Ford Trimotor that stunt pilot Harold Johnson looped, starting at an altitude of fifteen feet. The six-ton, fourteen-place ship was a standard airliner. Harold later did a complete aerobatic routine in a four-engine Lockheed Constellation airliner and was scheduled to do it for the Cleveland Air Race crowd. The act was even printed in the program, then mysteriously cancelled. The airlines probably didn't want Johnson showing their pilots what he could do with an airliner. (Bill Sweet collection)

pilot by the name of Gritton went along to keep the girl from getting tangled up in the props and the wires. He spotted her, and let her go.

"But her slight weight wouldn't pull the chute out of the bag! This gal was hanging twenty feet below the airplane. They couldn't land.

"Gritton got down in the landing gear. He tried to pull her up, but the rope was oily and he just wasn't strong enough with that wind force. They kept circling.

"Freddy Lund had been in the hospital. The authorities let him out for only one day to visit friends at the air show. Lund witnessed the predicament, got hold of another pilot, took off immediately in another plane, and came over close to Pangborn's airplane. Just out of the hospital and weaker than hell, Lund then actually walked from the wing of his plane onto the wing of Pangborn's aircraft!

"Those guys didn't use parachutes. Lund got down in the landing gear of Pangborn's airplane with Gritton, but not even the two of them could do the job.

"By this point, they were running low on gas. Lund climbed back up and walked back on the wing. Lund exchanged places in the cockpit with Pangborn. A big rawboned man from Montana, Pangborn went down in the landing gear. He and Gritton pulled her up through the landing gear before they ran out of gas. Upon landing, the trio simply rolled off the landing gear. They were hardly scratched."

Murphy laughed, punching his fist on the arm of his chair. "The utter nonchalance of one man going up and walking onto another airplane is typical of the first generation of barnstormers. Lund was to aerobatics what Caruso was to opera, and a little more."

"Those were marvelous days. Life was fun and giddy and every day was different. For awhile I flew in conjunction with a local carnival. The owner's good-looking wife sold tickets. She also participated in the girly show. You paid so much, they showed you a little. You paid more and retired to the back of the tent where one girl showed her all. The owner of the show had a sense of propriety. When it was his wife's turn to strip down, he'd say, 'Mike, please don't go in tonight.'

"I was single, and he would always try to get me girls, but I was broke. I often slept behind the horse on the merry-go-round. Girls at that time were down and out, too, but they had standards. Down behind the merry-go-round was pretty far down the road for them, and it wasn't the best thing for a backache.

"In barnstorming, it was frequently difficult to get home by sundown. Night flying was suicidal. The most promising temporary stopover was a farmer's pasture. It was good to ask permission to sleep in the haystack. Almost all the time, permission was granted. Maybe fifteen percent of the time they'd invite you to sleep in their barn.

"On one such occurrence I was almost asleep in that warm, dry barn, aware of how incredibly fortunate I had been. There was a gentle rap on the big barn door, and a lovely young girl suddenly appeared with a tray of food. At first she just stood there. Then such a sweet smile swept that youthful face. I was sure I was dreaming. 'Daddy says you might want a sandwich and some coffee,' she purred. She handed me the food but instead of turning on her heels and retiring, she knelt slowly in the hay at my elbow. 'If you want anything else,' she added in a whisper that was baby soft, yet almost guttural, 'we'll have to hurry.'

"She was just at that curious age.

"Several years later I passed through that town again. I found on good authority that she had married the local druggist and had two marvelous children. It seemed the best news I had heard in weeks.

"When I first went to Cleveland in 1936 with my 300-horsepower taperwing, I did straight aerobatics. The next year I was talking with acquaintances Cliff and Phil Henderson, who managed the big National Air Races. Cliff said, 'We ought to introduce something new.' I described an idea I was going to try in our own air show. I had been flying over Iowa one day in a small airplane when I spotted a freight train. I dropped down, put my wheels on a freight car, and just sat there for a little while. I figured I could land an airplane on top of an automobile in the same fashion, except that I would stop it altogether.

"Cliff said, 'If you'll do that, it'll be a world premier and that's how we'll introduce it. I'll give

One time U.S. power stunt champion Ray Miller taxies in from a National Air Show stunting routine in his clipped-wing Boeing Special. (Bill Sweet collection)

you a thousand dollars every year to introduce a world premier act in Cleveland.' That sounded like a hell of a lot of money then.

"I worked six months before I got the act down. I built a rack on top of the car and nailed two-by-four chocks around the wheel positions. We then put

the airplane in those chocks. Taking off worked, as I knew it would. Now how could I park the wheels right in those chocks? Even if I could do it, what would keep the plane from nosing over when the car slowed?

"I invented a few things to secure the tail on

Rod Jocelyn rolls in the wind somewhere over the state of Ohio in his famous clipped-wing Dart. The shortened wide-chord wings and big, closely cowled engine were his easily spotted trademarks. (Bill Sweet collection)

landing, but the arrangement still wasn't satisfactory. Finally the idea came to me in a dream. It was so simple. On top of the rack I cut two holes a half-inch larger in all dimensions than the tires. When the tires went down in those holes, the wheels were held so firmly that they couldn't move. Then the driver of the car just freewheeled it to a stop.

"Well at that point, it wasn't too much of a trick. It was, in fact, so easy that I had to make it look hard to make an act out of it. I came in, put a wheel on the car, and just rode there for a few seconds, sensing whether the car was at the right speed. If it wasn't, I pulled the wheel over to rock the car. I jumped off the car, came down, and bounded off again. I also gave a thumbs forward or back sign to tell the driver five miles per hour faster or slower.

"The second time I came on and again bounced around a little bit as if it was very difficult. On the third approach I put one wheel into the slot and just let it drop in.

"A few years later the world premier was my upside-down airplane. I had a cracked-up E-2 Cub in the hangar and a lot of extra parts. With the help of an engineer with whom I was doing test flights, I built an airplane with wheels top and bottom. In '39 I took off and landed in Cleveland upside down. There really wasn't too much trick to it. When we built the plane, we built it so that when I was upside-down, the engine was right side up and vice versa. Then we just reversed the fuselage — put the fuselage upside-down—but the wings had to be right side up for lift, because I was moving so fast. When I was upside-down I did have positive lift. It made a good act. So for that I got another thousand dollars.

"I tried to be reasonably careful. I wanted a safety pilot while perfecting the act, although I never used him in the act itself. A sheet of plywood was the seat. We called the plane the "cheek to cheek" because one guy sat on the top, the other on the bottom of the sheet. The controls ran straight through. The first few times I tried the top side, then I tried it on the bottom. The top cockpit was then closed and became part of the belly.

"Most people assume that taking off and landing upside down must be tricky. Well, I had had so much practice that it was just normal. There were a few problems I hadn't counted on, however. Personal fatigue came not from flying but from the exercise of getting into the bottom of the cockpit, pulling myself up into position, putting on the harness. I was tired before I started.

"I was never oriented while starting upside down. Until I got to two or three hundred feet, and could turn over, I was never oriented. I picked a landmark at the airport, like a smokestack, to move toward on takeoff.

"The approach was hardest because the field was hidden. Hanging head first, I couldn't see anything. I gunned the motor, pushed up the nose, took a look, pulled back the motor, let the nose down—until I was over the boundary and it was easy.

"For quite a few years I tried to keep ahead of the game in this world premier deal. The act nobody knows about, which we worked on for two years, was lowering an airplane by parachute. I bought a fifty-foot parachute from some guy on the West Coast, but was never successful with it. I sold it to some fellow in Cincinnati when I went into the Army. I saw him use it—I think it was in '46—in Miami. It worked, except that when the airplane hit ground, the parachute didn't collapse. Without a fast way to unhook the silk, the ground wind just jerked that airplane to pieces across the field.

"My early competitor, Joe Mackey, is inclined to tell people that in aerobatics if you wanted to go on living, you played to the crowd, not the other pilots. I never thought of it that way, but Joe was inclined to go out on a limb more than I. In order to stay in the business, you had to play to the other pilots, too, because their saying 'That guy is good,' meant everything in prestige and bookings.

"The best piece of advice I've ever had was what Wallace Beery told Roscoe Turner, 'Never turn the little kids away.' If you wish to ignore the adults, okay. If you choose to turn tail on your peers, fine and dandy. But never turn away the little kids. At the airports of yesteryear curious young people always wanted to talk to the pilot, to see and touch an airplane. I never turned down one who wanted to see my ship. I even made money by it, for years later people asked me to teach them to fly simply because I had been nice to them one afternoon when they were young.

"I've autographed bare backs a number of times,

arms, pieces of paper. The soles of slippers. I've autographed everything but a woman's breasts. You want to be noticed, but the people never stop crowding you. First one is jamming against you, then another and another. After a half hour or so it gets damn tiresome. You can't excuse yourself and come back another time. You do it then or never, and, dammit, you have to do it. I've done it until my head ached for an hour, and was sorry I ever got myself in such a mess."

8

The Press Called Me Superman on Page 1 while Shoveling Me into the Ground on Page 6

Roscoe Turner

Roscoe Turner was the most popular racing pilot who ever lived. He dressed the role of the hero, sponsored breakfast cereal and motor oil, and starred in his own radio show. He won three Thompson Trophy races, two more than anyone else except Cook Cleland, the Pacific war ace who notched two Thompson victories in the 1940s.

A sweltering, scary day at the tenth annual National Air Races, frozen in time, swam back into focus ten years ago in a little cement block museum in Indianapolis, a building the great flier called his Roscoe Turner Memorial to Speed. That day we found out what had really happened thirty-four years before when the sky hero's little bronze bullet shot into a cloud of smoke.

The aging Turner addressed a small group from behind a makeshift desk in a temporary office rigged up in his still new museum. Around its walls were scores of speed trophies, plaques, scrolls, mementos, memorabilia, shoe boxes of historic letters still to be put in place, and there, in the center of the floor, his 1939 Thompson Trophy-

winning airplane, looking hours old, regal, splendid, and proud.

Gray-white now, Turner's mustache was, as ever, meticulously waxed. His military tie had given way to an American eagle string tie and herringbone jacket, an American flag and military citation pin decorated his lapel. But the whole ensemble drooped and sagged on a sadly hollowed frame. His shoulders and head stooped. The feet, over a third of a century, had slowed to a painful shuffle.

"I was no different than Earl Ortman or Rudy Kling or Charlie Lindbergh—any of them—when it came to prerace jitters," Turner whispered, coughing into one fist. "No matter how many newspapers turn you into a superman, an immortal," he grinned weakly, "you're still a man inside, you don't quite feel like dying, and you're generally scared as hell."

Colonel Turner finished first in the Thompson Trophy 100-mile closed-course pylon race in 1934. When he came back to try again the following year, he was the darling of the crowd but the target of the press. "One win is enough," one writer snarled in

Roscoe with his first wife in Los Angeles in 1936. His mustache measured six inches and as he smiled, the waxed ends shot upwards like a bullfighter's banderillas. (Frederick C. Crawford Auto and Aviation Museum)

twenty-four point type. Some never had liked Turner, saying he was more a showboat and circus clown than serious aviator.

Roscoe always had a boundless enthusiasm, and incorrigible dash. In his barnstorming days he was the picture of sartorial splendor in whipcord riding trousers, Sam Browne belt, glistening boots, blue tunic, visored cap, and pointed mustache. It was not uncommon for his business suits to be vested, with gold watch chain, his freshly pressed ensemble complemented by spats, bowler, and gloves.

When popular cartoonist Zack Mosley looked

about him for a model to exemplify the noble, dashing American male (much as youthful radio listeners across the nation identified with Jack Armstrong, the "all-American boy") he decided on Roscoe Turner. He named his comics hero, "Smilin' Jack."

"Hero or no, at times superstition clawed at the gut despite all that reason and logic could do," Roscoe grunted, digging it all up again. "When I came back to try to win a second consecutive year in 1935, even I had a premonition. No one had won the Thompson Trophy twice—or had tried to. It asked too much of luck. One newspaper printed my obituary in advance and delivered it to my room at the Carter Hotel the night before the big one. They did that for as long as I raced in Cleveland.

"That anxious night in 1935 I had myself so boiled up about it, I couldn't sleep. I lay in bed trying to figure out what would happen if a wing came off or if I were sitting in a position where the wire would come back and chop my neck. I got up finally and went out to the airport about one in the morning and just stood there checking to see where everything was, whether the wires would catch me or not, whether I could get out.

"By morning I was so exhausted and feverish I would have had my backup fly the race if the newspaper hadn't made me into some kind of superhuman on page 1 even while their obituary writers were putting me into the ground on page 6."

There was fair and objective reporting, too.

"Colonel Turner knows perfectly well the odds are against him," one man wrote, "and that most racing pilots die in their cockpits. He doesn't deny that the glory and money are worth it, though winnings are immediately thrown into some bigger, faster, better ship with which to try it all over again next year. Racing is in his blood like a strong, intoxicating wine."

That afternoon in 1935, Turner led the grueling pylon classic all the way, setting a terrific pace. His tiny racer roared down the straightaway before the grandstand, starting its final lap. Then it happened. A black plume of smoke burst from the plane's underbelly. Then flames. With victory virtually within his grasp, his engine's supercharger threw a blade while turning thirty thousand revolutions a minute and chewed up the entrails of his engine.

The prop stopped and the motor belched oil and smoke which drenched his helmet and goggles.

Recalling the incident in the quiet of his museum thirty-four years later, excitement churned up in him again.

"I had the Thompson all sewed up. I even had it figured how to pay off my creditors with the $22,000 prize money. I said to myself, 'Roscoe, you show these rascals you've got *speed*' (because I hadn't had it wide open yet). I reached up and hit the throttle. The damn thing blew up. Smoke poured into the cockpit, blinding me. The air was choking. I couldn't breathe.

"Down below the crowd was yelling, 'Jump! Jump!' They could see the smoke trailing out of the plane. This was what they had come to see. Nobody had eyes for the winner Harold Neumann, flashing across the line. Everybody was watching my job in the sky. The race with death was the center of attraction.

"Jump? With that first squirt of oil I had instinctively pulled back on the stick, gunned the engine, climbed up to where I could get out all right with the parachute. But, hell, I thought, I just dropped the prize money. If I lose the ship, they'll put me in jail for life.

"With next to no engine left, I stuck with it. You don't want to see your ship go, if you can help it. And there was a chance. I headed down fast, and leveled off. The wheels hit. I thought surely the whole floor had fallen out. The plane bounced fifty feet in the air, and was heading for the stands so when she bounced a second time, I locked the right wheel and that turned her around, but still the big plane skidded to within a few feet of the crowds, right into that big white winners circle. I was down and safe.

"I heard the announcer say, 'Oh, my goodness, folks, that Turner is really putting on a *show* today.'

"Hell, I was glad to get down on the ground without killing anyone. Somebody took my picture showing my eyes big as fists."

He was pressed for autographs. "I'm sorry, boys," the champ said wearily, "I just can't make my wrist do it today."

"Tough luck, Turner," said a reporter racing up to the ship. "That's the damnedest luck we've ever

Roscoe in 1969: "When I get so old I can't come here and look over the field and hear the engines, I want to die."
(Photo by Bob Hull)

"The night before the Thompson in '35, I had myself so boiled up I couldn't sleep." (Photo by Bob Hull)

The all-time most incredible Bendix transcontinental race happened in 1935. Racing from Los Angeles to Cleveland, Ben O. Howard, in the center, beat Turner by twenty-three seconds. Vincent Bendix, sponsor of the cross-country speed race, stands at the right. (Frederick C. Crawford Auto and Aviation Museum)

Ben O. Howard

Winner Bendix Trophy Race 1935 Los Angeles to Cleveland 8 Hrs. 33 Min. 16.3 Sec.

Thompson Trophy victor in 1935, Harold Neumann, is congratulated by Roscoe Turner. The victory was a near miracle since the fuel lines of Harold's Benny Howard racer, Mr. Mulligan, *were so clogged at takeoff that he could barely clear the field. (Jim Borton collection)*

seen."

"What do you mean, tough luck?" said Turner, trying to be calm and making a mess of it. "Anytime you can get down and walk away from it, that's good luck. Hell, I'm just as happy as if I had sense."

Roscoe leaned back in his chair, closed his eyes momentarily. The juices were flowing now.

"I remember back in 1932," he sighed wearily. "I was talking with one of our foremost airplane manufacturers out at his plant. He expressed a typical opinion regarding the radial engine. 'Roscoe,' he said, 'you'll never build a 300 mile per hour airplane around a radial engine. And you know it.'

"Did I, though? That year Jimmy Wedell, another 'dummy', and I worked out a new scheme for streamlining the radial engine and making it fit better into our little racing jobs to cut down the big bulk of frontal resistance area—solely on the basis

The all-silver Laird-Turner Special. (*Rudy Profant collection*)

of what we hadn't learned and didn't know.

"Then came the races. We didn't get 300 miles per hour. But I made 270, and Jimmy got 280 out of his. Together we pushed Jimmy Doolittle, who won, up to 290 miles per hour with his in-line engine. It proved we were on the right track. Engineers weren't so sure it couldn't be done after that.

"Of course," he hesitated, "at first we overdid it. I mean the wing came off. It was too strong, too stiff. But we took care of that."

"Then came the famous NACA cowling which wrapped up the radial engine in a streamlined package. I tried it out on the new racer. And we got the extra ten miles per hour or better. It was at a time when neither the Army, the Navy, nor the National Advisory Committee for Aeronautics had much money to spend for experimentation. They welcomed our trying out ideas at the races."

Roscoe Turner really got down to business with the big, powerful *Laird-Turner Special* incorporating the know-how gained from hundreds of miles of pylon racing. Popular designers Larry Brown and Matty Laird both had a hand in building and rebuilding the ship to Turner's specifications. As a matter of routine, Laird registered the swift ship as the Laird-Turner Racer, an act which infuriated Turner as long as he lived. Nevertheless, the macho machine won the Thompson Trophy for Roscoe in 1938 (over 283 miles per hour) and in 1939 at better than 282 miles per hour. Pesco and the Champion Sparkplug Company paid the bills.

"Again, in 1939, the skeptics said I couldn't get two thousand horsepower out of a new Pratt & Whitney engine. I souped the thing up until everytime I ran it full throttle, even on the ground, I thought it would just take off, rip itself out, and leave the ship standing there, but it didn't. I won the Thompson that year with it. Even the engine manufacturers said it couldn't be done. But I had more than two thousand horsepower in that job. And the engine held together in the air.

"A few years later they were flying Thunderbolt fighter planes with more than two thousand horsepower, using the NACA improved cowling and knocking the Germans out of the sky with one of the best and the most famous fighter planes of World War II.

"The design for that plane, incidentally, was first conceived in the Seversky XP-35 pursuit. Jackie Cochran, the gal who always gave us males a big challenge for glory, proved this design in the cross-country Bendix race. Even the Army began looking favorably on it after her record.

"You can point to many other things, big and small. For a long time, for instance, military aircraft of all types had a big and cumbersome windshield design. It looked like somebody just threw up a bay window, and to hell with trying to streamline it. Racing pilots taught the designers how to do it. Probably more than anybody else, they are responsible for the bubble canopies of today.

"It's the same with landing gears. Some of the little racers introduced the wheel-pants streamlining device. They also incorporated some of the first retractable gears. Although these were never too successful in the races until the Army, the Navy, and industry had improved them, the racers pioneered the idea.

"They also pounded into some thick brains that propellers could stand a lot of redesign. Eliminate the big hub area, for example, to cut down on unnecessary air disturbance around the nose.

"I remember, too, that once while testing my racing plane, I accidentally got the prop in reverse. Still scared over the braking reaction, I went back up and tried it out intentionally. I think it was the first time that anybody included a report of mine in a suggestion to the Air Corps people at Wright Field.

"Today the use of the propeller as an air brake is a pretty big item. For instance, it made it possible for the big B-29s to land on short island runways in World War II.

"That's what air racing has done.

"The Jimmy Wedells, the Jimmy Doolittles, Art Chesters, Harold Neumanns, and all the others—some of them killed and forgotten, some of them still plugging away for aviation progress—those guys ran the biggest test laboratory of all. They took ideas proved well enough on the ground and put them up in the air, where ideas count."

Turner, the colorful eagle, was summoned to Washington where Congress presented him the Distinguished Flying Cross for air speed pioneering and achievement.

Colonel Roscoe Turner, fourteen years after his active racing career. He had given up the boots and puttees for more contemporary long trousers and dress shoes, but the diamond-studded wings stayed to the end.

In words somewhat more gritty than his response to the Congress, Roscoe later told the press, "Because of the bullheadedness and insistence of pilots, themselves, this country developed lubrication and better fuels that enabled us even to go to bat in World War II. The builders said, 'You can't get more horsepower from an air-cooled engine,' but I lived to fly engines that put out 3,600 horsepower. You see what happened? They were dead, dead wrong. If ever an expert comes calling where you live, you better hurry right over and count the silver."

The gray-haired man behind the desk of Mackey International Airlines in Fort Lauderdale, Florida, smiled sympathetically at the legends of the pompous braggart in the goggles and mirrored boots. Now president of the Florida-based airline, Colonel Joe Mackey was one of the few close flying friends the late Roscoe had.

"Sure, it's true," Joe laughed. "Roscoe Turner had the paraphernalia, all right, but it was only a ruse. It's what made him. It's why he was on top. It's why he was popular and why people paid their money to see him, because he was in the paper and he had his Packard, the lion, the boots, the whole bit. But I tell you it was an act. He was in the image business. It's all he had to sell and it made him a living, and without the image he never would have made it.

"But I've also been with him in Cleveland," said Mackey, somberly, "when we were all broke, and he had gotten something like a $2,000 prize. I saw him give it to stranded parachute jumpers to get home, when he himself needed it real bad."

But if Turner revealed his humanity to Joe Mackey, he proved to be exasperating, also.

"When Turner got his new Laird airplane," the Floridian recalled, "he asked me if I'd fly his Wedell-Williams in the transcontinental Bendix Race.

"I said, 'Sure.' I was at the height of my aerobatic career and I was sure I was the hottest pilot that ever came down the pike. There was nothing, I reasoned, that I couldn't do.

"I simply hopped in Roscoe's airplane and headed for the West Coast. First landing was in Saint Louis and I used the entire airport and a little bit more to get it down. Something was wrong. I couldn't handle it. Flying east again, I was out in front in the Bendix, but hadn't a ghost of an idea what the airplane was doing.

"A hundred miles north of Saint Louis I had the race in the bag when all of the oil flew out of the crankcase onto the windshield and my face and body. I limped into Saint Louis, but frantic airport mechanics could find nothing out of order. We simply refilled it with oil and I went on to Cleveland, but the race, and glory, had passed me by.

"Roscoe had had trouble, too, but he also managed to limp into Cleveland. I told him what had happened.

"Oh, hell," he said, "I forgot to tell you. That oil bath occurs every once in a while. Just ignore it. Just oil it up and go."

"Had I known that," Mackey sighed, "I would have won the race. But when ten gallons of oil hits you in the kisser, you think just maybe something's the matter. Then there was that little matter of the problem landings.

"'Look, Roscoe,' I said, 'I think I'm a hotshot pilot. I've flown about everything with wings on it, but I can't land your airplane and I've seen you land it all over the country. Now, what's happening?'

"Oh, that's something else I forgot to tell you," Turner drawled in his Corinth, Mississippi, twang. 'When I had it rebuilt, I had them raise the landing gear six inches because I thought it'd slow the air speed.'

"Well," Mackey said, "all it did was screw it up so nobody could handle it. Even after his explanation, I was all over the airport everytime I flew the Wedell. You had to try to land it on three points because if you didn't get that tail skid on the ground, you'd had it. In getting to that position, you stalled out on the wing so you were all over everybody."

And Turner is remembered by others, most of whom admire, some of whom disclaim him—persons such as Dudley Brumbach, retired photographer for the *Cleveland Plain Dealer*.

"People often ask me who I remember most in my lifetime of picture-taking," Brumbach laughed. "Of course Roscoe Turner was a lens louse of the first water. Why else would he carry a lion all the time? He wanted always to make sure somebody was around to record everything for posterity.

"Roscoe frequently came to the *Plain Dealer* office with his lion, Gilmore. In the old days in the newspaper business, it wasn't like it is now. They used to bring camels, lions, snakes, everything into the newspaper office. Tom Mix would ride his horse into the elevator and trot down the aisle of the city room, hat in hand. Monkeys, anteaters, you-name-it would come waltzing in there to try to grab a free headline and they'd shit all over the city room before leaving.

"What does a city room think when a lion strolls in with a fellow in blue pants and mirrored boots? It thinks here's a guy with an idea. It's crummy but people will buy a paper to read about it. So you give them something they'll pay money to read about, no matter how stupid you might think it is.

"On his behalf, however, I've got to say he was simply a generation and a half too early. Television would have eaten it up."

For many, the name Roscoe was synonomous with full-page ads like the following:

Boys! Girls! You're invited to join Colonel Roscoe Turner's Flying Corps! More than a quarter million boys and girls have joined this exciting club! You, too, can join. All you have to do is cut the figure "57" from a package of Heinz Rice Flakes and mail it with your name & address to Col. Roscoe Turner, H. J. Heinz Co., Pittsburgh, Pa. You'll get a thrill out of belonging to this corps headed by this famous flier who in one year broke both transcontinental air speed records and who has flown his pet lion Gilmore more than 25,000 miles in a year.

Fill out the coupon and write. Get your wings! Be a lieutenant. Get your certificate of membership, your pilot's license, SECRET PASSWORDS, secret salute! Learn how to become a captain and a major. You get all this equipment free!

Colonel Turner says, "You can't beat Heinz Rice Flakes. They keep you strong and healthy. They break all altitude records for wonderful flavor. These crisp, brown toasted flakes are my favorite cereal. Millions of wide-awake boys and girls eat them every day because they taste good and keep you keen and full of healthy energy for the fun you'll have in my Flying Corps.

So come on and join up now! Ask your grocer how you can get a Roscoe Turner "57" Special Airplane that *really flies!*

Don Young

9

I Couldn't Have Loved A Blood Brother More than This Man

To most, he was simply Roscoe Turner's mechanic, but Don Young still is considered one of the most brilliant minds of early aviation. After forty years, interest in Young among air historians has yet to peak. What makes him particularly interesting as a person is his long and faithful loyalty to a man whose manner greatly contrasted with Young's shy and retiring conduct.

"First, I would like to set the record straight on the Wedell-Williams airplane, since passage of years and the fusion of details may have caused some departure from the facts.

"You are aware by now that Roscoe and Joe Mackey were friends for many years and that Joe and I are still friends. Part of the friendship is based on a respect for Joe as a pilot that certainly has not diminished with time. On the other hand I am a bit protective about the reputation of the Wedell and the Twin-Row airplanes. Joe has told you that Roscoe hadn't said a thing about the Wedell's flying characteristics before Joe took off in it to fly the Bendix. I can assume that was true. Neverthe-

less, I had told him. I told Joe that he couldn't turn the Hornet engine over 2,250 revolutions per minute because he'd shed all the oil in the engine. The scavenger pump was not capable of taking care of all the oil that was being crowded in there at that speed. Joe said okay.

"But later that day I got a call from him in Saint Louis to tell me that he must have broken an oil line or a hose or something because he had lost all the oil. The plane was in the hangar and the boys had the cowling off and were looking for the leak.

"After I arrived in Cleveland and pinned him down on the subject, he said, 'Yeah, Don, everything was going so nicely and I had such a good lead that I poured the power to it and I shed all the oil.'

"Now that's as true as I sit here. I am not criticizing Joe's flying ability, but I think the record should be made clear.

"Joe also quotes Roscoe saying the landing gear had been lowered, resulting in godawful hazardous landings requiring 'all of the airport and a little bit more.' The only difference in the landing gear from what it ever was, regardless of what Roscoe or anyone else may have said, was that we had put on balloon tires. The length of the gear had not been altered.

"But Roscoe himself wouldn't make one good landing with that airplane out of a dozen attempts. You *couldn't*. That airplane had no flaps and a fixed gear, no shock absorber, whatsoever. No one could grease it onto the runway to save his soul. It was a murderous airplane to fly. No question about it.

"We built that airplane with a 300 horsepower Wasp Jr. that we souped to 550 horsepower. Pratt & Whitney was disturbed over the fact that we coaxed it so much. Even so, after we raced it the one year, we decided to put the big Wasp in it and we were pulling 800 horsepower out of the big Wasp. And after we had flown *that* a few years, we took that engine out and put in the big Hornet from which we pulled 1,030 horsepower. Now whenever you hang an engine that big out on the front of an airplane that size, it's going to have its faults. It was a good airplane in the air. Takeoffs were good, but landings could be anything but good.

"The three points had to hit ground at the same moment. Not only that, but your speed had to be just so, because if your power was a little bit low you were going to smack. If you pulled too much power as you touched down, it would try to take off again. It was a touchy airplane to fly. Now Roscoe could accomplish it and so could Mackey, and Mackey didn't do any poorer job flying it than Roscoe did, even if he says he did. He did a whale of a good job.

"Several persons, including Roscoe, have stated

Roscoe Turner's Wedell-Williams race plane, later piloted by Joe Mackey in a Bendix Trophy attempt, was painted gold with a red bull's-eye behind the garish 57 to resemble a box of Heinz Rice Flakes, Roscoe's latest sponsor. The plane was the Thompson Trophy winner in 1934, averaging better than 248 miles per hour. (Cleveland Chapter, American Aviation Historical Society)

Jimmy Wedell, the most discussed pilot-builder of his day, was a superb eyeball designer who ignored certain aeronautical assumptions. (Frederick C. Crawford Auto and Aviation Museum)

numerous things about the Wedell-Williams airplane, including the Number 44 that Doug Davis was killed in. Let me say something about our marvelous relationship with young Jimmy Wedell.

"You know, we saw Jimmy's airplane in Cleveland early in the game. He was having trouble with it. He had a fast airplane, pretty crudely put together, yet well put together, but he had aileron flutter. Roscoe and I decided that we could whip the aileron flutter by balanced ailerons and so we flew down to Patterson, Louisiana, to see if Wedell-Williams would build us an airplane.

"Now Harry Williams, the head of the operation, was an exceedingly wealthy man. He owned fifty-six airplanes. He told us that they didn't have time to build us an airplane. At that very moment, Jimmy himself was constructing the race plane that was soon to be flown by Mae and Jimmy Haizlip.

" 'But Jimmy will give you the prints,' Harry said over his shoulder, 'and you can build it yourself if you want.' With that much assurance, Roscoe took off for the West Coast and I stayed at Patterson for what proved to be quite an adventure.

"There *were* no prints for the Wedell-Williams

airplane. Jimmy had them in his head. Sure, he might have had a notebook in his hip pocket with the dimensions of a tube or something. I said to Jimmy, 'Well, where do I start?'

"He answered, 'There's some sawhorses out back of the hangar, and there's a stack of tubing.'

"Once I got started, there was no problem because I could visualize it. If I didn't have in mind what I was going to do, all I had to do was walk over and look at what Jimmy was doing. I might not have done everything just like he did, but the outcome was very similar.

"A young boy was assigned to me. He sawed tubing and I welded. Except for the engine, the wing panels, the gas tanks, pulleys, and cable, we built every stick of it, just the pair of us.

"We had completed the airplane when Roscoe returned. Jimmy took her up and tested her, and Roscoe accepted the craft. But before we left, Harry Williams came out to the field and said, 'Jimmy, I want you to fly that with Roscoe's equivalent weight.' Roscoe weighed 220 pounds and Jimmy probably weighed 150 wringing wet, and Harry Williams wanted the additional lead shot bags thrown in there to equal Roscoe's poundage.

"Then I walked down to the end of a measured mile with a stopwatch and Harry Williams and Roscoe went to the start of the measured mile to clock the new-built airplane.

"In the course of his maneuvers, Jimmy swung down across the field and I don't think he was hangar-top high when a wing blew up. How he ever

Jimmy Wedell in the cockpit of his famous Wedell-Williams Number 44 race plane in 1932. (Jim Borton collection)

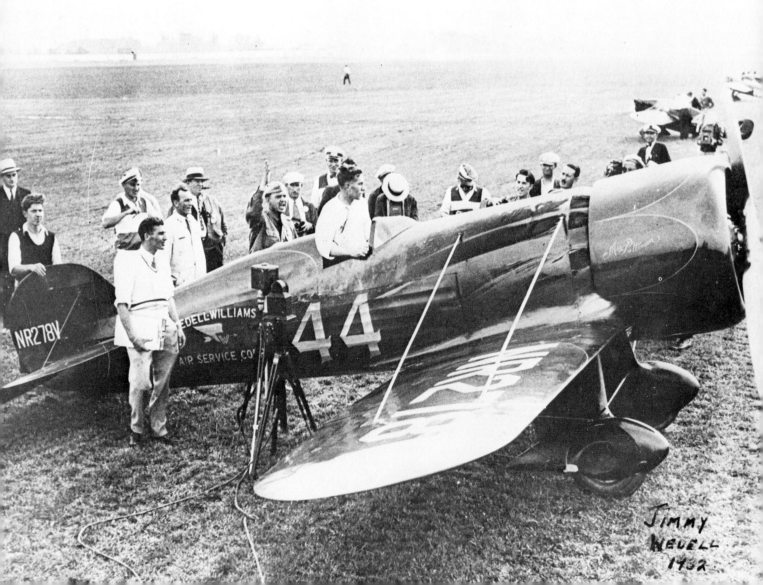

saved his life I'll never know. One very fortunate thing was there were individually opened aileron controls in the airplane. If you lost one open wing on one side, you still had aileron control on the other side.

"When the wing blew up on him, he pulled up and was able to hold that wing with the one aileron until that wing started to catch the lift. When it did, the wing came up and the nose went down, and Jimmy went out through the top hatch. At best he had no more than five hundred feet of altitude when he jumped free in his chute.

"When we got over to Jimmy on the ground, the airplane had gone straight in, making a hole like you've never seen before. We looked quite frantically at the young test pilot, surprised and overjoyed that he was not simply a shattered corpse. But Jimmy Wedell looked preoccupied. 'Have you fellows seen my other shoe?' he asked.

"Never in my life have I heard anyone say a bad thing about Jimmy Wedell, a truly great human being. His wife lived in New Orleans, ninety miles from Patterson. Jimmy told me he didn't like to have his wife live in Patterson because it was too small a town and there were too many gossips. So he flew the ninety miles in an Aristocrat. On some weekend flights, I rode home with him.

"First, however, he went to a certain store and bought trinkets—little dolls, not expensive things, maybe two or three yards of gingham. He tied these up in packages. Then he hunted up rocks or something to make the bundles heavier, and we headed out for New Orleans in the plane.

"There were people back in that bayou of Louisiana who never got out of there, who were deadly poor and lived in tarpaper shacks or worse. I believe the only chance those swamp folks had to buy or trade something was when a Frenchman maybe once or twice a year came in by boat and traded them gingham or bracelets or flour for muskrat pelts and softshell crabs.

"Jimmy had certain shacks picked out on his route to New Orleans. He turned around to me and said, 'Don, get that special package there ready to throw out, will you?' We were flying high, maybe eight or nine thousand feet. Then we cut the engine and started down for a shack way out in the marshes. He shoved the throttle forward and said,

'Okay, Don, kick it out.' Well, when he shoved the throttle forward, all sizes of kids swarmed out of that shack, each one calling out and waving his arms.

"He repeated this gift drop maybe a half-dozen times on his way home to wife and hearth. This was Jimmy's private delight. He never met those people but loved them in a quite special way.

"Jimmy's death a bit later on was a godawful loss. A boy over in Mobile or someplace wanted to buy one of Jimmy's planes. He came over on weekends to have Jimmy check him out in it. He'd been over a number of times but Jimmy was so busy that he simply couldn't leave what he was doing. Finally he said, 'Okay, come on, let's go.' The boy admitted that he had frozen on the stick. It was a duo-control plane and he just froze on the stick.

"Harry Williams was killed in a separate accident. Williams was a longtime close associate of Huey Long, and was highway commissioner in that section of Louisiana. Aviation was sort of a game with him. He was killed coming out of Baton Rouge one night with a friend. They were flying a Beechcraft, and, as I understand it, they had asked for lights. The field operator was apparently confused because he focused the illumination right in their eyes instead of ahead of them. Momentarily blinded, Williams flew into a tree with such terrible force that wood was forced clear through the engine cylinders and out spark plug holes.

"Since I spent so many years with Roscoe, people often ask what I did for a living before our paths crossed. I was first connected with the metal fittings department at Lockheed Aircraft. In those days there were no forged parts. We made by hand all the landing gear fittings, the motor mount fittings, the motor mounts, the tailskid, the exhaust stack.

"A boy by the name of Joe Moore and myself made the first exhaust stack, the first exhaust collector ring, and the very first motor mount ever made for Lockheed. Prior to that time, rings and exhausts were being shipped in from England. We decided we could do it cheaper, so the two of us made the first ones and from then on we made all of them. I learned a lot about metals. As Roscoe used to say, 'Don, if it looks strong enough, it just about has to be strong enough.' I became adept not only at making fittings, but also at welding fittings, plating them, sandblasting them, and putting them on the airplanes.

"People ask, 'Don, how would you even start to build an airplane?' I never thought of that as being very difficult, at least in the days of steel tubing fuselage with linen on the outside and wood fairings to hold it in shape.

"Jerry Voltee, chief engineer at Lockheed, used to come down from the engineering department to the metal fittings department. He said, 'Don, I want to make this,' and he'd sketch something out on his tablet. He said, 'You make this, *then* we'll take it to engineering and make a drawing. That way will be easiest for both of us, and cheaper, too.'

"We made many, many pieces for Lockheed by just having the idea of what was wanted. If they liked it, they made a print of it. That's how we did it—and it was fun.

"Roscoe Turner was a hell of a good pilot. He could come through on anything he attempted to do. When Roscoe and I first became associated, Roscoe flew the Lockheed Air Express for the Gilmore Oil people. The lion cub was given to

Roscoe Turner and passengers stand by Roscoe's famous Lockheed Air Express which transported Hollywood stars to Reno for quickie marriages. (Frederick C. Crawford Auto and Aviation Museum)

Roscoe by a lion farm in Agura. Of course he named it Gilmore after the oil company's president. They quickly adopted that name for their products: Lion Head Oil, Red Lion Gasoline.

"In our lean times, Roscoe could get the money, but he inevitably had to pay it back. The maddest Roscoe ever was with me was one time traveling from Cleveland to Chicago. For some reason we had to be in south Chicago by morning and we had driven all night. Roscoe said something to me and I said, 'Well, Roscoe, you're no businessman. You have the reputation of being a fast promoter, but you're not a promoter. You're just a hell of a good borrower. If Wilie Post, Amelia Earhart, or *anyone* I ever knew in the aircraft business were going to do something spectacular, somebody else would pick up the check—for the gasoline, the oil. You borrow it and you have to pay it back.' He blew his cork.

"He could get the money because he had the magic of magnetism. People basically liked Roscoe. Roscoe was a happy-go-lucky jovial guy and people loved to be with him. He had an attraction and the imagination that Earl Gilmore wanted. Roscoe didn't just fly Earl Gilmore, the president of Gilmore Oil Company, someplace. He didn't just fly Louis B. Mayer or Doug Fairbanks someplace and then just sit on the field and wait. He was with them and they wanted him with them. This was not true of many of the aviation people. Maybe they resented that.

"We flew at one time seventy-five percent of the celebrities of the motion picture business. I couldn't tell you how many times I sat alongside Will Rogers or Mary Pickford or so many others on a flight to New York.

"Roscoe had so many friends with the press in Los Angeles that he couldn't move without being front page news. Roscoe meant it to be that way.

"He realized this was an asset. I remember the morning Roscoe came into the hangar in Burbank. They were just starting a new airline out of Burbank called Century Airlines. Roscoe said, 'Don, do you know how many pilots checked into Century this morning for a job? Forty-two. As long as this doggy uniform will bring me in a couple thousand bucks a month and pay your salary, I'll continue to wear it.'

"His first uniform was adapted from the balloonist uniform of World War I. When Roscoe first came out to California, he tried to get all private pilots to wear a uniform, as a sign of pride to signify their profession. Of course that didn't go.

"Roscoe's first uniform included a Sam Browne belt and boots. This continued as late as 1930. Then he shed the boots and the belt and went with the blue tunic. He wore the tan trousers, whipcord trousers, and a cap.

"It all made good sense, too. How many people could fly in a business suit and get out of an airplane and go into the Waldorf-Astoria in New York and not look as if they had slept in their clothes in the park?

"There was only one Gilmore. After Roscoe bought the airplane from Gilmore Oil Company and he left the employment of Gilmore Oil, that company bought two or three other lions on their own, but were unsuccessful. One fell out of a window of a hotel up in Seattle. At least one was still living when Gilmore Oil was taken over by the Mobil Oil Company.

"Clyde Beatty, the lion trainer, regularly assured us that the lion was going to kill us for sure one day. He never believed you could fully domesticate a wild animal. He trained all his cats with fear, and he tried to drum into our heads that one day for sure Gilmore was going to turn on us and kill us both.

"Clyde didn't know that Gilmore had been very nasty once with Roscoe when he was very small. We had been trying to fit a parachute on the animal. The parachute bag always hung up in the top of the fuselage in the cabin, and we always put a harness on Gilmore with the notion in mind that if we ever had to ditch, we'd just snap the parachute riser to his harness and boot him out. Thank God, it never happened.

"As the cub grew, he had to be outfitted with bigger sizes of parachutes. One day in the Lockheed field hangar, we were outfitting Gilmore with his second chute and he was terribly mean. He just didn't want anybody fussing with him and he had teeth like daggers. Suddenly he bit through Roscoe's thumbnail. Roscoe grabbed him by the back of the neck, reached over for the lid off a forty-pound grease pail, and worked Gilmore over but good. Blood spurted out of Gilmore's nose as Roscoe's own blood gushed down his hand and

Roscoe Turner in his heyday is pictured with the lion cub, Gilmore. (Frederick Crawford Auto and Aviation Museum)

wrist. They were a pair.

"We all felt very sorry for Gilmore at that moment, but that cat would not leave Roscoe's side. From that instant, they were buddies. Wherever Roscoe went, Gilmore trailed at his heels, as desiring to be loved by his pal as any household tabby cat. In fact, he meowed all day long.

"The reputation of Roscoe, the loner, is totally exaggerated. I don't mean he wanted every pilot he knew to be with him, but Roscoe had telephonitus if any man ever did. When we hit a town, he'd get on that telephone and we never had dinner alone even if it was already the wee morning hours. He always had people around him.

"Robert Montgomery, young Doug Fairbanks, Mary Pickford, Betty Montgomery who played on television, and others were his dear friends. I used to hold Betty on my lap when she was a tiny thing. We took the lion over to Bob Montgomery's house I don't know how many times and let the kids play with him.

"This feud business, however, was not a publicity trick. There was a very great dislike for Ortman on Roscoe's part. Roscoe was justified in this because when they were competing at Oakland, Ortman cut Roscoe a couple of times on pylons and it made Roscoe so mad—we should have won hands down. Roscoe apologized to me. As soon as he landed he said, 'Don, there isn't enough money in this race for me to risk my neck and this airplane. But if that son of a bitch gets in my way in Cleveland, I'll chop him up.'

"Ortman had a group around him that was shooting its collective mouth off around the airport, badmouthing Roscoe. These things always get back to you. Roscoe was not a malicious man. If Roscoe disliked you, he just plain disliked you, but he never spoke about you. If you happened to mention someone to Roscoe, his only remark might be, 'Oh, *that* son of a bitch,' but it ended there.

"If people disliked Roscoe, on the other hand, he did everything he could to find out why, because it would disturb him. I don't care who it was. Here in California once a mechanic in a nearby hangar was spreading malicious talk about Roscoe. Roscoe searched him out and said, 'Do I know you?'

"The fellow said, 'Naw, I don't think you do.'

"Roscoe said, 'Do you know me?'

"The man answered, 'Well, no, I've only seen you.'

"Then Roscoe asked simply enough, 'Then why are you shooting your mouth off about me?' They left there good friends.

"On the other hand, he never felt he had to apologize for being a showman. That was his livelihood, pure and simple. Roscoe didn't make enough money out of all the actual races he won to pay for one airplane.

"The race years brought with them considerable pressure, some of which could be worked off or talked out, some of which was repressed. During this time Roscoe had terrible nightmares. They could come either before or after a race, but they would come.

"Roscoe flew from Detroit and broke a record from Detroit to New York one time. He landed at Floyd Bennett Field. The newspapers, carrying the news headline, were almost simultaneously on the streets. When he boarded a commercial plane later at Newark to fly to Toledo where I was to meet him, several passengers immediately recognized him and had him autograph their newspapers.

"Then he sat down and relaxed, fell asleep, and proceeded to have a nightmare. When he saw me in Toledo, he laughed. He said, 'Do you know what happened to me? I signed all those newspapers for people on the plane, then fell asleep. Suddenly I jumped up and said to everyone, "We've got to get out of here. Something terrible is happening." Of course the passengers thought, "Well, Jesus, this is Roscoe Turner, he ought to know." The stewardess had a heck of a time waking me up.'

"After World War II, the papers were comparing Cook Cleland to Roscoe, and I suppose in terms of intensity and determination, Cook probably was closer to him than anyone else. Still, Cook asked an unknown sponser for $35,000 minimum and he came home empty-handed. He wanted it all and desperately needed it to scrub up his three F2Gs.

"Well, jeepers, the glamour period, the day of drawing power, was long gone with the war. It was never the same after that, because in the thirties you pulled yourself up by your own pants pockets. You made these things—and they were hard to come by. You didn't have the facilities, and you didn't have the money, and you didn't have jet

Three famous Wedell-Williams racers in 1932. From right to left, Roscoe Turner's Gilmore Red Lion *Racer, Jimmy Haizlip's Number 92, which he flew to a first-place Bendix victory, and Number 44, Jimmy Wedell's personal racing plane. (Jim Borton collection)*

engines, and you didn't have big engines that had been proven by the military.

"In fact when we souped up the Hornet engine to 1030 horsepower and took it up to Pratt & Whitney and they put it on the engine stand, the boy on the engine stand turned around to Don Brown, president of the company, and said, 'Mr. Brown, we've never pulled this much horsepower out of a Hornet engine.'

"Brown said, 'Well, you're going to now if it holds together, so shove that throttle up there.'

"From World War II on, everything that was built was so far superior to anything we had to fly because of the metallurgy alone, and the facilities for proper stress analysis. We didn't have retractable gears on the Turner planes so we had that

Earl Ortman, in the dark shirt, enjoys his only triumph over Colonel Roscoe Turner. The scene was the major Oakland, California, race in the summer of 1938. Ortman led Turner over the finish line by 100 feet after a 200-mile chase. Though the photo shows all smiles, Turner claimed Ortman had fouled him several times, a charge still debated to this day. (Frederick C. Crawford Auto and Aviation Museum)

Motion picture actor Wallace Beery at left rests against his Travel Air airplane as he pals with Walter Beech, creator of the still important Beechcraft airplanes. (Frederick C. Crawford Auto and Aviation Museum)

hanging out there restricting the speed. I really think that if the Twin-Row job had had retractable gears, we probably would have had a 500 mile per hour airplane.

"Roscoe looked after other people's engines, too. There was a fellow out here who had worked for one of the big engine companies. If somebody had engine trouble, he went after the job. Roscoe was close friend of the roughneck comic actor, Wallace Beery. Wally flew a beautiful Bellanca and kept it in the hanger with our ship. One day Wally told this fellow to give his engine a top overhaul.

"On that day a Santa Anna sandstorm was blowing. They come from out of the desert, generally, with a lot of wind and a lot of heat. The whole sky fills with sand. Paxton removed all of the cylinders from Wally Beery's engine, and was grinding the valves. Here was the naked engine with nine cylinder ports open and a Santa Anna going like nothing you've ever seen and the sand just boiling through the hangar.

"Roscoe walks through the hangar and he says, 'Don, who the hell is working on that engine?' I told him and he searched out the man. He said, 'You get out there and you get those cylinders filled with rags and you get that engine covered up and I'll tell you one thing, you'll never work on an engine of mine, but you get *that* engine covered up.'

"Now this wasn't Roscoe's engine. By God, he looked after other people's interests, too.

"The Thompson in 1938 was one of the first times I didn't have to work on the plane the whole night before. Roscoe said, 'Don, let's go to town.'

"We passed the hangar where Tony LeVier and Bill Schoenfeldt had their airplane. Tony was flying the Schoenfeldt *Firecracker* Larry Brown had built for Roy Minor. After Minor died, I guess Schoenfeldt took possession of her.

"We stopped to talk to the boys and were told they had burnt a piston in the engine, and there was no way of getting the engine rebuilt in time for the Greve Race the next day. Roscoe looked at me and said, 'Don, what do you think?'

"I said, 'I don't know where we'd get a piston.'

"He said, 'You leave that to me. You and Tony work on the engine. I'll take Bill Schoenfeldt with me to town.'

"Tony and I stripped the engine down and we found three bad pistons. We disassembled the engine piece by piece and cleaned it thoroughly. We worked all night. About daylight, up drove the Packard with Roscoe and Bill Schoenfeldt. Roscoe had the Thompson Products people call out a group of men to machine a complete set of pistons and a set of rings for this engine. Tony and I put the engine back together.

"Tony went out at ten o'clock that morning and qualified, then proceeded to win the Greve Race and its $12,000 prize that day, and he gave us a hell of a run in the Thompson the next day.

"The cash prize meant everything to us that year, but Roscoe put every penny of it right on the line for a competitor.

"Now throughout the thirties the pit crews used assorted ways and means to assist the racing pilot in the air. Roscoe had a habit of missing pylons. If he had won a race for every pylon he missed, he wouldn't have been only a three-time winner of the Thompson. So one night in the car I said to him, 'Roscoe, we can win this race.'

"He looked at me and said, 'What do you mean, we can win this race.'

" 'First, we don't know if you have enough fuel to run this 300-mile race. If you'll come out to the field tomorrow morning and fly, I'll put in two different gas tanks. When you hit the course, if you'll switch to the new tank and run three laps on that, then switch back to your other tank to come in, I'll check the fuel and we'll know for certain just how much we have.'

"We were using 184 gallons of fuel an hour and we had capacity for 205 gallons. If everything went right, the race would last an hour and two minutes to an hour, three minutes. So it was close.

"Then I said, 'If you'll come out to the airport in the evening, we'll take one of the small rental airplanes and you and I will fly the course. We'll become familiar with it to the point that if the pylon blows down or all the bunting blows off of it, you'll know from farmer Jones's barn or alfalfa field that you're on course.

" 'Also, I've painted large numbers on huge pieces of white plywood to help you count laps.'

"My plan was to put the large plywood counters right in his line of vision after the turn on the home pylon.

"We kept stop watches on Earl Ortman, Steve Wittman, and Roscoe. We had a chart set up for the thirty laps, showing current positions of the contenders. If he was hard-pressed, we'd keep the card for his place and the one for the number of his lap close together. If he had a wide margin, we'd spread them out—probably twenty feet—which he could still see easily.

"I told Roscoe, 'You won't have to worry about your lap. We'll be telling you what your lap is and we'll tell you what your place is.'

"Everything was just going great, when all of the sudden—no Roscoe. I started running toward the grandstand because we were way out there and there were no walkie-talkies in those days. I ran and ran and *ran,* hoping to find out quickly where to go to pick up the body. I knew he had crashed. Everything else had gone by.

"I ran my heart out. Suddenly I heard an airplane flying fast behind me. Here comes Roscoe, and in another two or three laps he was out leading the pack again. He had lost a lap, missed a pylon again. Well, it was easy to do.

"Very few people can understand how close Roscoe and I were associated, how very deep our mutual respect. It was teamwork.

"The first time I met race competitor Benny Howard was at the Curtiss-Reynolds Field in Chicago at a race. I looked up and saw two guys on the wing of our racer, and I chased them the hell out of there. They turned out to be two of Benny Howard's mechanics. They went back over and told Benny what I had said and he said, 'If that son of a bitch comes over here, hit him in the head with a prop bar.'

"I was so keyed up because it was my part to see that that racer was ready to go. If Roscoe didn't win that day, we both would be eating beans for still another year.

"When I was leaving the hangar one night, the prop on the Wedell was sitting crossways and I just walked into it. It could have scalped me. Well, as I went by it I just halfheartedly pulled the prop down so it wouldn't hit someone in the face. As I pulled it down, it didn't feel right. Normally, it will bounce back a little on compression. I played with the prop for a minute.

"Roscoe had already scheduled a speed dash for the next day because he had built a new type of cowling as a result of some cooling problems. I called Roscoe on the phone, told him there was something wrong with the engine. Roscoe came to the field and Wilbur Thomas, a Pratt & Whitney man, came over to look at this thing. By the time he got there I had the prop and the nose housing off the airplane. Thomas said, 'Well, Roscoe, you just have had a bad cam ring gear. I'll have them send you over a new cam ring gear and some new cam followers and you'll be all set.'

"He left and I said, 'Roscoe, he's wrong. *Something* caused that ring gear to go sour. *Something* in this engine changed the clearance in that cam ring gear.

"Roscoe really got upset with me. He said, 'Wilbur Thomas knows his business.'

"I said, 'He should know his business, Roscoe, but there's something wrong with this engine.'

"I took it apart to the point where I had nothing but the crankshaft. The crankshaft had broken and a bolt had stretched and had changed the clearance in the nose section. Had Roscoe Turner run a speed dash with that airplane, he almost certainly would have been killed.

"Another time he was going to Sacramento to bring the governor of California down to Los Angeles on the Air Express. I had just gassed up the airplane. While I was on top of the fuselage, I asked the boy who was helping me to bring me a five-gallon can of oil, because it was easier to pour the oil from where I was than to try to do it standing on a wheel.

"He handed me the can of oil. I put in the funnel and started to pour. That's when something strange went into the tank, but it went in so quickly that I couldn't determine what it was. I immediately stopped pouring, handed the can back to Bill, and asked, 'Bill, did you check this can before you put oil in it?'

" 'Yeah,' he said, 'it was clean.'

"I said, 'Something has gone in the tank.'

"He said again, 'Well, nothing was in the can.'

"By this time there was a mob of people around the airplane, which was typical whenever Roscoe went anywhere in those days.

"Roscoe had been standing by the car talking with Mrs. Turner. He walked over and I explained about the oil tank. I went into the hangar and got a piece of rod and probed, but found nothing. We had baffle plates in there and an eighteen-gallon tank. With the thick, heavy oil, it was difficult to feel anything. Finally Roscoe said, 'Don, button it up. I've got to go.'

"I said, 'Well, you're *not* going.'

"He said, 'What do you mean I'm not going? What do you think I'm going to do?'

"I said, 'Roscoe, I don't know what you're going to do but this airplane's going back in the hangar and the oil tank's coming out of it.' Now this meant pulling off the engine, pulling off the fire wall, pulling out the 300-gallon gas tank and then the oil tank—a good five- or six-hour job just to get the tank out.

"Roscoe walked over to the car and said to Mrs. Turner, 'Well, what am I going to do?'

"I could have kissed her. She said, 'Turner, for once it looks like you're going to listen.'

"Roscoe came back and said, 'Okay, Don, I'll call the governor and tell him I'll be there at eight o'clock in the morning. But I'll need the airplane at six.'

"I said, 'Okay, you'll have it.' I got the oil tank out and walked over to the bench with it. I shook it—nothing. I thought to myself, 'God, I haven't goofed, have I?' When I got the tank to the bench I turned a flashlight in there. There, glued to the bottom of the tank, was a full-sized oil-soaked cigar. Had that gone into the oil pump and the screen, Roscoe might well have gone down in the mountains without a trace.

"Roscoe called the boy helper to the table, saying, 'Come over here. I want to show you how goddam careless you really are.' Apparently someone had laid a cigar on the bench and it had fallen into the empty can. When Bill picked up the can, he simply poured oil on top of it.

"These are the little things that made Roscoe say, 'I need him.'

"I'm not trying to pin laurels on Don Young, but these were the kinds of things that made our relationship incredibly close. It got to where if *I* wasn't satisfied with something, Roscoe would say, 'Okay, do it your way.' I had to get to the bottom of a thing. I had to find out what made it do this and do that. We had a few fusses, and they were dillies.

Sometimes he'd feel I was being a little too cautious, and if he wanted to go, then it was 'Don, goddam it, you can't do this.'

"Roscoe really didn't care to fly without me in the cockpit alongside him because of this long association. We might fly for hours and never say a word. It made no difference. Roscoe and I went on innumerable trips together and we inevitably got a suite of rooms or a twin bedroom because there were always things to discuss.

"Once we'd been away on business for two whole months. When we hit Burbank, someone from his family was there to meet us. Yet he stood there by the car and said, 'Don, come over to the house tonight, will you? I want to talk to you.'

"The family always saved Roscoe's newspapers, the oldest one on top of a stack perhaps three feet high. He sorted down through and got up to date. I walked in and said, 'Hi, Roscoe.'

"He replied, 'Hi, Don,' and went back to his newspapers. I went down to the playroom and played Ping-Pong and shot billiards with Mrs. Turner, her sister, or a friend. When it was time to leave, I came back upstairs and Roscoe still sat there buried in his newspapers. I said, 'Good night, Roscoe,' and he said, 'Good night, Don.' Other than that, he never said a word. He wanted me there just *in case he thought of something.*

"Roscoe never talked to anyone about me, but he knew what we meant to each other. In 1940 the racing was over. I went back to Indianapolis to help Roscoe set up his new business at the airport that he had recently purchased. You'll never know what a mess that hangar was. The windows were so dirty that we had to have lights on all the time.

"I resurfaced all of the benches, scraped scads of paint off the floor, cleaned the filth-encrusted windows, stocked some new parts, and worked out some organization to the place. I worked my heart out, but nevertheless decided that I'd return to the West Coast and the Lockheed Company.

"I went to work for Roscoe as a mechanic, but I ended up his goodwill ambassador. Long after I returned to Lockheed during the war years, I went through Indianapolis one time on my way to New York. I wanted to have breakfast with Roscoe one more time. Roscoe said, 'Don, we should be together again. We were a team.'

"When they built the Lockheed general offices on the site of the animal's arena we had to move Gilmore back to the lion farm.

"My wife and I visited him there.

"My wife first walked up to the arena where the sign said Roscoe Turner's Flying Lion. She called his name. If he opened one eye as recognition, it was a surprise. Then I stood out behind a tree. He was all stretched out there sunning himself, mostly asleep. From behind my tree several yards away, I hollered 'Hey!' Boy, how the dirt flew. He was on his feet in an instant. He immediately had my scent and he wouldn't take his eyes off my tree until I stepped out. Then he would simply quiver and shake like he was going to fall down, then he would bounce and jump like a kitten.

"I saw Roscoe for the last time in 1969. His race plane had been hanging on chains on the hangar for twenty-nine years. Would I come back and restore the racer? I told him whenever he was ready.

"Well, it was a dog, the worst looking thing I ever saw. I got up at four in the morning and went over to Roscoe's museum-in-the-making and worked until ten or midnight. If I needed rivets or screws or pieces, Roscoe's brother Bill was there to help me. (Bill Turner was head of the aviation department of Shell Oil Company by the time he retired.)

"Roscoe had just come up from Florida at the time. For some time nobody knew what really was wrong with his health. He complained of his back but he also coughed an awful lot. Later the doctors learned the score but they never told Roscoe how bad he was because Mrs. Turner asked them not to. Anyway, Roscoe had just come up from Florida and he walked into the museum while his brother Bill was working with me.

"I heard Roscoe say to Bill, 'I told you that son of a bitch was miraculous.'

"During those last evenings together, restoring the racer, I had cause to recall that Roscoe loved to cook. He used to come over to the museum and invite me to the house. Donna might be in Florida. He could fry sausage and hominy that was out of this world.

"When we got ready to go to bed, his master bedroom had two large double beds. I always took a *Time* magazine or a newspaper. Roscoe took noth-

ing, but when he got in his bed he reached down on the nightstand for his Bible. There was never a night he didn't read it.

"I didn't go back for the funeral. I knew he would understand and nobody else mattered.

"Later when I did go back there, a friend of mine took me out to the place. He's got a beautiful crypt in the mausoleum. It couldn't be nicer if Don Young had designed it.

"His little museum was beautiful. It was red carpeted throughout. It had Roscoe's Packard. I had gone back and restored the Packard, too. Then there were the beautiful cases. I couldn't say how much money Mrs. Turner put out for the cases that went around the posts, filled with Roscoe's mementos.

"I had nursed Roscoe's lion since he was a tiny cub. He died at nineteen years and Roscoe had him mounted and kept him in his den at home. When the museum was started, the airplane sat over there in the corner with the plastic over it, and under one wing Gilmore sat on his platform. I thought that was a hell of a looking animal to be sitting out there all by himself so I went downtown and I must have bought a hundred chrome shower curtain rods and I built him a cage with gold base, gold top, and chrome bars. Then I placed some Astroturf around him so that it appeared that the cage was on a hilltop.

"Roscoe was a fighter, a scrapper. When he went after something, he was tenacious. He had great ideas as to how his museum was to be sustained. Roscoe was the kind who could have gone to Pratt & Whitney and said, 'Look, I want $25,000 toward this museum. We've always used your engines. We've done this, that, and the other. Now come on, boys, kick through.' They probably would have.

"But Mrs. Turner got no support, whatsoever. She said to me one day, 'Don, I'm going to go two years with this and support it all I can.' On the day of dedication, the governor of Indiana was there, the mayor of Indianapolis, and more bigwigs than you could shake a stick at. Boy, they were going to do everything for that museum. Then they went home and completely forgot it existed.

"So Donna Turner had a losing battle from the word go, and one morning one of the boys back at the Smithsonian Institution called me in Chula Vista and asked me how to take the airplane apart. Donna, herself, called me a few hours later. She said she knew I would be upset about selling the airplane."

"I wasn't really. I think the Smithsonian is the place for it, where millions of people can see it down through the ages. Nothing can happen to it there. Hell, it would take an atom bomb to do away with the Smithsonian Institution.

"I never thought that Gilmore would go to the Smithsonian Institution, but there he is today, standing under the wing of Roscoe Turner's fastest airplane."

10

What on Earth Am I Doing Here

Mary Haizlip

A crack pilot married a girl who had never seen the inside of a cockpit and rapidly molded her into a trophy winner and holder of the women's world air speed record. Among air race historians, Jimmy Haizlip probably is as popular for his cartwheel crash of the Gee Bee race plane as he is for bettering Jimmy Doolittle's record in his smooth-as-silk 1932 Bendix Trophy win. Nevertheless, this is about his wife.

"I was fortunate to break the women's world speed record and I was the first person to use 100 octane gas," laughed petite and provocative Mary Haizlip. *Everybody* stood around waiting for me to blow up. They thought that was the most daring thing. I thought it was pretty daring, too.

"*Time* magazine was notoriously inaccurate in those days, at least as far as we were concerned, but they did say one thing about me that was quite factual. They told of my taxiing to the corner of the field and opening the throttle for better or for worse. Indeed, that was the only time I ever had the feeling just for an instant, 'What on earth am I

doing here, in a rigid landing gear airplane that everybody says is this, that, and the other thing.'

"It was after World War I that I met Jim Haizlip. Jim was, from the very start, a very distinguished charmer. His mother wanted him to quit flying and do something worthwhile, so he went back to school at the University of Norman. He started a flying service there to help with expenses. It is in no way an exaggeration to say that he was the most popular boy in the school. He was president of everything. Every last one of the twenty coeds was after him.

"The chaps weren't allowed to have cars in those days, so Jim had an enormous motorcycle, a Harley with a sidecar for when he needed it (which was often) and later on, an Indian Ace. I had seen Jim in the air. One of the local people had commented to me, 'Oh, look at Jimmy Haizlip doing them flip-flops. He's going to kill himself for sure.'

"I don't know when I began wanting to fly. Perhaps I was born with the idea, but I expect not. I'd never been around any flying stalls, in those

131

days there just weren't any. I spent winters in Pasadena with my family and summers at Colorado Springs.

"My father was very successful in the mining field. He had invested in some oil wells that turned out to be 'dusters,' so we went to see what had happened to his money. Then I heard about this flying school.

"We phoned and Roy Hunt who was Jim's assistant in the school, and who subsequently became a

well-known pilot, came to talk to me. He told me he was a student of the great Jimmy Haizlip. He said, 'I personally am going to teach you to fly.' Oh, how lucky could a young girl be.

"Mother and I and the whole entourage went down and met the great Haizlip. In barely two minutes time it was clear that the great and marvelous Haizlip outranked Mr. Hunt and *he* taught me to fly.

"From the moment we met portal to portal we

Petite Mary Haizlip stands beside the Wedell-Williams race plane in which she earned the women's air speed record of the world in 1933. (Jim Borton collection)

were married in fourteen days. It would have been sooner, but we waited for my parents to leave town. I hardly considered it a rash thing to do. He was delightful, charming, erudite, suave, came from a privileged and delightful family, and had the only airplane in town. He had everything any girl could want; they all wanted him and I got him.

"To hear Jim tell it, unfortunately, it was at least partly a professional experiment. He nursed the idea that he could teach a girl to fly and was determined to make good. It is true that one girl in the physical education department had successfully stirred his masculine yearnings. She was, to hear him tell it, 'a sturdy, lovely, attractive girl.' Fortunately, the Haizlip flying operation was built to survive on cash dollars, and the sturdy young thing was broke.

"Meanwhile, I was scoring points where they counted. Jim told his friends, 'I got her in the cockpit and saw how quickly she took instructions. She told me later she had been in a kind of swoon there. Nevertheless, she took instructions and did exactly what I told her. She absorbed them. I instantly got a measure of her overall intelligence that I couldn't have obtained any other way. I had flown as a combat pilot in World War I, so when she was in my medium, I could just see that here was all this intelligence.' He also told people I was pretty. For whichever reason, he paid for my flying lessons.

"I do not wish to suggest that Jim was simply enamored. I am sure that I did have what the French call extra lucidity, sensitivity to his very thoughts. People are either that way or they're not. I still read his mind with the greatest of ease.

"My first air race was in 1930. Naturally, those thirty-degree pylon turns seemed pretty steep. I still was on student status with Jim (I still am) and I did exactly what he had told me. My airplane was simply slower than my competitors' and I had to make it up by flying less distance.

"I may have been the only bride ever to learn about racing airplanes in the bedroom. Our bedpost was the pylon. Looping string around it, Jim taught strategy clearly and precisely. The Haizlip method was to stay out just far enough, take aim on the pylon, and let my thermals (this race was in the afternoon) push me a hundred feet or so, so that I would then dive on the pylon with a little more altitude to spare.

"'Keep your eye on that pylon and come just as close as you want to that,' Jim would shout from the foot of the bed. 'Don't think about a bank too soon. Come to this aiming point—no, you're not going to run into the ground while you're looking at it—and level out at twenty-five or thirty feet.'

"I'm sure I passed in my nightie more diving, turning, and just general fast flying instruction than any other race pilot in the world. Jim couldn't pass the bedpost without thinking of pylons.

"Once, in Cleveland, during the women's 800 cubic inch race (races were categorized by the size and power of the aircraft engines) Jim and Walter Beech, the airplane manufacturer, were watching me fly. I was racing Earl Rollin's little mid-wing Cessna, and Walter said, 'Good God. She's going to kill herself.'

"Jim countered with 'Good girl. You're doing just as I said.' Because I could read his mind, I heard every word.

"Once there was talk around about whether I had ever jumped. I said, 'No.'

"They said, 'Well, why not?'

"I said, 'Well, I guess the answer to that is that I don't own a parachute.' Well, with that, about ten persons ran in and brought out parachutes. Someone helped me into the thing. It wasn't packed properly. Jim wasn't there, needless to say. We went to three thousand feet. I fell about five hundred feet and began to wonder if it was going to open.

"It finally did and, of all things, there were great blotches of blood on the canopy. The chap who had used it the Sunday before had been killed. It jerked me terribly. I wasn't very big, and it wasn't properly fitted. I was black and blue. I just waited and waited holding my breath. Then finally it opened and I thought, 'Oh, isn't this nice.'

"In 1932, the package arrangement with Mr. Harry Williams, owner of the plane, was that my opportunity to attempt a world's speed record in Cleveland was dependent on Jim making a good showing in the cross-country Bendix from Los Angeles to New York. Jim often said he wished he could simply erase from his mind that trip west from Patterson, Louisiana. Taking off, the plane became progressively erratic.

"On a takeoff at midday in 130 degree temperature in Pueblo, Colorado, the Wedell's direction became uncontrollable. It left the runway too fast to stop without cracking up and burning.

"In the next three hours Jim surrendered about half of his remaining life expectancy worrying about the coming landing at Burbank. When he did land, it was reported to me as a crash, but in reality the Wedell suffered only two scraped wing-tips.

"Nevertheless, Jim and Jimmy Wedell spent all of the next two days working feverishly to add extra bracing to the landing gear struts. They didn't know until the last few hours before starting time whether the airplane would be at all usable. Even then, Jim might have elected to throw in the sponge. He had never been at all keen on flying the long Bendix. In the fast and furious Thompson Trophy skirmish, his knowledge of combat flying could be put to better use.

"With considerable effort, some excellent groundwork, and two refueling stops where 290 gallons of fuel were added in fourteen minutes, Jim flashed by the finish line and the crowd-filled

An absorbed James D. Hartshorne, second from right, former Plain Dealer *aviation editor, extracts tomorrow's lead sports story from a happy Jimmy Haizlip who has just won the 1932 Bendix. (Jim Borton collection)*

stands at Cleveland with a time well ahead of the other contestants. He beat the transcontinental speed record that Jimmy Doolittle had set the previous year.

"Back in Cleveland, it was then my turn. Those times and associations were so close and intimate. The whole core of the industry attended the races; I had to make good. The requirements of the speed run were to fly over a specific measured course upwind and downwind with no diving start, carrying a barograph to record altitude and distance flown.

"The biggest difficulty was that because of the uncertainty all that summer (Harry Williams hated any notion of women flying his airplanes) I had never even sat in the Wedell-Williams up to that moment. I was given fifteen minutes to fit myself into the cockpit alone, take off safely, make a familiarization flight, and land in one piece—immediately after which recording instruments were installed for my attempt on the world speed record.

"I soon discovered that the airplane and cockpit controls were different from any other model of aircraft I had known. In the early developmental days, if a need for a control arose, it was added wherever a convenient place could be found. Planes were not like automobiles, which have standard controls and brakes that all work the same.

"The brakes on Number 92 were operated by two little pads, each about the size of a dollar, inboard of the rudder pedal. They required so much pressure that when Jim flew the airplane for the first time, he wore heavy basketball shoes to keep from bruising his heels. Jim passed on other details such as adjusting the longitudinal trim for takeoff, high speeds, and landings. However, there was next to no opportunity to test such preflight information where it counted—in the air.

"Jim said later, 'The instant her airplane started rolling, I was trembling. She was strapped in and all by herself. She hardly knew the racer well enough, but it was do or die, as the plane's owner could well deny a second chance. I knew in my heart that whatever happened on that dangerous flight, she would be able to cope.'

"I set a new world's speed record for women that lasted for seven years.

"To show what any world's record means, four years later Jim and I were visiting in France and stopped at the formal headquarters in Paris of the Federacione Aeronautique Internationale, where all world records were made official and filed. We discovered that the directors had never heard of the great and noble charmer James Haizlip, but immediately greeted Mary Haizlip as the holder of three flying records, two for altitude, and the prestigious women's speed record, formerly held by a French woman.

"On the Sunday before Labor Day was the climax for the women's races that year, the free-for-all for the Cleveland Pneumatic Tool Company Aerol Trophy. Because of the superior speed of Number 92 both Jim and I felt more than reasonably assured of victory. The race was scheduled as ten laps around a triangular course. Because my only other flight in the Wedell had amounted to less than a half-hour, Jim urged that I start well outside the slower airplanes and take it easy for the first few laps until I had some practice on pylon turns.

"Busy with other things on the ground, we neglected to clean the dust and trash that had entered at the tailskid opening during earlier flights. This dust had been pulled forward by the suction over the cockpit and was under the pilot's seat. As the race started, a thundershower was gathering over the western field boundary. The rush of cool air just ahead of the rain caused a sharp bump that shook a handful of dust right up into my face and under my goggles.

"Having very long legs but a short torso, I could just barely see over the top of the cockpit. Some well-meaning person had wired the air tube so that it went right in my face. Thus, all this dust continued to pour into my eyes, nose, and mouth. I tried in vain to bend the tube or tear it off but it was wired too securely.

"During this initial distraction, I momentarily lost sight of the first pylon. To make certain I hadn't cut the corner of it, which would disqualify me, I made another circuit. I could spare the slight delay. But during the second lap, the thunderstorm covered the field of the five-mile race course.

"Had the race continued for the full ten laps, or even been allowed six laps as the regulations provided, I easily would have been in the lead. As it was, we were flagged down during the fourth lap. Though I had flown exactly as planned for the ten-lap race, we had to be content with second place. Gladys O'Donnell, who happened to be leading in the fourth lap, was given the win. They would not reschedule the contest.

Number 92 was a lucky airplane for both Jim and wife Mary. The single-engine Wedell-Williams Special allowed just enough room for the pilot and an extra pair of shoes. (Rudy Profant collection)

"This seemed so grossly unfair at the time that Mr. Harry Williams, following the race results over the radio in Patterson, Louisiana, came into the picture. Mr. Harry, by this time, had become my ardent fan, and his true southern gallantry deeply resented such 'ineptness' to a lady he admired. A

Mary Haizlip slips into the cockpit of Number 92, filled with the 100 octane gasoline no pilot had ever used. Time *magazine reporters and the public turned out on the sidelines to watch her blow up, but instead she achieved a world speed record for women. (Mary Haizlip collection)*

man of action, he instructed a prominent Cleveland attorney to get a court injunction that would halt that particular race decision and possibly force a rerun. He also alerted one of his top pilots to fly him immediately to Cleveland to stop the whole show if necessary.

"However, there were of course the feelings of the other contestants to consider, and also those of the race officials, who meant well, though they had bent the rules. Hearing of Mr. Harry's reaction on the radio, I rushed to a telephone and calmed him down before he could depart for Cleveland. I successfully urged him to call off his orders so that the races could continue as scheduled the next day.

"I was disappointed but not undaunted. The next year the Aerol Trophy Race was flown in both Los Angeles and Chicago. I was fortunate enough to

win the crown both times.

"One incident occurred that year that neither Jim nor I can ever forget. It was a Sunday afternoon and we both were napping after the usual ceremonial noon dinner. We were still living in Ferguson, a suburb of Saint Louis. About four o'clock I awoke badly shaken by a vivid dream. I told Jim I had seen Jim Wedell crash in an airplane on the far side of the field at Patterson. While it was fresh in my mind, Jim asked for all of the details. I told him that it was not one of the racers. It was a biplane and looked like a British Moth. Jim countered that that was hardly likely because the only Moth he had seen in the hangar was stored far in the back with the wings folded. He had never seen it flown.

"That evening around seven o'clock, Jim had a call from the *Saint Louis Globe Democrat* telling him that news had just come over the wire that Jim Wedell had suffered a fatal crash. The airplane was a Moth.

"One beautiful competitor of mine, a German girl, was Florence Klingensmith from Minneapolis. At one time, Florence had a truly fast airplane, a big 300 horsepower Cessna. In one particular race she pounced on my tail and just followed me around. When trash developed in my fuel line and I sputtered in the final moments, Florence sailed by and won the race. Our poor mechanic had bet a hundred dollars on me (1931 dollars!) and I had some trouble holding my head high for awhile.

"Back in Saint Louis I was despondent for a time because I had let myself down, but Jim cooled me off. Jim was always cooling me off, and heating me up. 'Now, Mary,' he shrugged, 'in the next race you're simply going to have to be far enough ahead that Florence won't be right on your tail. You know she can't make those turns without someone to follow.'

"In two minutes I had completely forgotten my earlier oath to quit racing altogether.

"For awhile I was chief test pilot of a subsidiary of the Ford Motor Company of Detroit. There were four of us, three fellows and myself. Within two months, the three men all were killed in air crashes. That automatically made me chief pilot. That's how to succeed without really trying.

"Would I have liked to compete in the Thompson? Oh, if they had let me, of course. I've never particularly been a women's libber. I've had a very fine relationship with men. I can't recall one ever giving me a harsh word. Like Will Rogers, I never met a man I didn't like. Yes, if they'd opened up the Thompson, I would have competed, but I never had a belligerent feeling about it. I was glad to get in wherever I could.

"There was talk among males that the physical stresses of the Thompson Race—like the airplane sandwiches—were just too physically exerting for women. I do not accept that at all. As a matter of fact, I think it's absurd. It's in the same class as everyone thinking I was going to blow up when I was the first person to use 100 octane gasoline. It's in the category of fairy tales. We had a good snicker over talk of the effects of the menstrual cycle during stressful air racing. I never had any

problems, but I'm hardly medically qualified. I hear some people, at that particular time, are quite emotional, nervous, and upset. It's just been completely beyond anything that's ever touched me.

"I have always been surprised by the question, 'Was it at all difficult to fly to win, with the ever present possibility that your efforts might endanger the very lives of your friends?' The answer, of course, was 'not in the slightest.' I never endangered anyone. I was extremely careful. I never cut in or came too close. I would have had that in mind whether they'd been absolute strangers or sisters, so there was never that feeling of concern. Naturally I went in to win.

"Some writers of the day said that the women flew a little higher, a little wider, a little safer than the men. I think that's fair. It was partly from inexperience. Most women had no instructor to show them how to go around the bedposts as Jim did. The others suffered simply because they didn't have as good a mentor. I knew he was the best and he knew. I knew that if I could absorb what he was telling me, that was precisely what I should do.

"Florence Klingensmith was eager to get into the men's race that was the big race of the 1933 Fourth of July meet in Chicago.

"Something was the matter with the cockpit enclosure on her plane. For a quick fix, someone got the idea of using an old Army stunt—wire-lacing hooks on the enclosure, like lacing your boots. I saw the piece of wing fabric go just as she turned the home pylon. She pulled up for altitude and headed off southeast. Jim watched to see her trim the plane as she circled around and came back.

"She just went on and on. About a mile and a half from the field, from a height of some four hundred feet, she went straight into the ground.

"I know she was unfamiliar with that particular airplane. I believe this was her very first flight in it, except perhaps for practice. Usually we trimmed it with a pretty heavy nose and then changed the trim for landing, but for racing the stabilizer was far forward. When she slowed down, the plane became noseheavy. She likely didn't realize that all she had to do was add a little power. I think she cut her power as she flew away from the field, hoping that she could free herself from the plane.

In 1931, young Dorothy Hester had plenty of headlines and the backing money of the B.F. Goodrich Rubber Company. As "Miss Silvertown," she promoted a Goodrich tire. Dorothy performed aviation's most hazardous stunt, the outside loop, every day at the Cleveland air races, her record being sixty-two such loops in succession. (Photo by Dudley Brumbach)

"Jim says she struggled to get out. We do remember watching them wire that damn thing on. It had to be undone from the outside. It was absolutely the worst gerry-fix we'd ever seen for a cockpit. Someone—the owner, probably—said, 'Bolt her in. I want her to stay.' Everyone seemed to be in high spirits. I'm not sure about Florence.

"Probably her ghost is still around because she had a very bad time in her last minutes. Everyone thought it was pilot error. They were wrong. It was lack of general briefing and general experience, and the fact that she could at least have gotten out if it had been a detachable canopy.

"Florence was a dear person, certainly a beautiful young woman, and the irony of the tragedy, in Jim's view, at least, was that she ordinarily could have

One of the loveliest of women pilots was Florence Klingensmith, pictured here shortly before she crashed and died in a traditionally men's air race in Chicago in 1930 when fabric peeled from her wing. The incident clamped a lid on further consideration of women race pilots in the Thompson free-for-all. (Rudy Profant collection)

landed the airplane with twice the fabric gone. Apparently the paralysis of panic set in as the horrible shaking sensation increased.

"I might add that I flew that race, too, and won it. Another pilot had been flying my plane earlier, and the landing gear hadn't been inspected. I was rolling across the runway, having touched down at the conclusion of the race, and it gave way on me.

"Jim probably could tell the accurate, correct details of about seven or eight fatal crashes, but there's no purpose. We very much played them down at the time. Our whole effort then was toward building up the industry. Being with Shell Oil Company, we wanted to popularize flying.

"Air racing was one way to convince the other pilots—Jim's potential customers—that what he told them was truthful. If you beat them in a race, then they believed you. It was just like any other sales promotion.

"Racing was actually a hobby for us. Jim was a Shell Company executive and this was just a very part-time thing. I totally sympathize with those other poor chaps who were so hungry and desperate. We were fortunate that our racing was really for fun. I don't think either of us was very frightened. I'm sure I wasn't or I wouldn't have been there, because I'm a coward.

"I suppose it *was* fairly daring for a young girl of eighteen or nineteen in the early thirties to suddenly declare to God and the World, 'I'm going to go race airplanes.' I think most of the women pilots were a little boyish, athletic and all that. Today they'd be women's libbers. That was never my posture. I loved being a girl. I think I was just born with the idea I'd like to fly and meeting Jimmy Haizlip simply brought it to fruition. It certainly wasn't a question of being masculine or feminine. It was just an inherent love of flight.

"I think this was true of several of the women. I'm sure it was true of Amelia Earhart, whom I knew very well. She was a very sweet, nice person. Whenever she came through Saint Louis, she stayed with us.

"It was beastly hot in Saint Louis. This one evening we were all going out somewhere. Jim said, 'I'm going to make you three girls a nice punch to cool you off.' We all thought that was fine. Jim made the punch with some very, very strong sloe

gin. Of course it was difficult to detect. The minute I tasted it, I raised one eyebrow and Jim nodded his head.

"In those early days, Amelia never drank a drop of spirits. Neither did my mother. My mother's admonition to me when I went off to a house party was, 'Now, dear, you must drink only one cocktail.' My parents lived in Washington at the time and moved in diplomatic circles. My mother would tell me ever so seriously, 'Now, dear, if you find yourself forced to drink champagne, put a cracker in it. It'll absorb the alcohol.' You know me and champagne —I ate the cracker and everything.

"Well, Amelia and mother thought it was just great. They drank and drank. They started talking and I don't think Jim or I said anything all evening. Neither of our victims was ever the wiser.

"Amelia generally was shy, but she let her hair down with me and was very outspoken. I have a strong theory on what happened to her.

"You know, of course, that a little late in life Amelia married G. P. Putnam, the press agent. He took over Amelia's public relations. He cooked up her going around the world. Her navigator wasn't too hot. Nevertheless, they got around fairly successfully until the last stop.

"In those days we didn't have radio aids and navigation aids. But G. P. Putnam (Amelia significantly called him Gyp) arranged for Amelia to land at an island and then come into San Francisco at a time that was to coincide with some civic celebration. I think her personal judgment would have quickly vetoed such grandstanding.

"She started out for that dot in the ocean in very bad weather. Jim has flown over it several times and says the island is nearly impossible to locate even in clear, sunny weather. He nearly missed it in blue, cloudless skies.

"My theory is that Amelia missed her island rendezvous, flew on, ran out of gas, and died in the sea.

"This theory about her landing in the hands of the Japanese is pure moonshine. I think some eager person wanted to write a book.

"You say Roscoe Turner grew misty eyed talking about Amelia? He was emotional about everything. They were not close friends. A romance? They hardly knew one another. She asked *Roscoe* to be her navigator? Roscoe wasn't about to take second billing, and, as I say, I don't believe Amelia knew him that well. God bless Roscoe, but I don't believe many of his stories. He was, however, an experienced pilot and could guess just as I am guessing what happened.

"The Earhart craze was inevitable because she was the first woman to cross the Atlantic alone. We all knew she would be the heroine.

"Incidentally, she looked exactly like Lindbergh. There was a very strong resemblance, and G. P. had her cut her hair like Lindbergh. She was *known* as Lady Lindbergh, which was all G. P.'s doing. Lindbergh was a handsome man. Amelia was an acceptable looking woman, though not that good looking. Of course I madly envied her because she weighed about 90 pounds wringing wet, and was tall. I wasn't fat, either, but I was about 110. I always wanted to be emaciated.

"Several of us in the thirties received much acclaim in a very short time span. Real five-day wonders, all of us. You know, 'Look, a woman pilot!' When Ruth Nichols no longer had all this prestige and press, I think it was too much for her. It is an adjustment to be up there and then, just as quickly, to discover that you are nobody. Another dear friend of mine, the first woman pilot, took her own life, also, after some years. Incredibly sad.

"I never really cared one way or another, so it was no adjustment for me. As long as I had Jim Haizlip, I needed very little more.

"Jim spent a long time in the Philippines. He brought back a genuine, old, headhunter's axe. Even had blood all over it. He cleaned it and said, 'Let's try this on for size' and hung it up over my head on a tiny hook.

Amelia Earhart, second from left, in 1931. (Jim Borton collection)

"I said, 'Why do you hang a huge axe on such a tiny hook right above my head?'

"He never answers but simply goes out slamming the door and comes back slamming the door. He looks up at the hook now and then and simply shakes his head. Now and then I think he loosens it a bit but nothing happens. I don't understand it at all, but that's the way it goes. Who am I to question the master?"

As Mary described, her husband Jimmy Haizlip won the Bendix Trophy in the 1932 National Air Races, flying from what is now Lockheed Airport in Los Angeles to Cleveland. Diving across the finish line without touching down, he went on to New York and set a coast-to-coast record of ten hours and nineteen minutes, including stops for gasoline.

Because fuels were not developed then as they are now, his gasoline had to be specially filtered. He had spotted ground crews and gasoline at seven places across the country for this event. That he only required two stops was something of a record in itself.

His plane was a single engine Wedell-Williams Special with just enough room for himself and an extra pair of shoes. The compass was mounted on the cockpit floor and was read by flashlight. Without modern instruments, Jim navigated the western mountains by the late moon, remembering to allow for the moon's apparent travel of fifteen degrees per hour, plus an added seven degrees or so because the plane was traveling faster than the earth was turning, and in the opposite direction. His speed averaged out to 240 miles per hour. Jim remembers it all as a singularly long ten hours and nineteen minutes.

Each has had an accident. Mary's was most serious. When she was testing an experimental monocoupe, the entire tail assembly disintegrated. She credits Jim with saving her life. As he had instructed her, she cut the switch, braced her feet against the panel, and blocked with her arm. Jim had fastened her into the plane so securely, she said, that it was like "falling three stories strapped to a chair."

She suffered a broken back, but not for long. After two months, she became so bored with her bed that she walked off and left it. She has never returned.

Jim was hospitalized one Sunday afternoon for an hour and a half. He had been on his way to an air show to stage an exhibition. Taking off into a strong wind and toward a number of obstructions, he had attained an altitude of 400 feet when his motor died. He switched to his reserve gas tank and hit the wobble pump, but finally realized that the engine was not going to start again. By now, his speed had dropped from 120 to 65 miles per hour. He was down to 200 feet, too low to clear the trees and buildings ahead. He maneuvered his plane into four vertical wing slips and touched ground directly under the point at which he had started down. He breathed a sigh of relief—then taxied the plane into a ditch hidden in the weeds and broke his nose.

In 1919, he was assigned to lead an air formation over the welcome home parade for hero Eddy Rickenbacker. After the parade, Jim was invited to lunch at the staid and elegant Los Angeles Country Club. He wore his uniform, and admits he might have swaggered about a bit, but after lunch he began to wonder if his hosts and their friends took his tales of flying seriously.

He decided to prove them by landing on the golf course. He came in low, touched his wheels to the ground, and discovered that the number one fairway had just been thoroughly watered. Golfers scattered in all directions. His wheels stuck. He managed to pull his plane up just in time to miss the clubhouse.

On another occasion he was assigned to Air Patrol in McAllen, Texas. Land development on the border was in full swing, but there had been unfortunate episodes with banditos and many potential buyers were apprehensive. One of the land developers asked Jim if, when he next led a land excursion into the area, Jim might fly over and do a few stunts to reassure the people that the border was indeed patrolled. Of course Jim would.

Outside Mercedes, Texas, there was a filtered water canal built mostly above ground. It was 125 feet wide and 20 feet deep, its banks straight up and planted with poplars. Three hundred or so members of the land party were gathered on the banks listening to a sales talk and watching Jim perform. They seemed enthusiastic. Jim decided to do his favorite stunt. He would come in low, skip the water in the canal to a fine spray and dart away

THIS IS THE CROSS ATLANTIC PLANE

AMELIA EARHARS
SHIP BEING SERVICED.
1932.

Thompson Aeronautical servicemen attend to the needs of the Lockheed Vega airplane that carried Amelia Earhart, alone, across the Atlantic Ocean. (Jim Borton collection)

again, the better to reassure these prospective land owners.

As he approached the water, he observed that his plane was not performing quite as he had expected. It was slightly tail heavy. The wind currents seemed unusual. In order to touch the water, he had to reduce his speed. When he did, his wheels went too deep and the propeller bit. "We came to a complete stop. I looked back to see if Jerry, my observer, was all right, and he wasn't even there. I stood up on the seat to look over the center section and saw him pop up from the water fifty feet ahead."

Jim jumped into the water—flight boots, jacket, silk scarf and all—and floundered with Jerry to the levee opposite where all the people were watching agape.

Later, while Jerry was having his broken arm mended at a nearby cavalry post, Jim apologized and explained that no one had ever been hurt flying

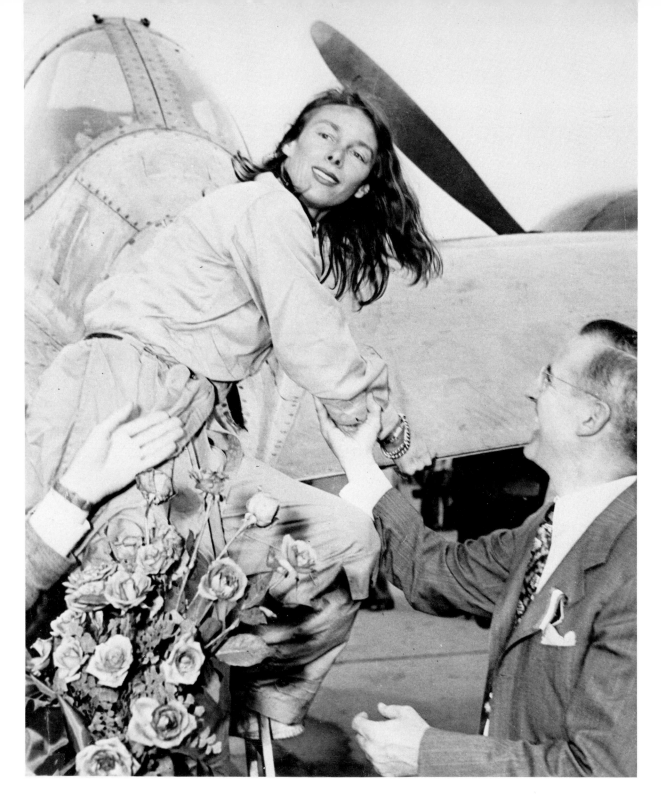

A professional charter service pilot, Jane Page lost first place in the 1946 Halle Trophy race to Marge Hurlbert by just four seconds. Marge died ten months later, stunting for an Iowa air show. Jane's grace and vivaciousness caused many to regard her as the postwar Amelia Earhart. (Bill Sweet collection)

Arlene Davis of Lakewood, Ohio, was perhaps the most well-liked and dignified racing pilot of either sex. She is shown here with her Arlene Davis Dream Ship, a Spartan airplane purchased from an Oklahoma oil firm. (Bill Sweet collection)

with him before. Jerry finally admitted it had not been all Jim's fault. When he had seen the crowd, he said, he climbed onto the tail of the plane to sit and blow kisses to the people.

In 1947 Jimmy Haizlip retired from the Air Force and the couple moved to Los Angeles. Mary became a realtor. Jim went on the special projects at Northrup Aviation as chief engineer and test pilot.

Mary said, "My memories of the races all are very pleasant. I enjoyed every minute. I am often asked, 'Do you fly anymore?'

"My standard answer is, 'No, there seems to be very little demand for the services of an elderly lady test pilot.' "

The couple's home was destroyed in the Malibu fire many years ago, and the mementos of a pair of lifetimes were lost in the blaze—the trophies and plaques, the certificates and awards, the photographs and letters from dear friends—Amelia Earhart, Jimmy Doolittle, Wiley Post, Doug Davis, Lowell Bayles.

"Well," Mary said, almost smiling, "When they are in your memory, you don't have to dust them."

The War Machines

Cook Cleland

The war gave a whole new dimension to the imagination-stirring aerial free-for-alls. Fighter planes that had won air victories over the world's battlefields were converted to superb racing craft.

After World War II, Turner was old. The souped-up surplus war craft were piloted by a new generation of racing pilots, veterans who competed with Messerschmitts and Zeroes for the biggest stakes in anybody's race. Roscoe, veteran of ten years in speed flying, became an official observer and along with General Jimmy Doolittle, Tony LeVier, and Jacqueline Cochran helped to formulate regulations for the postwar events.

In 1946, the first year of peace, the number of Thompson applicants swelled to more than one hundred pilots. In past years the great expense of designing and building racing planes had kept the number of entries to a handful. Turner had once said: "The greatest obstacle a racing pilot has to overcome is to keep from starving to death. It is a profession in which one gets little or no encouragement. Your friends beg you to quit before it is too late, and your creditors try to collect before you take off on the basis that you likely won't get back alive."

After the war, surplus fighter planes were available for a fraction of the price of the homemade varieties.

Not everybody was ecstatic about the newly found discount super race planes and their effect on the meaning of the National Air Races.

"I never even felt that the postwar contests were national in scope," said Thompson Trophy contestant Dick Becker. "Yes, guys like LeVier, Chester, and Wittman—the grand veterans—were there, but somehow their showing up in military aircraft shattered the romance and glamour completely, I think.

"A P-51 is a P-51. You can paint it purple if you choose, it's still a P-51. Get two in a race and you've got two North American P-51s in a race. There's nothing unique about the damn things."

Some, such as current racing pilot Nick Jones, deny that the very good war plane was necessarily a very good racing plane.

"They're one and the same," Cook Cleland

As test pilot for the P-38 during World War II, Tony LeVier was just the man to offer an aerobatic act with a war plane that National Air Race crowds talk about to this day. (Frederick C. Crawford Auto and Aviation Museum)

shouted with characteristic fire, "particularly with a prop plane. When I first got into racing, I talked to an old engineer at Pratt & Whitney. I said, 'I want to change this fighter into a racer.'

"He just looked down his nose and said, 'Young man, you have a racer to start with. That's just what a fighter is.'

"Becker and I got along as a business and racing team. He was a damn good man. There was good chemistry between us.

"Our third team member, Ben Jacoby, was a superb pilot. Although he had flown that ship in Navy combat, his plane didn't have nearly as many modifications as mine or Becker's. We ran out of money and the three of us discussed this many times. I was reluctant to let Jacoby race, though I was perfectly aware of his record and his skill.

"We didn't have the bucks to modify his prop. He was pulling everything out of his engine. He went in on about the eighth lap. I did not see the crash. I'm told he came around on the eighth and appeared totally dazed, disoriented, weaving se-

No job for an amateur was the overhaul and maintenance of WW II bombers and fighters turned race planes. (Frederick C. Crawford Auto and Aviation Museum)

verely—clear signs of monoxide poisoning. I'm told he did not appear to know whether he was going to take the pylon on the inside or outside. He finally slid down the outside of it and went into the ground.

"Tests showed his blood to be full of carbon monoxide.

"We received our three F-2Gs from the government over a period of time. There were fourteen Corsair F-2Gs built, four experimental and ten semi-production planes, at a cost of some eighteen million. They all were made at Goodyear. There were more than enough airplanes for experimental use and not enough for squadron use. I asked them, why not let a Navy carrier airplane win the Thompson Trophy race? It'd made a lot of people turn their head. Which it did.

"The first F-2G cost me $1,250, but I'll tell

Lieutenant E. F. Roth was one of the performing Navy Blue Angel pilots in 1948. The crack Navy exhibition team appeared at both the National Air Races and Bill Sweet's National Air Shows. At the World's Fair of Aviation at Omaha in 1946, Bill named them when he spilled into the mike, "Look at those great Navy pilots fly. They're flying like blue angels." (U.S. Navy)

you how the government works. I immediately wanted an improved carburetor with a little larger throat for more manifold pressure. The government wanted $1,375 for the carburetor. They wanted more for the carburetor than for the whole damn airplane.

"The Air Force didn't have to come aboard ship slowly. They didn't need the folding wings, didn't have all that extra weight. The Navy airplane is just a fantastic bit of engineering, but its wings have to

Cook Cleland: "In '46 the Navy hadn't yet declared Corsairs as surplus but they made an exception with mine. It was a Marine plane, a combat veteran with 900 hours, 400 on the engine, and it had been built by Goodyear." (Frederick C. Crawford Auto and Aviation Museum)

fold. It has to be able to come down the elevators. The Air Force can build an airplane to just go, land, and take off.

"Everything imaginable had to be stripped off," Cook grinned. "A Navy airplane had heavy trap-pings. The wing-fold mechanism had to go, plus the tail hook mechanism, all of the armament, the oxygen, and the instruments, including the radio. Some persons blamed the carbon monoxide problem on extensive stripping. That's not a fair statement. The problem was that a race like the Thompson was more taxing on the engine and the airplane than normal combat dogfights simply because of the duration of the race.

"In the service, our engines were allowed to be operated at 3,000 horsepower for three minutes. In the Thompson, we operated them wide open—close to 4,500 horsepower—for forty-one minutes! I don't remember how many exhaust stacks Becker broke on his plane. I broke eighteen on mine."

Optimism that the team of Cook Cleland, Dick Becker, and Ben Jacoby would win big in their Navy F-2G war planes was hardly unanimous.

Among the skeptics were important suppliers.

"For example, I wanted BG spark plugs. They were good platinum-pointed plugs and they cost eight bucks apiece. We had twenty-eight cylinders; with two plugs per cylinder, that's fifty-six plugs per airplane. At $400 per airplane, for our three airplanes, that was $1,200 just for good spark plugs.

"Everybody was getting new plugs, either from Champion or somebody and the company would put a little decal on your plane. I asked the BG man for some plugs and he said they didn't have enough to go around, besides, the expenditure would have

Tex Johnston is shown with his bright yellow 1946 Thompson-winning P-39 Airacobra Cobra II. His flightmate, Jack Woolams, flying a second P-39, Cobra I, was killed three days earlier while testing his ship over Lake Ontario. It caused racing veteran Benny Howard to warn against "damn fool alterations of surplus military craft to a point where they were too dangerous to fly." (Frederick C. Crawford Auto and Aviation Museum)

to be okayed from the home office. In 1947 I qualified at 417 miles per hour. Mind you, when you're doing 417 on the pylons, you're really doing about 100 miles per hour faster on the straightaway. Doing 500 miles per hour at sea level in a prop plane is a very heady situation. I don't think very many planes can do it today.

"Anyway I taxied up to the hangar, and cut the switch, and there stood a BG spark plug man with a brand-new set of plugs. I never had any trouble after that. Everybody wants to get in on a win. He who has, gets.

"You see, a lot of people didn't think we could do it. We even tried to glean some bucks from Howard Hughes. We got to him through a fellow who dated Jane Russell. He was a big man on campus at Case Tech and he once had secured a pair of panties autographed by the actress. He got to know her *real* well then. So, we got to her and she got to Howard Hughes. He still didn't back our airplanes, nor did anybody ever back them. Becker and I were good mechanics and fliers, but lousy salesmen.

"One problem we did have with the F-2Gs was their center of gravity. We never broadcast it around too much because the technical committee would have raised hell. We had a hundred gallons

Dick Becker was closest friend and teammate to Cook Cleland in a Navy squadron and in the postwar National Air Races. With the money they dreamed of winning, Dick and Cook planned to open a charter air service for Alaska-bound fishermen. The venture went the way of broken dreams. (Dudley Brumbach and Bud Yassanye collection)

of water back in the plane where there was a void. That meant eight hundred pounds in a compartment where there had been nothing. Believe me, the first two or three laps were hairy.

"I used to experience 'stick reversal' at seventy-five feet when I was pulling back with both hands going around the pylon. You heard a lot of chatter, then the nose came up and the stick went into my lap. Before I spun out, I had to put both hands on that stick and push. At about the end of the third lap, enough of the water was transferred up forward as it was used up, and the plane settled down. If we had ever let the technical committee know that our center of gravity was way back there where it was unhealthy and unholy, they never would have let us fly the airplane."

In the postwar years, every detail of the racing plane was critical, right down to the paint job.

"Chance Vought painted one airplane for me," Cook said. "They estimated 300 hours. When they were through they said, 'Do you know we spent 1,200 hours on that thing?' I don't know what they paid a man up there then. I suppose it cost the factory twenty dollars an hour.

"After a pilot qualified his plane he had to put it in the barn. He couldn't move it or do anything to it until the day of the race. All you *could* do at that point was work on the paint. The reason for that rule was that somebody made a mistake in the '47 Thompson. A P-51 wanted to get his wheels up in a hurry. He thought that by jumping the gun, he might get out in front. He put an extra cumulator on the system after he qualified. On a retractable landing gear, the doors are closed when the wheels are down. The doors have to open, the wheels come up, then the doors close. This guy screwed up his timing. The doors came just half open, the wheels came up—crunch. He finally had to drop out of the race with that insufferable drag, but his sin was fooling around with the mechanical part without testhopping.

"As I remember the most spaceworthy story in the press about Cleland and Becker had to do with our cowlings in 1948. We had redesigned our cowling to pick up 250 or 300 horsepower. In the race we were pulling such tremendous power that the fuel burned a little slowly. It wouldn't happen in an air race today because they probably have something to monitor the fuel. In those days we just had one carburetor setting.

"Suddenly the whole cowling blew ajar in flight. It felt like someone had thrown a hand grenade into the cockpit. My entire dazed mind was bent on getting down. After the initial shock of the thing I said to myself, 'It's all right, old Becker will take the race. He's right behind me.'

"Then I landed and taxied up to the hangar and there was Beck. He had blown up, too, the lap ahead of me.

"It blew the induction manifold hoses, too. We were lucky we didn't have a fire. We were burning menthol triptane. Shell made it—150, 200 plus

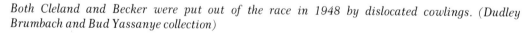

Both Cleland and Becker were put out of the race in 1948 by dislocated cowlings. (Dudley Brumbach and Bud Yassanye collection)

Paul Mantz with his daughter, Tevita, 17, just as he was announced the first three-time winner in Bendix Trophy Race history, in 1948. Known for his penchant for brilliant ties and loud sportscoats, Mantz's big money profits came from furnishing planes and his own fortitude for movie stunt work. By '48, Mantz owned five hundred planes, the seventh largest air force in the world. Paul Mantz was technical advisor to Amelia Earhart for all of her famous flights, and popular accounts of the relationship infer a romance. (Frederick C. Crawford Auto and Aviation Museum)

fuel. We paid a dollar seventy-five a gallon for it, and burned about five hundred gallons during the race in each airplane. Several pilots threatened to lodge a protest to bar us from the race when they heard we were sneaking in such a super weapon fuel. They were just jealous as all hell.

"Shell kept saying, 'Boys, this is the stuff. If you really want something, this is it.'

"Of course, it was our undoing in '48. It literally tore up our airplanes. It blew our air scoops all to hell. We were both lucky we got back. That Shell guy is probably still running because he knew I'd kill him. I'm only sorry we didn't share a little of our fuel with all those complainers before the curtain rang down on the 1948 Thompson Trophy try."

In years to come, Cook selected a calmer avocation to while away his hours: teaching pretty young women who own their own airplanes to fly. Occasionally, he teaches them even if they don't own their own airplanes. "I taught one of the Blue Angels' wives to fly last year," Cook grinned in 1976. "It's surprising how many customers I get."

It was Cook who gave the celebrated aviatrix Marge Hurbert her basic instruction in not quite the prescribed manner.

"I'll never forget it," sighed Cook. Marge was a lovely little lady with a lot of moxy, a load of talent.

"I coached Marge at my old Willoughby airport in the Navy Corsair I raced in '46. The runway at my airfield was real short—2,000 feet tops. You really should check someone out on a big, safe runway, but I thought I'd teach her to do it right. Anyway, it was the only field I had. Things were crowded in that cockpit so I took out the seat and cut a big hole in the armor plate to cut the weight down. I crawled back through the hole in the armor plate so that I was able to sit precariously directly behind Marge.

"I held a broom handle with a cup on it over Marge's shoulder, fastened to the stick. I shouted instructions to her from the same position.

"Of course she had the rudder and the brake pedals and everything. She could have clobbered us both. If we had cracked up, it would have taken a pair of cranes and crowbars a couple of hours to free us from all that metal, if we hadn't burned first.

"I was disgustingly brave in those days.

"Unfortunately, she was killed not too long after at the untimely age of thirty-two. She had been a school teacher in Painesville, Ohio, and died scooping out of a slow roll before 2,500 spectators at a show at Decorah, Iowa. Those slow rolls are hellishly more dangerous than people know. You must keep your nose up. She scooped out.

"The races are coming back again. The sport really went downhill after they knocked out the Nationals. The Professional Race Pilots Association (now USARA, the United States Air Racing Association) is doing a great job promoting it again. I sure was hoping they would put on one here in Pensacola. I'd just love to promote one for the people here, and have it be continuous.

"For that matter I'd still love to get hold of an airplane, redo it, and whip the socks off those people out in California. I still believe I have the stuff.

"Some guy in northeastern Ohio has my F-2G in a museum, one of my engines and one of my props are in the Crawford Museum, and some parts to one of my airplanes are in the Smithsonian Institution."

"I'm just scattered to hell and back."

Author, left, and Cook Cleland wax nostalgic with Cook's bulging scrapbook of the glory days of the Thompson air races.

William P. Odom

12

Bill Odom
Is Down

My world ended in that crash." A sorrowing Bradley Laird, his world shattered in the wreckage of his new Berea home, was taking the bodies of his wife and baby to their native Minneapolis that night of September 6, 1949.

Just six days earlier, the Lairds had moved into the ranch style house, the first they had ever owned.

"We were all wrapped up in our new place," he added. "Jeanne was such a good mother. We were so completely happy. Why did this awful thing have to happen?"

Bradley Laird was in the Army when he and Jeanne married in 1943. She lived with him at three camps before he went overseas in May 1946. After his service in the Phillipines and Japan, they went immediately to Kalamazoo, Michigan, where Laird worked with a paper firm. Meantime, young Bradley David, now five, had been born, and Laird jumped at the offer of a better job by a Kalamazoo stationery company.

That company transferred him to the Cleveland territory in June of 1949.

"Jeanne and I picked out this place on July Fourth on a weekend visit," he recalled. "It still was being built out on West Street. We loved the place right away. It was finished Wednesday and we went right in."

Laird, still shocked but recovered from the hysteria that rocked him when William P. Odom's plane plummeted into the roof, paused a moment. "You know we weren't even interested in the air races? Our big excitement was our home. I was washing windows and sort of watching the planes. As I recall, Jeanne was in the house. Baby Craig, 13 months, was in his playpen in front of the house. Young Bradley was playing on the lawn with his toys. His grandfather was watching him.

"I called to Jeanne to get her sunglasses and come outside to see the race. She didn't seem too interested. She said she could see the race through a window as she worked. Jeanne came to the door to tell Bradley to stop playing with the hose. Then she went back inside. That was the last I saw her. I never heard the roar of the motor. I just felt a terrific explosion and saw a sheet of flame whip off the roof.

"I was stunned but I dashed into the house calling Jeanne's name. Flames in the utility room blocked my way to the master bedroom where I thought Jeanne had gone to get her glasses, so I ran back through the dinette to a hallway. I got as far as the bathroom but the flames stopped me again.

"I didn't know Jeanne was in the bathroom. The fire was roaring and it forced me outside. I saw my father-in-law running with little Craig toward the street. The flames showered the baby's playpen and Mr. Hoffman, Jeanne's father, was burned snatching Craig free. Young Bradley was sort of standing there and I grabbed him and ran with the grandfather. We went to a neighbor's home. They took us all to the hospital.

"That's where I was when they told me Jeanne was dead. I never saw her at all. Baby Craig died three hours later."

Mrs. Laird was a former Minneapolis department store model. She would have been 24 in twelve more days. Two nights earlier a few relatives had come to Berea from out of town to celebrate the housewarming.

The house, as Laird said, was their life.

Plain Dealer reporter Robert Roach later called the smoke and the scream of sirens, "part of the darker side of the National Air Races."

West Street neighbors hurredly moved furniture from the west side of the house. They couldn't get close to the scorching heat of the east side.

State highway patrolmen and police from Cleveland, Berea, and Westview tried in vain to keep the rapidly forming crowd out of the way of the firemen and volunteer workers. Souvenir hunters picked up pieces of scattered wreckage that littered the street and the front lawn of the Raymond Novak home across the street from the flaming mass.

A wheel of the wrecked plane had landed on the porch of the Novak house, waking the baby sleeping in the front room.

Seemingly in minutes, a crowd of some two thousand gathered. Spectators were standing seven and eight deep behind the ropes put up by police.

It took a half hour, by some reports, to drown the fire. The engine of Odom's plane had torn through both house and foundation and was buried six to eight feet deep in hard dirt and shale.

Berea patrolman A. J. Yanke was cut in the right arm and left leg when he broke through a front window in an unsuccessful attempt to find Mrs. Laird.

Odom's remains were uncovered at eight o'clock. A bulldozer was used to remove the debris and wreckage and some remains at the bottom of the hole, according to Berea fire chief George A. Smith.

Laird concluded, "The thing I cherish most in the world is my wife and I've lost her. In my forty-seven months in the war I never experienced anything like this."

William Paul Odom of Teterboro, New Jersey, was the last pilot to enter the 1949 National Air Races. Captain Bill Odom, noted around-the-world flyer and long distance solo record holder, was to fly a radically modified F-51 Mustang fighter plane in the Thompson Trophy race for Jacqueline Cochran, considered the leading U.S. woman flier in 1949.

It was Odom's first attempt at closed-course racing. He was one of four pilots who topped 400 miles per hour in the qualifying trials. His trial speed was 405.565. He had come within a mile of equaling it in the third lap of the Sohio race (which he won) when he flew 404.676 a day or so before the Thompson.

In 1946 Bill Odom had first cracked the around-the-world record set by the late Wilie Post in 1933 when he and Milton Reynolds, Chicago pen manufacturer, circled the globe in 78 hours, 55 minutes. A year later, flying solo, he cut this time to just under 73 hours. Early in 1949 he established a new long distance solo record for all types of planes when he flew his small Beechcraft *Bonanza* nonstop from Hawaii to Teterboro, New Jersey, a distance of more than five thousand miles.

Bill Odom had two children. His wife had divorced him the previous September.

In all his adventures, the New Jersey pilot managed to obtain substantial backing and marvelous equipment. Milton Reynolds, his around-the-world backer, was a millionaire. The *Reynolds Bombshell* was equipped with every safety device and aid to navigation that money could buy.

An inferno on West Street, Berea, Ohio, was caused when the F-51 race plane of pilot Bill Odom crashed through this modest new home of Bradley Laird, killing his pretty wife and infant son. (Frederick C. Crawford Auto and Aviation Museum)

Jackie Cochran's green *Beguine,* which Odom would pilot, was the envy of every competing Thompson pilot simply because of its exquisite equipment and superb condition.

Miss Cochran had purchased Bill's racing plane from J. D. Reed of Houston, Texas. Reed reportedly spent $100,000 streamlining the already fast wartime fighter. The air scoop and radiator were removed from the belly of the fuselage and cooling equipment was installed in the wingtip tanks. Miss Cochran said she believed this alteration alone would add about thirty miles an hour to the plane's speed.

It had been widely advertised that the F-51 (or P-51) renovated fighter had been turned into the finest and most successful race plane in existence. It was the envy of every race pilot flying the Thompson and everybody else who knew airplanes. With that kind of press, private guards were hired, in case of attempts of theft or sabotage.

However, there was uneasiness from the very beginning. Odom was dissatisfied with the comparatively recent change in the shape of the big plane race course, which, ironically, had been altered in the interest of safety. He told *Cleveland Press* aviation editor Chuck Tracy, "The new seven-pylon speed course may be designed to cause less strain on the pilots, but it well may prove harder on them than the four-pylon quadrangle flown last year. Race officials should have given

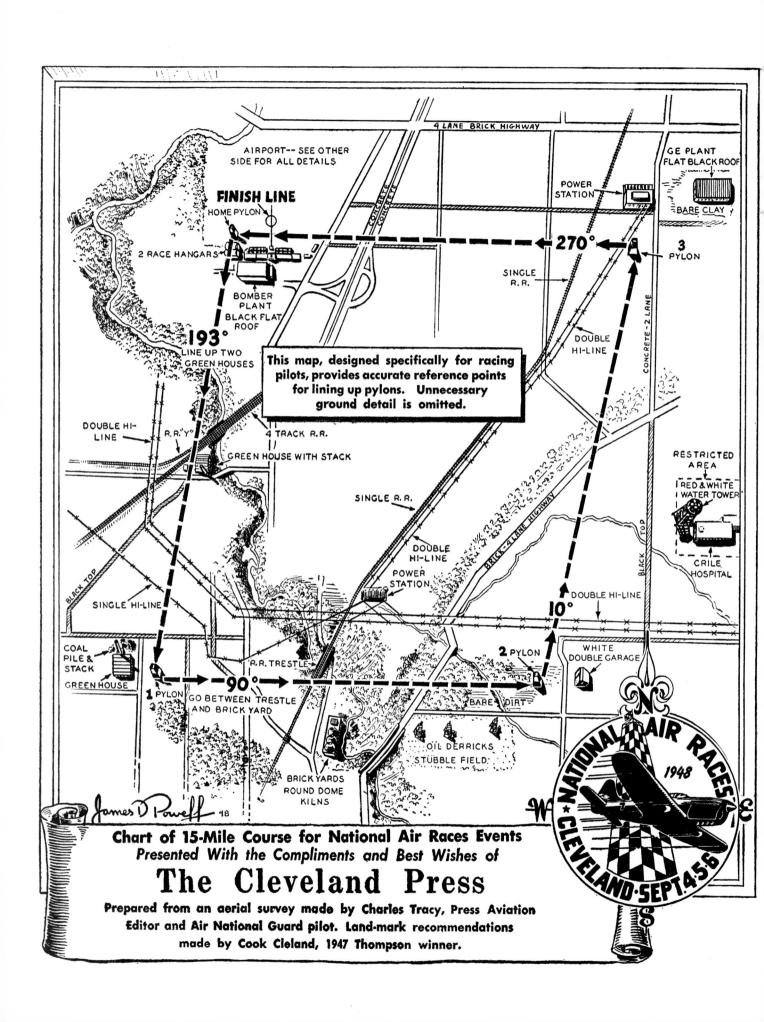

AIRPORT-- SEE OTHER SIDE FOR ALL DETAILS

4 LANE BRICK HIGHWAY

FINISH LINE
HOME PYLON

GE PLANT FLAT BLACK ROOF

POWER STATION

BARE CLAY

2 RACE HANGARS

270°

SINGLE R.R.

3 PYLON

BOMBER PLANT BLACK FLAT ROOF

193°
LINE UP TWO GREEN HOUSES

DOUBLE HI-LINE

CONCRETE - 2 LANE

This map, designed specifically for racing pilots, provides accurate reference points for lining up pylons. Unnecessary ground detail is omitted.

DOUBLE HI-LINE

R.R. "Y"

4 TRACK R.R.

GREEN HOUSE WITH STACK

RESTRICTED AREA

RED & WHITE WATER TOWER

SINGLE R.R.

DOUBLE HI-LINE

BLACK TOP

POWER STATION

BRICK - 4 LANE HIGHWAY

CRILE HOSPITAL

BLACK TOP

SINGLE HI-LINE

DOUBLE HI-LINE

10°

COAL PILE & STACK

GREEN HOUSE

R.R. TRESTLE

2 PYLON

WHITE DOUBLE GARAGE

1 PYLON

90°
GO BETWEEN TRESTLE AND BRICK YARD

BARE DIRT

OIL DERRICKS STUBBLE FIELD

BRICK YARDS ROUND DOME KILNS

James D. Powell 48

NATIONAL AIR RACES 1948 CLEVELAND · SEPT.4·5·6

Chart of 15-Mile Course for National Air Races Events
Presented With the Compliments and Best Wishes of

The Cleveland Press

Prepared from an aerial survey made by Charles Tracy, Press Aviation
Editor and Air National Guard pilot. Land-mark recommendations
made by Cook Cleland, 1947 Thompson winner.

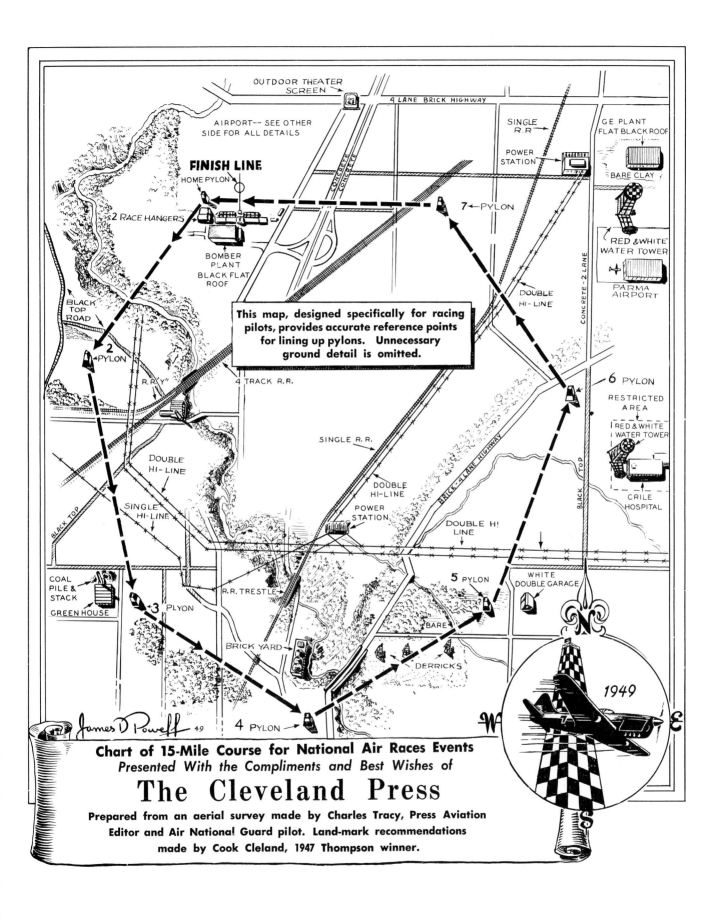

OUTDOOR THEATER SCREEN

4 LANE BRICK HIGHWAY

SINGLE R.R

POWER STATION

GE PLANT FLAT BLACK ROOF

BARE CLAY

AIRPORT-- SEE OTHER SIDE FOR ALL DETAILS

FINISH LINE

HOME PYLON

2 RACE HANGERS

BOMBER PLANT BLACK FLAT ROOF

CONCRETE CONCRETE

7←PYLON

DOUBLE HI-LINE

CONCRETE - 2 LANE

RED & WHITE WATER TOWER

PARMA AIRPORT

BLACK TOP ROAD

This map, designed specifically for racing pilots, provides accurate reference points for lining up pylons. Unnecessary ground detail is omitted.

←2 PYLON

R.R "Y"

4 TRACK R.R.

SINGLE R.R.

DOUBLE HI-LINE

6 PYLON

RESTRICTED AREA

RED & WHITE WATER TOWER

CRILE HOSPITAL

DOUBLE HI-LINE

SINGLE HI-LINE

BLACK TOP

DOUBLE HI-LINE

POWER STATION

BRICK 4 LANE HIGHWAY

DOUBLE HI LINE

BLACK TOP

COAL PILE & STACK

GREEN HOUSE

←3 PLYON

R.R. TRESTLE

5 PYLON

BARE

WHITE DOUBLE GARAGE

BRICK YARD

DERRICKS

James D Powell 49

4 PYLON

Chart of 15-Mile Course for National Air Races Events
Presented With the Compliments and Best Wishes of

The Cleveland Press

Prepared from an aerial survey made by Charles Tracy, Press Aviation
Editor and Air National Guard pilot. Land-mark recommendations
made by Cook Cleland, 1947 Thompson winner.

N

1949

W E

S

entrants at least a year's notice if they planned to change the shape of the course." His plane reportedly was designed for the four-pylon, ninety-degree turns circuit.

"High-speed turns of any angle are tiring, and the more pylons there are, the greater chance there is to miss one."

Mike Kusenda of NASA in Cleveland recalls that J. D. Reed actually duplicated the 1948 air race course in Houston, Texas, and part of the $100,000 reconditioning cost went to rebuild the plane according to the shape of that course.

"Reed had been most anxious to win the Thompson Trophy and had had the airplane modified according to the shape of the 1948 race course, figuring that his *Beguine* would be constantly banking. Had that been the case in 1949, it wouldn't have been necessary to have as much wing area on the outside of the turn as there was on the inside.

"The airplane was actually built with one wing eighteen inches shorter than the other specifically for that round pylon course. Then, ironically, over the winter the air race officials altered the shape of the official course to seven pylons to prevent crashes.

"When Reed heard this, he put the airplane up for sale and Jacqueline Cochran bought it. Of course she couldn't fly it in the Thompson because there was a ruling prohibiting women participants. But she could hire Bill Odom.

"At the races in Cleveland that tragic September, a couple of Bill's competitors, looking over the *Beguine,* realized that one wing was shorter than the other. I'm not sure whether an official protest was filed. There *was* controversy, but apparently it died down and he was able to get into the Thompson. That eventually was the cause of the accident.

"He turned inside the course slightly and when he saw the pylon coming up on his right, he tried to turn back into it. He turned into that short wing and rolled over. By the time his reflexes caught up, he had it in a climb, but the climb was upside down. He crashed into the house upside down at a forty-five-degree angle."

A reporter of the *Plain Dealer's* society department had been flying as an observer on a pilot training program of James R. "Bud" Harrington's flying school at Cleveland Airport. On September 6 she was an observer in a plane used for radio contact for Bill Odom. This was her report:

"Bill Odom apparently had no time to turn on his plane radio before he crashed to his death. Those of us in his radio contact plane had no hint of trouble until he failed to come by the stands to complete a second lap. Seconds later we saw smoke on the horizon to our right as we sat in the plane parked on runway 31 facing the grandstand.

"Before the crash, Odom had been flying according to a flight plan prepared for him by a close friend and former air race pilot, Benny Howard. Howard was to radio Odom from the contact plane after the first nine laps and give him the position of each plane in the Thompson.

"Until then, Odom was to take third place and stay there. He was not to turn on his radio until the ninth lap. At the end of ten laps he was to push the ship into first place and stay there.

"For Odom, the tenth lap never came.

"He had been asked on his arrival here, 'How much do you know about pylon racing?'

"'Not a damn thing,' he replied. 'But between now and Labor Day, I'm going to learn a lot.'

"He did learn a lot.

"The day of the race he conferred with James R. 'Bud' Harrington in whose hangar he was based on whether or not he should wear an oxygen mask to help prevent a blackout. The notion was nixed since none of the turns were steep and because any additional equipment might prove hazardous.

"Forty minutes before the Thompson, the DC-3 radio contact ship was towed into position on the field. Two mechanics and I were aboard when Howard arrived, hoisting himself through the hatch. He pulled on his radio earphones and got out his charts. He briefed us on the flight plan and assigned me to help the mechanics check off the laps of each plane and operate the radio controls.

"The planes roared off with Odom in seventh position, but when they came by the stands on the first lap he had pulled into third place. We saw the plane race west, flying low, and then drop from view. As the field came by completing the second lap, the big whine was not with them.

"Howard's face paled. 'Where's Odom?' he screamed. The radio was still silent. Smoke rose on the horizon to our right. 'I don't like the looks of that smoke,' Howard said. Seconds later after the rest of the planes had completed the third lap, Howard slid down through the hatch. 'I'm afraid that's it,' he said as he climbed into a jeep that carried him to the race officials' booth.

"Later in the Harrington hangar, people were speaking in whispers of the pilot who had joked with his bystanders—not a cocky pilot but one eager to chalk up another victory after winning the Sohio race. A few remarked about his enthusiasm as he confided his plans to fly around the world a third time, this time flying over both the north and south poles."

When the remains of the home had partially cooled, firemen and council president Henry Barr entered the bedrooms and lavatory calling for Mrs. Laird. Rescuers ultimately grabbed picks and shovels and discovered Jeannie Laird under the floor. (Frederick C. Crawford Auto and Aviation Museum)

Jim Hartshorne of the *Plain Dealer* recalled the panic as if it were yesterday.

"Odom never came back after the first round. Right away, we alerted all our newsmen. It took a few minutes because air race officials hate like the devil to announce a death. They wanted to be damn certain. We got the word from our people. The Associated Press guy in the stands finally took my word for it that Bill was dead because he had no one else and he couldn't leave the pressbox.

"It was Bob Drake's first year out there. I really had to get him going.

"'Hey, the guy's dead. Call the city desk.'"

Arthur C. Young, 32, former copilot with Odom was one of the first to reach the crash site. Ironically Young lived at 376 West Street, and was sitting with his wife Lois in their backyard when the *Beguine* went in three houses away in the new residential section off Lindbergh Boulevard.

Young had flown with Odom to China in March 1948. He stayed there after Odom flew on and began air-lifting for the Chinese Nationalist Government. After his return, he started a sign-painting business.

"At the fire, everything was scattered," he said. "One wingtip radiator was in the bathroom of the house. Parts were scattered all over the corner. There was no way to get to the back bedroom and bathroom. The man thought his wife was in there and he was screaming his heart out."

Mrs. Evelyn Novak, 30, who was standing in her front yard, fifty feet from where the race plane struck, said the impact made her stagger.

Cleveland Press aviation editor Chuck Tracy quoted most of the competing pilots as saying Odom suffered "a simple high speed stall."

"Any airplane will do that," said Tracy, "if you snap those controls that quickly. Odom was not an

Charred wreckage of the Laird home and remnants of the Odom race plane are all that's left in this picture of 432 West Street about two hours after the crash. (Frederick C. Crawford Auto and Aviation Museum)

experienced fighter pilot. He had been a transport pilot."

Tracy even phoned the Pentagon, attempting to get a rundown on Bill Odom's military career in the Air Force to see if he ever had flown a fighter plane. The Pentagon, as usual, was pretty tight-lipped.

"A fighter pilot has a lot of inherent training," said Tracy. "He does things automatically. I've had enough personal experience with a P-51 to know that there's a lot to that.

"It was a high-powered engine. I flew a P-51 for awhile during my last tour in the Air Force. The torque, the engine noise, and the heat from the engine just scare the hell out of you.

"A nonfighter pilot who finds himself suddenly upside down quickly panics and starts pulling back on the stick, which is fatal. Yet I don't think he had a lot of choice, anyway, because it happened in a flash. When an airplane hits a high speed stall, everything stops working for awhile. The wings don't lift. It just flips out of control.

"The guys who worked on Odom's plane were good men. I knew them well. If any one of them had been flying that plane the accident wouldn't have happened. A student commits many errors by not looking before he turns. Odom didn't see the pylon he was going after, and the reason he didn't see it was that he was so wrapped up in his airplane and the excitement of the race. He wasn't settled down.

"That airplane was a beauty. I don't believe there was a thing wrong with the ship. I doubt if anyone had ever done such an incredibly good job on an airplane as J. D. Reed did on the *Beguine*. It was the most sensible modification I've ever seen on a P-51; they all ought to be that way. These boys put a lot of thought into it, right down to the paint. It may well have been the best racing plane ever put together. Had they had a pilot to go with it, the airplane would have waltzed away with the Thompson Trophy.

"On the other hand, Bill Odom was no jerk. He was a gentleman. He figured out everything scientifically and precisely for the race. A swashbuckler like Cook Cleland relied on brute force. Odom was refined and clever.

"For instance, one of the things that happens to a race pilot during a race is that he gets cotton-mouthed. The extreme thirst affects his physical fitness. So Odom had an iced tea system in his plane (he would tell you about this and laugh). He sucked on a tube in his mouth, and the iced tea was just the ticket."

After Odom crashed, the other nine planes flew steadily on. Cook Cleland crossed the finish line thirty minutes after the crash to win the race and $19,100 with a speed of 397.071 miles per hour. He broke the Thompson record of 396.131 he had set in 1947.

The daring winner received his laurels. The races were over. Already exit roads were glutted with cars. There was still no word of Bill Odom, but the crowd sensed he was dead. Air race fans are intent and seldom at a loss, but now they were almost somber.

It was evening before Mrs. Dorothy Odom could be located and advised. She immediately went into seclusion.

Just before the Thompson planes had been towed from the hangar, Jackie Cochran had gone to the hangar to wish Bill luck. She had given him a rosary to carry and said she would say a prayer for him every lap of the race. Upon word of the tragedy, Jackie was reported "broken up." That evening she telephoned Odom's parents in Columbus, Mississippi.

"At the time of the races," recalled Ray Novak, who lived across the street from his new neighbor, Bradley Laird, "we had company here. The pastor of our church loved the Thompson Trophy race and he drove over from Elyria with his family. We put his one-year-old girl on the davenport in the living room for a nap.

"When the race started, the pastor and I were in the backyard pitching horseshoes. On the second lap we looked up and saw Bill Odom on the inside of Number 1 pylon. Then he simply inverted and dove into the house across the street. The first thought I had was that he had struck our home. The whole front of my home was on fire from the explosion of Odom's fuel tanks. His landing gear landed on my porch and was also in flames.

"Everything was confusion. I remembered that my wife had been standing in the front yard, and I couldn't find her. I kept shouting her name. The yard and street were cluttered with debris and articles from the inside of the Laird home. I saw a pair of women's shoes lying in the yard and for a minute I thought they were my wife's.

"In awhile the police screened off the area with canvas. They started to dig with tractors for the plane and pilot. I was told that Odom wore a huge diamond ring valued at approximately fifteen to twenty thousand dollars. They claim that the part of the hand that had the diamond was supposed to have landed in this area. It is creepy that it could still be out here under the sod.

"Our place had at least two thousand dollars damage. The porch burned and all of our trees and shrubs were trampled or burned.

"The crowd was surly. I asked them to please move; so did the police. The mob wanted to stay all night if necessary. They kept hoping the tractors would arrive, and start to dig immediately, so they might quickly view the gore. The mob started to thin out around three o'clock in the morning. They enjoyed the spectacle.

"It took four hours to get everything out of the hole the police were interested in. The only visible part of the plane was its tail. The rest was simply gone. The police had been ordered to prohibit pictures. I saw them actually pull film from people's cameras and hand back the cameras amid boos and jeers.

"They found a part of the hand above ground. Parts of the fingers were gone. The finger that bore the ring was missing. One of the airplane's wing tanks came off and went right up over the house. Someone probably picked it up and ran home with it. The other tank was under the house."

Bud Duresky, a neighbor of the Novaks, recalls "the house seemed to rise off its foundation, take a deep breath, and settle back." Fires burned everywhere on both sides of the street. Even the trees were blazing.

"When the plane exploded, there was an incredible spray of metal. The whole front of Novak's house was pockmarked by flying pieces. I later found a part of the prop on my front lawn more than two hundred feet from the point of impact.

"All hell was breaking loose. Fire department. Police Department. Ambulances. Wires burning everywhere. Everybody was on West Street but the U.S. Marines, and I don't know what kept *them*

from coming. Fire engines couldn't get down the street. The mobs didn't care.

"Then Jay Beswick, Berea reporter for the *Plain Dealer,* came in and asked to use my phone. He'd shout to me every few minutes, 'What's happening out there now?'

"While the police pulled stuff out of that hole in the ground, I stood on my porch. Hell, I could have sold admissions to the porch for five dollars apiece.

"A guy in a business suit yelled, 'Mister, can I borrow a pair of pliers?' I thought he was probably from the illuminating company and had seen a dangerous sparking wire. I started into the house. Then I saw that he wanted to snip a hose off a clamp he was holding. He said, 'It's off Odom's plane! Look what I've got!' I backed him out the door.

"The police and others tore the house completely down. Three or four nights later, all that remained was a chimney—someone put a big canvas around that, why, I'll never know.

"Twenty years after all this happened, I was hunting pheasant way out behind my place and I found even more parts and debris from that plane. Homes are built there now, over still more of the parts, I'm sure."

"When he struck that house," retired coroner chief investigator Ray Keefe said, "he moved it a good four inches off the foundation all around. The bathroom where the woman was was adjacent to the side of the garage. The airplane drove her right through the floor and the bathtub was flung through the side of the house into the yard."

Coroner Samuel Gerber added, "In our examinations, we would try to find out as much as we could, especially if carbon monoxide poisoning could have caused the crash. In the Odom case where there was no fluid blood available, we tested a muscle for carbon monoxide. The result was negative. We also established that he hadn't been drinking.

"After the physical examination, I went to the Statler Hotel where Odom had stayed. I secured the room to protect his possessions. On his desk were numerous letters of correspondence from oil companies and other businesses all anxious to have Bill Odom sanction their products—*if* he won the Thompson Trophy race."

This portion of the engine of Bill Odom's doomed F-51 race plane was five feet in the ground. (Frederick C. Crawford Auto and Aviation Museum)

13

People Will Always Race Airplanes

Immediately after the Odom crash, the air race critics struck. Typical in tone and comment were the words of *Plain Dealer* columnist Philip Porter:

"I nearly said it was the most horrible thing that could have happened to the National Air Races, but it was not. The worst thing would be for a plane to crash into a grandstand full of thousands of people. Don't think plenty of people who have been mighty close to the air show year after year haven't believed it possible, particularly the reporters and photographers.

"Poor Bill Odom might have lost control of his ship while turning the pylon in the front of the grandstand instead of the pylon in Berea. I shudder when I think of the possibilities. What did happen in Berea was bad enough. Death and destruction were farthest from the thoughts of young Bradley Laird. The next second a plane shot out of the sky into his house and his world fell in.

"It brings up a question again that has often come up—why *have* this so-called race with its dangerous possibilities? A decade or more ago there might have been some point to it—to demonstrate the speed and maneuverability of the fastest planes in the country—but the fastest planes no longer are in this event and haven't been since the war.

"The fastest planes are the jets but they shouldn't race. They staged a race for Air Force jet pilots Monday but it was far from a success. The winner almost had to bail out because his tail control broke off. The second man had unusual trouble when a small door flew open, dragging his left wing, and he almost ran out of gas. The third man's seat broke loose and he had to pull out and land while in a crouching position. The fourth entry didn't get off the ground.

"Fliers don't need to race jets to prove their speed. The maneuverability of a warplane is much more important at 20,000 to 40,000 feet where the battles are usually fought than down near the ground. What is the military benefit of sheer pylon turns, anyhow? The most important military developments of the last few years have been the flying

This P-35 was part of a squadron that took off from Cleveland, headed for Buffalo, in 1930. Radioed to return to base because of increasing foul weather to the east, the squadron complied, but one pilot became confused in the fog and crashed. The big engine, cleanly severed upon impact, came to rest on the front porch of a Cleveland home.

of the jets faster than the speed of sound, the building of the B-36 bomber which flies 10,000 miles nonstop, the Berlin airlift.

"But you can't fly a supersonic jet close enough for a grandstand crowd to see it with any safety at all. Neither can you demonstrate for a crowd the possibilities of the B-36. How could you show the airlift flying C-54s through a cloud three minutes apart, twenty-four hours a day, loading and unloading ten tons of coal in fifteen minutes flat.

"In other words, air technology and air performance are past the show stage. The air race promoters should face it. Of course there will continue to be air shows, little regional ones all over the country and the big one which has been held here practically from the beginning, even if they do little but provide a gathering place for flying enthusiasts.

"They perform a useful function. But isn't it time for the folks who plan the shows and those who put up the money to review the whole concept of air racing?

"The tragedy that descended on the Lairds of Berea might not happen again in fifty years, but it happened once. That's too much."

Henry Barr, who was a photographer and president of the Berea City Council in 1949, was standing a mere two blocks from the Laird home when the trouble struck.

"The Laird child was in its crib. The driveway faced on West Street which was to the south of the house. The gasoline immediately ignited when it was splashed or thrown toward West Street by the ruptured and disintegrated airplane. The liquid flame flew over the baby like a blanket. The grandfather ran over and began to beat at the flames and I managed to grab the child and pull him from the crib.

"I had been a spectator to the race and went

nowhere in those days without my camera. I immediately began to snap pictures of the smoke pouring up and people throwing things out of the windows. Those photos went all over the United States.

"I went into the house with the firemen and we walked back and forth looking for this woman. The plaster and debris in the bathroom had covered up

What easily could have resulted in the first deaths of air race fans in 1949 was avoided thanks to the skill of Jack Becker who brought down this F-38 warbird racer, flames streaming from her left engine housing, exactly where the people, planes, and cars were not. Jack Becker walked away. The near-tragedy occurred during time trials for the Thompson Trophy race. (Dudley Brumbach and Bud Yassanye collection)

her body and we actually were walking over her legs without knowing. It suddenly dawned on somebody what might have happened. That's how they found her.

"My recollection of Odom, himself, when they dug everything out, was that his head was completely pushed up into his helmet.

Jet bolts popped and pieces disintegrated at nearly ground level altitudes and unheard of speeds. Joseph McDowell examines an elevator that has just come apart in a race. (Dudley Brumbach and Bud Yassanye collection)

"I was president of the Berea City Council at the time. You can understand that there was a great deal of feeling in Berea after this happened that the races were out of hand. After years of threats to these nonparticipants, Berea finally had experienced the long-prophesied tragedy.

"I reacted, as president, to the strong community

feeling. We devised an ordinance. We soon decided we couldn't do it alone, so I took the ordinance to the Olmsted Falls council and they, of course, passed it. Then I took it to Brookpark. Brookpark was less impressed with it because they felt they had a good thing over there. They had been granted firefighting equipment, police cars, and so on, because the races took place in the middle of their community. Ultimately, I think they did pass it and Middleburg Heights passed it.

"At the time there was a great deal of talk about moving the whole works out over Lake Erie. The planes could just fly by. The majority of pilots didn't like the plan at all.

"Our ordinance was surely one of the final stakes through the heart of the National Air Races, because it also gave the local administrations any federal muscle necessary to keep any future racers from flying.

"To a large extent I hated to be part of this. The races were a great institution in their day, but they had outlived the speed for that type of flying.

"I had known air race director Ben Franklin personally for a number of years. I had worked for the Chamber of Commerce before the war. Ben's desk was just two desks over from my own. Of course his heart and soul were in the promotion of the National Air Races.

"After the petition, Ben called me once and asked straight out, 'Henry, what are you trying to do to my baby? Bury it?'

"I quietly said, 'No, Ben. But Berea's my hometown. I've got to look after those people.'

"You know, Franklin still tells people that he had to go into the City of Berea in disguise after the 1949 tragedy. Oh, no! I always liked the old boy. He had his heart and soul in those races."

Ben Franklin has his own version of the demise of the races.

"We didn't have any air show in 1950 because Louie Johnson was secretary of defense at the time, and Louie Johnson was down on *everything*. He said, 'What do we want to spend the money for? We have so many B-25s. Why do we need anything else?' "

From the very beginning of the 1929 races when Lindbergh, Doolittle, and Al Williams performed in military planes before the crowds, the branches of the military carried a leading role at the races in terms of formation flying, mass parachute jumps, helicopter demonstrations, formation fly-bys, ground exhibits, air maneuvers, and jet races. The civilian events alone would not have been sufficient to fill up three days of entertainment and the show most certainly would have lost considerable money. The secretary of defense had Korea to contend with and did not feel he needed additional public support at that time.

Franklin continued, "Flying over Berea definitely was out. For weeks and months after the '49 tragedy, I'd be as welcome at a Berea meeting as a skunk at a lawn party. However, Claude King and I had already worked all winter laying out a new course that would have missed the city of Berea altogether. It would have been located over pure countryside, but of course the planes would have had to approach the field and return the back way. The new course plans were all ready to go, but Johnson killed them. For that matter, the '49 course had been a tremendous improvement. It was far more circular, with no hairpin turns. It was a damn good course.

"We had a deal with Detroit for 1951 and '52. Well, the 1951 show lost about five thousand dollars for Detroit and five thousand for us. The fellow over there didn't get out any publicity. Detroit then backed out. Jack Reece of Continental Motors was at the head of that Aero Club of Michigan, which backed out of their '52 deal.

"I could see what was happening. To start with, everyone figured that everybody who came back from the Air Force in 1946 would certainly buy his own airplane. That just didn't happen and so a lot of airplane companies didn't exist for very long without fat government contracts. Cessna and Beechcraft withstood the times, as did a few others.

"I met with Crawford and Malcolm Ferguson, president of the Bendix Corporation. I told them that civilian air racing was a thing of the past, and I urged them to form a National Aircraft *Show*, eliminating air racing altogether. I suggested a jet event for the Bendix with Air Force jets, because the Navy didn't have anything fast enough to race at that time. Talbot was secretary of the Air Force at the time, so the first two shows were in Dayton and the next was in Philadelphia. We lost about five

Smiling but shaky, Air Force Captain Bruce Cunningham talks to fellow officers after winning the 1949 jet division of the Thompson Trophy race at a speed of nearly 587 miles per hour. It nearly cost him his life. When chunks of his tail assembly fell off in flight, he almost decided on a catapult escape from his F-86 Sabre. Finishing after Cunningham was Captain Martin C. Johansen, who was given a scare when a small metal inspection door flew open in flight, causing a tremendous drag which resulted in the left wing becoming heavy. When he stopped in front of the stands, Johansen had only 20 gallons of fuel left, not enough to taxi across the airport. Still another Thompson jet entrant, Captain Vernon J. Henderson, pulled out of the race after a steep pylon turn. The turn was so violent at treetop height that his seat broke loose in the cockpit. Crouched in a precarious kneeling position, it was a near miracle that Henderson could even land the jet airplane traveling at missile speed. (Dudley Brumbach and Bud Yassanye collection)

thousand dollars in Philadelphia, too, because they didn't hold up their end. I had a heart attack there which I fortunately recovered from.

"Our last show was in Oklahoma City. One of the finest men I ever worked with was Stanley Draper who headed the Chamber of Commerce—a real live wire. Stanley made one phone call and said, "Stop over at the bank. There's $50,000 lying there for you to start with." That started the show off at Oklahoma City. We had some sonic boom trouble out there but we paid off the claims. I think we made a little money out of Oklahoma City.

"I wondered how some of the planes these guys brought could fly. Ultimately, the NAA made us limit the number of planes in any race.

"Rosy O'Donnell was the general in charge of the first year we had a jet race event around the pylons. The jets were popping their rivets. Rosy was standing at the foot of one pylon. The perspiration was just rolling off of him. He said, 'I'll be all right as soon as I get this last jet down.' He didn't want any more of that.

"A woman was reading a newspaper in her yard in a western suburb when an airplane canopy floated down. It landed some ten feet from where she was sunning herself. Her newspaper went flying and she nearly had a coronary. The Air Force, hat in hand, went to pick it up and to say they were sorry.

"In the thirties and forties, everything having to do with water, land, and sky was in its formative stages. Now we've arrived, and I don't see how they can improve to any major degree. To be sure, the moon walk would have made a nice finale on the third day of the races."

The faltering public air shows after 1949 in Cleveland were hardly the end of the story. A favorite response to the old question, "When was the first air race flown?" is, "When the first two airplanes were built." Similarly, the last air race will be staged when only two airplanes are left.

Midget racing planes had won instant popularity with nearly everybody when the Goodyear-sponsored event was introduced in Cleveland in 1947. It was conceived as an event to bring the race closer to the spectator, and limited to stock engines of not more than 190 cubic inches displacement.

What the midgets lacked in power, they packed

A plane flying fast and low toward Cleveland Airport in late August, 1946, dropped this 12-foot gasoline tank on the roof of a Lakewood resident. (Frederick C. Crawford Auto/Aviation Museum)

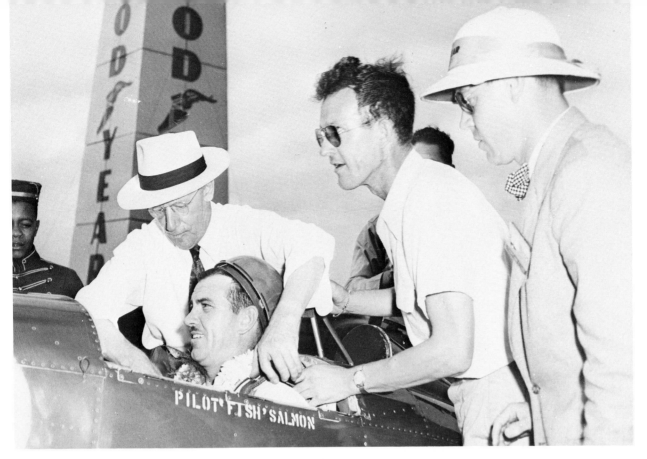

Tony LeVier (in dark glasses) and Goodyear race officials cluster around pilot "Fish" Salmon in Minnow, one of two midget monoplanes designed and built by LeVier & Associates for the 1947 Goodyear race. Only 16 feet long, with a wingspan of only 18½ feet, each was powered by an 85 horsepower Continental engine and had a design top speed of 200 miles per hour. (Dudley Brumbach and Bud Yassanye collection)

in know-how. Some weighed less than three good-sized men, yet they offered a new day for air racing. Techniques and devices born of backyard workshops of the nation might never have been uncovered by our great engineering laboratories.

This midget racing developed into the Formula One and Formula Vee racing that are growing in popularity all over America today.

A few persistent, hard-hitting individuals convinced Cleveland in the sixties, and again in the seventies, that Burke Lakefront Airport was the safest and best place in the nation to stage an air race. Formula One and Formula Vee racing is again a major part of the lineup of the annual Cleveland National Air Shows.

The Professional Race Pilots Association is now the United States Air Racing Association with branches on both coasts and an enlarged membership which includes writers, bankers, attorneys and just all-out fans, who, in their own ways, contribute to air racing, even if they, themselves,

have never crawled inside a cockpit. All over the country, cities who have never put on such a sport are discovering brand-new excitement in watching small, fleet airplanes whip around pylons.

Are the primary difficulties posed by air racing much different today than in the '30s and '40s?

"Well," grinned Don Berliner, popular writer on modern air racing, "there is only one class today that permits unlimited power, the converted warbirds, as in the postwar Thompson. These terribly strong airplanes were designed to fly when shot full of holes.

"Racing still has the problem of souped-up engines blowing up. My big fist has been through any number of holes in the side of crankcases, for picture-taking.

"In the other classes power is limited. They concentrate on designing a good airplane, and perfecting it. The variety of problems certainly has been reduced since the '30s.

"Had someone been clever enough to have in-

The popular new midgets lined up for the 1947 Goodyear race. (Frederick C. Crawford Auto and Aviation Museum)

vented a jet engine, he could have run a jet in the prewar Thompson. He could have used an atomic engine or a steam engine. If he could have figured out some way that an airplane did not need a landing gear even though it would have been demolished at every landing, it would have been legal in the Thompson Trophy race. Give people a very wide open opportunity like that, plus a lot of money and a lot of attention, and they are going to do foolish things. There were some terrible prewar racers that were at best barely flyable.

"Reckless pilots are still the concern. Also, as long as rookies have to break in at the major air races, the sport will be in trouble.

"Today, we still have the competitors, the crews, the officials, the organizers, and the backers. Even if today's racers aren't potentially as interesting as the home-built jobs before World War II, they're still the most interesting planes in flying today.

"The average pilot today is probably less colorful than in the '30s. He wants to survive, for one thing. Racing isn't quite so flamboyant today, as it doesn't attract the wild man. Also, you can't make a living racing. Reno, today, doesn't pay any more dollars

than Cleveland did forty years ago. You might be able to stretch a year's worth of income by winning a big race in Cleveland in the '30s; today, you're extremely lucky to break even.

"Aviation is grown up, and is therefore more staid. A 747 flight is not as physically exciting as a Ford Trimotor flight. All of aviation is more stable than it once was, but if air racing planes are the most interesting airplanes around, therefore their use and the people who surround them are also the most interesting.

"The game has retained its relative position."

Howell "Nick" Jones said, "We certainly are not pioneers like Wittman, Turner, the Granville brothers, and Jimmy Wedell in the 1930s. However, we who race airplanes in the late 1970s are doing many of the same things. We are building airplanes in barns, living rooms, carports, and garages. We are building them much as they did, and we race very much as they did. The difference is that they were the fastest men on earth and we certainly are not.

"While the pioneer racing pilots could put a lot of horsepower in a small air frame, in the formula one class of small airplanes, we cannot. We must use a hundred horsepower Continental engine, which is a very standard, staid little engine. We *have* proved that you can turn that Continental 4,000 revolutions a minute without tearing it up, and we have proved that a properly designed small airplane can fly 275 miles per hour on 140 to 150 horsepower.

"I am designing my current racing plane with the free assistance of a number of highly qualified aeronautical engineers and other experts. Air racing still excites people of this type. They still love to see how fast you can go with limited horsepower.

"My new design is going to be radical, but whether it will be better has yet to be proven. Steve Wittman is flying a Tailwind with an Oldsmobile engine at Oshkosh. An Oldsmobile engine costs one-tenth of a similar horsepower airplane engine, and is three times as dependable. General Motors makes more engines in one day than the airplane manufacturers make all year, so in three weeks they have twenty years of experience with that engine. These automobile engines are great, but the auto engine turns at a speed not consistent with a propeller.

"If you could use two propellers then you would have the same disc loading and your tip speed would allow any revolutions a minute you might choose.

"I can see a four-place airplane with very short, stubby retractable landing gear and two pusher props being driven by a Cadillac or an Olds engine. These engines cost six hundred brand new, and a 200-horsepower airplane engine can cost five thousand. Ridiculous. It is often from the hard position of financial necessity that the racing pilot of today says, as did Fagin in *Oliver,* 'I think I better think it out again.'

"I don't think we have contributed enough to warrant Dick, Hugh, Leo, Eb, and the long line of friends who have died on the course. It hasn't been worth it. However, those guys were going to race whether I ever raced or not. None of them was the first to get killed in this game. They knew that it could always happen, and that it probably would. I know it, too, and feel terribly selfish that I continue to race. I'm going to race beyond this new airplane and probably quit. I've got these children to raise, which is more important.

"But people will always race airplanes."

Art Chester, early president of the Professional Race Pilots Association, was one of the most ardent proponents of midget air racing. (Frederick Crawford Auto and Aviation Museum)

March winds splashing against his nostrils, blood draining to his temples, pilot Tom Poberezny is one with his Bücker Jungmeister airplane. Aerobatics still enliven the pace of any air race, stirring the crowd's expectation of the inconceivably dangerous or ridiculously slapstick routine, both seasoned by the never distant possibility of a single fatal error. (Bill Sweet collection)

Added Dave Garber, current racing pilot in the unlimited race plane class, "We still race to go fast, we race to win, and there's no criteria set up on how to do it. Frankly, the reason I got into unlimited racing was to prove that the warbirds—the P-51s and the Bearcats—can be beaten. Some of those guys are spending a hundred thousand dollars or better to build up a P-51 or a Bearcat to make it competitive, and it knocks out a whole segment of us little guys. I intend to prove with the airplane I am currently building that it doesn't take all that money to win. My new ship also will be stronger than the P-51. If a racing pilot today can go 450

miles per hour on less than 700 horsepower, that's accomplishment.

"I've been in air racing longer than I care to remember. The point is that I enjoy it. I don't have a single regret. I feel I have contributed to the state of the art. I feel to have airplanes and to have wings is to say, 'I have been involved.'

"If you had found me two hundred years ago, I probably would have been aboard a sailing ship, looking for a new island.

"My new airplane will be the first home-built unlimited in the world."

Rudy Profant

14

My Love Affair with the Ortman Racer

Sometime after the following interview, the Keith Rider R-3 racing plane, the *Marcoux-Bromberg Special,* that sleek yellow and black ship once raced by Earl H. Ortman, was purchased by the Bradley Air Museum in Connecticut from air historian Rudy Profant of Cleveland. The Pratt & Whitney Co. is currently restoring its engine while the Bradley Museum refurbishes the once proud plane for public display. When he was still its guardian, Rudy Profant recounted its fate, the story of one hero airplane after its moments of glory.

"My first dealings with the famous *Marcoux-Bromberg* airplane occurred in the 1950s. Believe me, buying a historic airplane happens only in dreams.

"The racer had been left on the field following the last great 1939 Thompson Trophy classic. So, apparently, was Roscoe Turner's *Golden Bullet* Wedell-Williams speed plane. In time, both craft were rolled into the General Airmotive hangar belonging to Jim Borton of Olmsted Falls, and remained there throughout World War II.

"It didn't take terribly long for Jim to get riled, familiar with the instinctive traits of racing pilots. He contacted both men and threatened to sell their no longer shiny airplanes for hangar rent, hoping for a quick show of the pilots' faces. When that didn't occur, Jim did sell the golden Turner Wedell-Williams to Fred Crawford who donated the historic airplane to the Crawford Auto and Aviation Museum where it remains to this day.

"Strangely enough, the *Marcoux* must not have been of sufficient historic or romantic interest to Crawford to give that still regal airplane a safe and lasting berth next to the Turner racer for centuries to come, a fact that has left aviation preservationists shaking their heads for years.

"Instead, the *Marcoux* was sold to two brothers who had hopes of restoring the craft and flying it in the next year's pylon battles. Unfortunately due to the war, the next race wasn't to occur until 1946. Planes competing then had billions of taxpayer dollars of engineering savvy behind them and could easily cruise at a brisker pace than the *Marcoux's*

The awesome Marcoux-Bromberg race plane, steed of pilot Earl Ortman throughout the 1930s. In the final Thompson Trophy battle before World War II, the big yellow racer shot into the lead on takeoff, was nip and tuck for five laps. Three laps from the finish, Ortman's oil pressure dropped to zero. He radioed the tower to clear the field. His motor was burning up. "I'm afraid she's ruined," he said. (Photo by Bill Yeager)

top speed mark.

"The brothers' dream was abandoned and they dumped the airplane. Quite by accident, some months later, I discovered the black and yellow airplane packed up on a trailer on Cleveland's west side. It soon was mine.

"Many have told me how nervous the *Marcoux's* pilot, Earl Ortman, used to be. He would sit up on the headrest of his airplane and smoke cigarettes as if life depended on it. In between the packs of Luckies, he'd go through roll after roll of hard candies.

"In race competition, there were so *many* things Earl had to do besides simply steering this racer—determining speed and turning strategy and avoiding collisions with almost everybody.

"Despite the now colorful stories of Earl's drinking, this man not only had to be sober, he also had to be incredibly skillful to race the *Marcoux* at its best. Quite often he placed high in the money when this airplane had terrible problems and shouldn't even have been in the air.

"Earl Ortman was a fun guy, a little on the wild side. He was the kind of guy who would have more speeding tickets than he could pay. But I almost pale everytime I think what torture it must have been to race 200 pylon miles in a race plane cockpit in the 1930s, and particularly racing the 2,500 miles cross-country, sitting in a confined area with no more elbow room than a sitting coffin. The cockpit area was pared down to the extreme, significantly cutting frontal vision and body room for the sake of streamlining. It simply would have driven me mad to have sat in that single position hour after hour. He also ran the chance of going to sleep due either to sheer boredom, drowsiness, fatigue, or exhaust fumes.

"There was no interior in those planes, no padding, no sound deadener, because all of that meant extra weight. I doubt they took any safety measures to curb that horrendous roar. Racing pilot Tony LeVier wrote in his biography that he was so cramped in his Schoenfeldt *Firecracker* that when he emerged, he was certain his back was broken. His competitor, Harold Neumann, carried a hacksaw with him in case he flipped over in one of Benny Howard's tiny race planes, both of which had a fuselage narrower than a man's shoulders. It's no mystery why so few racing pilots ever saved their lives by parachuting.

"All in all, despite the consistent money-making racing by Earl Ortman in the late '30s, it is almost unbelievable that he didn't die a very young man.

"Historical museums already have expressed interest in the Ortman racer. It is one of a kind, part of a once incredible dream of unconquerable speeds in the air over Cleveland.

"One outfit wanted to buy it fully assembled but with a guarantee that it would fly and not crash. That upset me. In its last Thompson Race in Cleveland, the *Marcoux-Bromberg's* giant Pratt & Whitney engine stopped three times at three hundred mile per hour speeds. If this plane or any plane is flown enough, the odds are that it will eventually crash, then what is left for air racing history?

"It's like taking the original painting of *Whistler's Mother* and throwing it back and forth between two buildings, figuring someone's going to catch it most of the time. The Ortman racer never should be flown again.

"A slight exaggeration would be to say that everything was reversed on this ship. It would be a little like stepping into a strange car and discovering that when you pressed on the brake, you went faster and when you switched on the wiper blades, your lights flashed on.

"This is why it is clearly possible that even Cook Cleland, the Navy ace of the 1940s who won the Thompson Trophy race in 1947 and 1949 in his tiger of a souped-up F-2G warplane, might take it up and kill himself. I believe that any of the best Blue Angel jet pilots might also hop in the *Marcoux* and crash. He is a better pilot than Ortman, but he doesn't know this airplane. Ortman is dead and can't tell him. There's no way to learn how to fly this airplane because there's nothing else like it.

"It isn't suffering from wear and exposure. It's not rusting in some scrap pile. I haven't painted it half a trillion unauthentic colors. Too few of these famous airplanes are left, forty years after the fact, and some that are bear little resemblance to their original splendor. They've been added to, altered, and generally tinkered with to death.

"People sometimes ask why I'm so satisfied owning this big yellow relic. I pay rent for its storage and infrequently have time to visit the monster, stored among two cars, some bicycles, and a

Rare portrait of racing pilot Earl Ortman beside his flying money-maker, the Marcoux-Bromberg, *in the 1930s. (Photo by Bill Yeager)*

lawnmower. I guess it's just the idea that anytime I do want to look at it, I can. I just feel I was lucky enough to finally track it down and purchase it outright. I was only eight years old when Earl Ortman raced it. I've hung on to the plane for twenty years and while I haven't had the funds to fully restore it, at least I've been a keeper of the flame. No harm has come to her in the past fifth-century. Sure, I hope to see her restored, hear that powerful engine roar, and at least be able to taxi her onto an airfield.

"For now, however, my reward is simply standing

Rudy Profant illustrates the compactness of the cockpit, scarcely as wide as a man's shoulders. (Photo by Bob Hull)

there looking up at her or hopping up to perch in the cockpit. I look at it and I say, 'Well, now, I have something that the whole world once read about!' No one, of course, can collect air racing pilots. You can't own them, and even if you could, they grow old. But this airplane is ageless, and with care it will survive far longer than I shall."

Nearly forty years after Earl Ortman raced this battling race plane, former owner Rudy Profant finds it easy to imagine jitters before the Thompson race—where participation separated men from boys. (Photo by Bob Hull)

Souvenir Program

Airplane Maneuvers

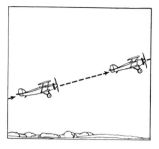

CLIMB—To ascend at a normal angle in an airplane, not a steep angle.

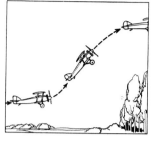

ZOOM—To climb at an angle greater than that which can be maintained in steady flight.

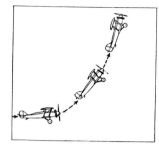

STALL—A climb so steep that flying speed is lost, sometimes resulting in a spin.

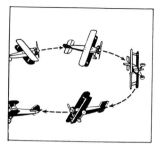

VERTICAL BANK—To turn in a circle with the wings in a position vertical to the earth.

SPIRAL—To descend in large circles not unlike the coils of a spring.

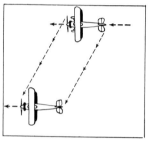

SIDE SLIP—A maneuver in a steep banked position. The airplane slips sideways faster than forward.

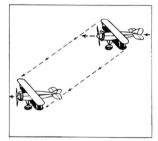

FORWARD SLIP—Similar to the side slip with less bank. Sideward and forward speed are about equal.

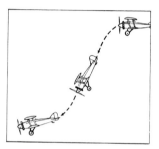

DIVE—To descend steeply with or without power.

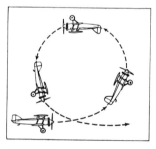

INSIDE LOOP—To describe a vertical circle in which the nose comes up and over.

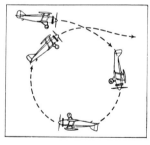

OUTSIDE LOOP—To describe a vertical circle, nose down and under.

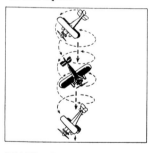

TAIL SPIN—Resulting from loss of air speed. The ship spins nose down.

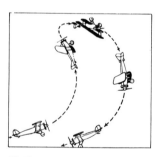

IMMELMAN TURN—Starting as a loop, concluded in a turn coming out in opposite direction.

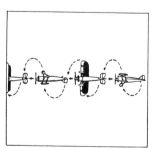

ROLL—To make a complete revolution about the fore and aft axis of an airplane.

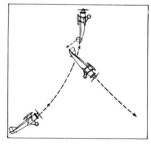

WHIP STALL—Resulting from a stall wherein the nose whips down and under beyond a vertical position.

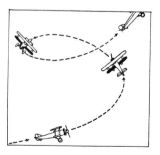

CLIMBING TURN—To ascend at an angle and turn while climbing.

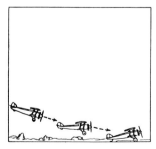

3 POINT LANDING—To land an airplane on the wheels and tail skid at the same time.

Illustrations Courtesy of Standard Oil Co. (Ohio)

1931
NATIONAL AIR RACES
CLEVELAND

OFFICIAL PROGRAM
PRICE 25¢

Daily Program of Events---1931 National Air Races

Events of necessity may not be run off in the order listed.   Watch the Score Board.

SATURDAY, AUGUST 29th

Inaugural Day—Flower Pageant Day—Derby Day.
1:00 P. M. to 9:15 P. M.

Event

- Informal Opening Ceremony.
- **A** Arrival Boardman and Polando (made longest non-stop flight in history).
- **B** Navy Planes—Tactical Maneuvers.
- **C** Marine Planes—Tactical Maneuvers.
- **D** Army Pursuit Planes—Tactical Maneuvers.
- **E** Event No. 31—Civilian Acrobatics Exhibition.
- **F** Autogiro Exhibition—Autogiro Co., of America, Pitcairn Aircraft Corp., Kellet Aircraft Corp.
- **G** Formal Inaugural Ceremonial—1931 National Air Races.
  Dedication 4 to 5 P. M.—Flower Pageant (Cleveland Plain Dealer) Massed Bands, Flag Ceremonial.
- **H** Al. Williams and the International Team.
- **I** Glider Exhibition—Hawley Bowlus.
- **J** Miss Silvertown (Dorothy Hester).
- **K** Event No. 39—Parachute Jumping Contest.
- **L** Band Concert.
- **M** Navy Corps Night Flight.
  Fireworks Spectacle.
  Army Comet Fireworks Flight.

SUNDAY, AUGUST 30th

All Ohio Day
1:00 P. M. to 9:15 P. M.

Event

- Opening Ceremony.
- **A** Marine Planes—Tactical Maneuvers.
- **B** Autogiro Exhibition—Autogiro Co. of America, Pitcairn Aircraft Corp., Kellet Aircraft Corp.
- **C** Event No. 31—Civilian Acrobatic Exhibition.
- **D** Arrival Transcontinental Handicap Air Derby for Men and Women from Santa Monica, Cal.
- **E** Miss Silvertown (Dorothy Hester).
- **F** Shell Trophy Special Event No. 100—Men's 115 cu. in. Straightaway Speed Dash.
- **G** Event No. 17—Sportsman Pilot Race—120 cu. in. A. T. C.
- **H** Event No. 34—Men's Dead Stick Landing Contest (with brakes).
- **I** Army Pursuit Planes—Tactical Maneuvers.
- **J** Shell Trophy Special Event No. 101—Men's 275 cu. in. Straightaway Speed Dash.
- **K** Event No. 25—Women's Free-for-all 510 cu. in.
- **L** Navy Planes—Tactical Maneuvers.
- **M** Event No. 35—Women's Dead Stick Landing Contest (with brakes).
- **N** Al. Williams and the International Team.
- **O** Event No. 39—Parachute Jumping Contest.
- **P** Band Concert.
- **Q** Marine Corps Night Flight.
  Fireworks Spectacle.
  Army Comet Fireworks Flight.

MONDAY, AUGUST 31st

Exchange Club Day—Knights of Pythias Day—American Boy Scout Day—British Day—Bucyrus Day
12:00 M. to 9:15 P. M.

Event

- **A** Arrival of Lieut. Walter Hinton with the Exchange Club Plane.
- **B** Event No. 34—Men's Dead Stick Landing Contest (without brakes).
- **C** Event No. 35—Women's Dead Stick Landing Contest (without brakes).
- **D** Opening Ceremony.
- **E** Event No. 6—A. T. C. 510 cu. in. Race for Men Pilots.
- **F** Shell Trophy Special Event No. 111—Free-for-all Straightaway Speed Dash for Women—Qualifying for Aerol Trophy Race.
- **G** Navy Planes—Tactical Maneuvers.
- **H** Event "B"—Men's 115 cu. in. Race—A. T. C.
- **I** Autogiro Exhibition—Autogiro Co. of America, Pitcairn Aircraft Corp., Kellet Aircraft Corp.
- **J** Miss Silvertown (Dorothy Hester).
- **K** Shell Trophy Special Event No. 102—Men's 400 cu. in. Straightaway Speed Dash.
- **L** Event No. 26—Women's A. T. C. 650 cu. in. Race.
- **M** Event No. 31—Civilian Acrobatic Exhibition.
- **N** Shell Trophy Special Event No. 103—Men's 510 cu. in. Straightaway Speed Dash.
- **O** Marine Planes—Tactical Maneuvers.
- **P** Goodyear "Doughnut" Tire Plane Demonstration.
- **Q** Al Williams and the International Team.
- **R** Army Planes—Tactical Maneuvers.
- **S** Event "A"—Men's Free-for-all 115 cu. in. Race.
- **T** Arrival (Bendix Trophy Race), Transcontinental Free-for-all Speed Dash from Los Angeles, Cal. (Weather Permitting).
- **U** Event No. 39—Parachute Jumping Contest.
- **V** Band Concert.
- **W** Army Corps Night Flight.
  Fireworks Spectacle.
  Army Comet Fireworks Flight.

TUESDAY, SEPTEMBER 1st

Army Day—Cleveland Ad. Club Day—Lorain Day—Sportsman Pilot Day—Italian Day—Youngstown Day—Early Birds Day—Demolay Day—Sandusky Day—Famous Flyers Day
12:00 M. to 9:15 P. M.

Event

- **A** Event No. 34—Men's Dead Stick Landing Contest (with brakes).
- **B** Event No. 35—Women's Dead Stick Landing Contest (with brakes).
- **C** Opening Ceremony.
- **D** Arrival of Entire Army First Pursuit Group.
- **E** Shell Trophy Special Event No. 108—Free-for-all Straightaway Speed Dash for Men Qualifying for Thompson Trophy Race.

By 1931, the Cleveland National Air Races had attained global significance. From left to right, these crack pilots are Matio De Bernardi of Italy; Captain Boleslaw Orlinski, Polish ace; Al Williams, holder of the American land plane speed record; Ernst Udet, later one of Hitler's generals; and Major Aloas Kaubita of Czechoslovakia. (Jim Borton collection)

Wilie Post and Harold Gatty, New Zealand navigator, appeared at the 1931 races fresh from the publicity of their round-the-world flight in the *Winnie-Mae*. (Bud Yassanye collection)

Daily Program of Events---Continued

Tuesday, September 1st—Continued

Event

F   Event No. 8—Men's A. T. C. 650 cu. in. Race.

G   Event No. 31—Civilian Acrobatic Exhibition.

H   Al Williams and the International Team.

I   Event No. 20—Sportsman Pilot—450 cu. in. Race.

J   Shell Trophy Special Event No. 104—Men's 650 cu. in. Straightaway Speed Dash.

K   Autogiro Exhibition—Autogiro Co. of America, Pitcairn Aircraft Corp., Kellet Aircraft Corp.

L   Shell Trophy Special Event No. 109—Women's 510 cu. in. Straightaway Speed Dash.

M   Miss Silvertown (Dorothy Hester).

N   Army Planes—Tactical Maneuvers.

O   Amphibian Novelty Race.

P   Army Trio—Three Turtles.

Q   Event No. 5—Men's Free-for-all 510 cu. in. Race.

R   Event No. 39—Parachute Jumping Contest.

S   Band Concert.

T   Army Corps Maneuvers.
Fireworks Spectacle.
Army Comet Fireworks Flight.

WEDNESDAY, SEPTEMBER 2nd

All Kiwanis Day—Q. B. Day—Governors Day—Lake County Day—Mansfield Day—German Day—Marion Day

12:00 M. to 9:15 P. M.

Event

A   Event No. 34—Men's Dead Stick Landing Contest (without brakes).

B   Event No. 35—Women's Dead Stick Landing Contest (without brakes).

C   Opening Ceremony.

D   Navy Planes—Tactical Maneuvers.

E   Event No. 21—Sportsman Pilot Race—650 cu. in.

F   Al Williams and the International Team.

G   Event No. 4—Men's A. T. C. Race—400 cu. in.

H   Army Planes—Tactical Maneuvers.

I   Event No. 12—Men's A. T. C. Race—1000 cu. in.

J   Goodyear "Doughnut" Tire Plane Demonstration.

K   Miss Silvertown (Dorothy Hester).

L   Event No. 31—Civilian Acrobatic Exhibition.

M   Event No. 22—Sportsman Pilot Race 800 cu. in.

N   Shell Trophy Special Event No. 106—Men's 1000 cu. in. Straightaway Speed Dash.

O   Miss Silvertown (Dorothy Hester).

P   Mead Glider.

Q   Autogiro Exhibition—Autogiro Co. of America, Pitcairn Aircraft Corp., Kellet Aircraft Corp.

R   Event No. 7—Men's Free-for-all—650 cu. in.

S   Event No. 39—Parachute Jumping Contest.

T   Band Concert.

U   Navy or Marine Corps Night Flight.
Fireworks Spectacle.
Army Comet Fireworks Flight.

THURSDAY, SEPTEMBER 3rd

Navy Day—S. A. E. Day—Elks Day—American Legion Day—Rotary Day—Buffalo Day—Polish Day.

12:00 M. to 9:15 P. M.

Event

A   Event No. 34—Men's Dead Stick Landing Contest (with brakes).

B   Event No. 35—Women's Dead Stick Landing Contest (with brakes).

C   Opening Ceremony.

D   Shell Trophy Special Event No. 105—Men's 800 cu. in. Straightaway Speed Dash.

E   Navy Planes—Tactical Maneuvers.

F   Shell Trophy Special Event No. 110—Women's 800 cu. in. Straightaway Speed Dash.

G   Marine Planes—Tactical Maneuvers.

H   Event No. 10—Men's A. T. C. 400 cu. in. Race.

I   Autogiro Exhibition—Autogiro Co. of America, Pitcairn Aircraft Corp., Kellet Aircraft Corp.

J   Miss Silvertown (Dorothy Hester).

K   Shell Trophy Special Event No. 107—Men's 1875 cu. in. Straightaway Speed Dash.

L   Event No. 36-A—Air Transport Speed and Efficiency Contest for Single Motored Planes (For Speed).

M   Civilian Acrobatic Exhibition.

N   Event No. 19—Sportsman Pilot Race—350 cu. in.

O   Al Williams and the Internatonal Team.

P   Event No. 13—Men's Free-for-all—1200 cu. in.

Q   Goodyear "Doughnut" Tire Plane Demonstration.

R   Miss Silvertown (Dorothy Hester).

S   Event No. 39—Parachute Jumping Contest.

T   Band Concert.

U   Navy or Marine Corps Night Flight.
Fireworks Spectacle.
Army Comet Fireworks Flight.

FRIDAY, SEPTEMBER 4th

Engineers Day—American Girls Day—Ladies Day—Moose Day—Toledo Day—Shrine-Grotto Day—Czech Day—Canada Day.

12:00 M. to 9:15 P. M.

Event

A   Arrival of Famous Siskin Flight Canadian Royal Air Force and 15 Planes, Trans-Canada Air Pageant.

B   Event No. 34—Men's Dead Stick Landing Contest (without brakes).

C   Event No. 35—Women's Dead Stick Landing Contest (without brakes).

D   Arrival Post and Gatty (around the world flyers)

E   Opening Ceremony.

F   Army Planes—Tactical Maneuvers.

G   Shell Trophy Special Event No. 111—Free-for-all Straightaway Speed Dash for Women Qualifying for Aerol Trophy Race.

H   Al Williams and the International Team.

I   Event No. 27—Women's Free-for-all—800 cu. in. Race.

First To Loop Autogyro

Johnny Miller 1931

Miss Silvertown

IN presenting "Miss Silvertown" (Dorothy Hester) at the 1931 National Air Races, the B. F. Goodrich Rubber Company hopes to further the cause of aviation, particularly among women. The ease with which this young aviatrix performs her many difficult maneuvers proves that aviation holds no secrets or handicaps for any woman who yearns to fly.

Many of the aerobatic maneuvers with which Miss Hester will entertain each day of the races, were developed and used during the World War as means of attack and escape.

Aerobatics are essential to safe flying, since without them the pilot of an airplane might not be able to meet successfully any emergencies which may confront him. Before commercial or transport pilots are licensed by the Department of Commerce, they must successfully perform many of the maneuvers demonstrated by Miss Hester.

"Miss Silvertown" was born at Portland, Oregon, September 14th, 1910. She learned to fly at The Rankin School of Flying in that city and has to her credit approximately 350 hours in the air.

She holds the women's world record for aviation's most hazardous stunt—the Outside Loop—making 62 consecutively at Omaha Air Races, May 17th, 1931. Miss Hester also holds the world record for either men or women for aviation's most difficult stunt—the Upside Down Barrel Roll. She also performed consecutively 56 of these maneuvers at Omaha Air Races this year.

Miss Hester considers each of her more than forty different aerial gyrations a contribution to safe flying.

THE B. F. GOODRICH RUBBER COMPANY

AKRON ◇G◇ OHIO

Goodrich Low Pressure Airplane Tires and Aeronautical Accessories

Atcherley English Stunt Pilot 1932

Crowd-pleasers at the 1931 National Air Races: Johnny Miller looped an Autogiro while hovering no higher than a house roof; military airplanes over Lake Erie were a novel sight; clown Major R. L. R. Atcherley from England as the Oxford Professor.

Daily Program of Events---Continued

(Friday, September 5th Continued)

Event

J Miss Silvertown (Dorothy Hester).

K Autogiro Exhibition—Autogiro Co. of America, Pitcairn Aircraft Corp., Kellet Aircraft Corp.

L Glider Exhibition.

M Canadian Pageant of Canadian Royal Flying Corps.

N Event No. 28—Women's A. T. C. 100 cu. in. Race.

O Marine Planes—Tactical Maneuvers.

P Canadian Civilian Aircraft Exhibition.

Q Event No. 30—Men and Women Pilots Mixed Race by Invitation.

R Goodyear Blimp Landing.

S Event No. 33—Cleveland Pneumatic Aerol Trophy Race. Introduction of Aerol Trophy Winner.

T Event No. 39—Parachute Jumping Contest.

U Band Concert.

V Army, Navy or Marine Corps Night Flight. Fireworks Spectacle. Army Comet Fireworks Flight.

SATURDAY, SEPTEMBER 5th

Akron Day.

12:00 M. to 9:15 P. M.

Event

A Event No. 34—Men's Dead Stick Landing Contest (with brakes).

B Event No. 35—Women's Dead Stick Landing Contest (with brakes).

C Opening Ceremony.

D Event No. 36—Air Transport Speed and Efficiency Contest for Multi-Motored Planes (Stick and Unstick).

E Navy Planes—Tactical Maneuvers.

F Miss Silvertown (Dorothy Hester).

G Marine Planes—Tactical Maneuvers.

H Event No. 36—Air Transport Speed and Efficiency Contest for Multi-Motored Planes (for speed).

I Shell Trophy Special Event No. 108—Free-for-all Straightaway Speed Dash for Men Qualifying for Thompson Trophy Race. (Qualifying Speed 175 miles per hour).

J Event No. 14—Men's A. T. C. 1200 cu. in. Race

K Event No. 36-A—Air Transport Speed and Efficiency Contest for Single Motored Planes (Stick and unstick).

L Army Planes—Tactical Maneuvers.

M Al Williams and the International Team.

N Autogiro Exhibition—Autogiro Co. of America, Pitcairn Aircraft Corp., Kellet Aircraft Corp.

O Event No. 11—Men's Free-for-all 1000 cu. in. Race.

P Event No. 39—Parachute Jumping Contest.

Q Band Concert.

R Navy and Marine Corps Maneuvers. Fireworks Spectacle. Army Comet Fireworks Flight.

SUNDAY, SEPTEMBER 6th

All Nations Day.

12:00 M. to 9:15 P. M.

Event

A Event No. 34—Men's Dead Stick Landing Contest (without brakes).

B Event No. 35—Women's Dead Stick Landing Contest (without brakes).

C Opening Ceremony.

D Navy Planes—Tactical Maneuvers.

E Event No. 23—Sportsman Pilot Race—1000 cu. in.

F Marine Planes—Tactical Maneuvers.

G Event No. 24—Women's A. T. C. 350 cu. in. Race.

H Al Williams and the International Team.

I Event No. 29—Women's A. T. C. 1875 cu. in. Race.

J Goodyear "Doughnut" Tire Plane Demonstration—and Glider Exhibition.

K Novelty Flying.

L Event No. 1—Men's Free-for-all 275 cu. in. Race.

M Navy Planes—Tactical Maneuvers.

N Autogiro Exhibition—Autogiro Co. of America, Pitcairn Aircraft Corp., Kellet Aircraft Corp.

O Miss Silvertown (Dorothy Hester).

P Event No. 9—Men's Free-for-all—800 cu. in. Race.

Q Event No. 39—Parachute Jumping Contest.

R Band Concert.

S Navy or Marine Corps Night Flight. Fireworks Spectacle.

MONDAY, SEPTEMBER 7th

Labor Day—Wooster Day.

12:00 M. to 9:15 P. M.

Event

A Event No. 34—Men's Dead Stick Landing Contest (with brakes).

B Event No. 35—Women's Dead Stick Landing Contest (with brakes).

C Opening Ceremony.

D Army Planes—Tactical Maneuvers.

E Event No. 2—Men's A. T. C. 275 cu. in. Race.

F Navy Planes—Tactical Maneuvers.

G Al Williams and the International Team.

H Event No. 3—Men's Free-for-all 400 cu. in. Race.

I Novelty Flying.

J Glider Exhibition.

K Landing of Goodyear Blimp.

L Manufacturers Demonstration.

M Marine Planes—Tactical Maneuvers.

N Autogiro Exhibition—Autogiro Co. of America, Pitcairn Aircraft Corp., Kellet Aircraft Corp.

O Event No. 18—Sportsman Pilot Race—275 cu. in.

P Event No. 32—Charles E. Thompson Trophy Race—Free-for-all for Men.

Q Introduction of Charles E. Thompson Trophy Race Winner.

R Event No. 39—Parachute Jumping Contest.

S Band Concert—Presentation of Trophies.

T Navy or Marine Corps Night Flight. Fireworks Spectacle. Army Comet Fireworks Flight.

Above, Shy, young Lowell Bayles with the *City of Springfield,* the winning team for the Thompson in 1931. Soon afterward, the Gee Bee was demolished in Detroit when Lowell fatally attempted a new world speed record. (Frederick C. Crawford Auto-Aviation Museum) *Below left,* Pratt & Whitney Wasp engine. (Jim Borton collection)

Thompson Trophy Winners

1930

100-mile race

prize purse, $10,000

LAIRD SOLUTION, black and gold, powered by a Pratt & Whitney Wasp Jr. engine. Charles W. "Speed" Holman substituted at the last moment for Lee Shoenhair of B. F. Goodrich to win at 201.91 m.p.h. after Arthur Page crashed his formidable Curtiss Xf6C 6 monoplane early in the race.

Travel Air *Mystery Ship,* James Haizlip

Howard DGA-3 *Pete,* Ben Howard

1931

100-mile race

prize purse, $15,000

GEE BEE SUPER SPORTSTER, MODEL Z, black and lemon yellow, Pratt & Whitney Wasp Jr. engine. Lowell R. Bayles purchased stock in the Springfield Air Racing Association and arranged to fly this stubby Gee Bee against a field dominated by Doolittle's Laird Super Solution. Doolittle's engine went sour and Bayles had the race to himself, finishing with an average speed of 236.23 m.p.h.

Wedell-Williams, James Wedell

Laird Lc-Dw-300 Solution, Dale Jackson

1932

100-mile race

prize purse, $10,000

GEE BEE SUPER SPORTSTER, MODEL R-1, red and white, powered by a Pratt & Whitney Warp engine. Jimmy Doolittle completely dominated, finishing with an average speed of 252.68 m.p.h.

Wedell-Williams, James Wedell

Wedell-Williams, Roscoe Turner

Airplane photographs courtesy Cleveland Chapter, American Aviation Historical Society; Model photographs courtesy Cleveland Model & Supply Company

Thompson Trophy Winners

1933

100-mile race

prize purse, $9,500

WEDELL-WILLIAMS 44, black and red, Pratt & Whitney Wasp Jr. engine. Roscoe Turner finished first and had the trophy in his arms when he was disqualified for cutting a pylon. The race went to Jimmy Wedell, who had finished second at 237.95 m.p.h.

Wedell-Williams, Lee Gehlbach

Howard DGA-5 *Ike*, Roy Minor

1934

100-mile race

prize purse, $10,000

WEDELL-WILLIAMS SPECIAL, gold, Pratt & Whitney Hornet engine. Roscoe Turner staged a blistering battle with Doug Davis, in the Wedell-Williams 44, until Davis power-stalled on a pylon turn and dived into the ground. Turner's average speed was 248.12 m.p.h.

Brown *Miss Los Angeles*, Roy Minor

Wedell-Williams, J. A. Wortham

1935

150-mile race

prize purse, $15,000

HOWARD MR. MULLIGAN, all white, Pratt & Whitney Wasp engine. Roscoe Turner outclassed the field until his engine blew up, forcing him to execute his famous dead-stick landing in front of the grandstands. Harold Newuman went on to win, with an average speed of 220.19 m.p.h.

Wittman *Bonzo*, Steve Wittman

Rider R-1, Roger Don Rae

Thompson Trophy Winners

1936

150-mile race

prize purse, $20,000

CAUDRON C-460, blue, Renault engine. Michel Detroyat of France, familiar to fans as an acrobatic pilot, easily won in his slim monoplane at 264.26 m.p.h.

Rider, Earl Ortman

Rider, Roger Don Rae

1937

200-mile race

prize purse, $20,550

FOLKERTS SPECIAL JUPITER, light cream with red trim, Menasco C-6S4 engine. When Earl Ortman was pacing his engine as his crew told him he had the race won, Rudy Kling nosed him out at the finish line to win at an average speed of 256.91.

Marcoux-Bromberg, Earl Ortman

Laird Turner LTR-14, Roscoe Turner

1938

300-mile race

prize purse, $41,200

LAIRD-TURNER SPECIAL, all silver, Pratt & Whitney Twin-Wasp Sr. engine. Roscoe Turner really got down to business with this big, powerful ship, winning at 283.419 m.p.h.

Marcoux-Bromberg, Earl Ortman

Wittman Bonzo, Steve Wittman

1939

300-mile race

prize purse, $35,500

LAIRD-TURNER SPECIAL, in which Roscoe Turner became the only three-time winner. Average speed, 283.53 m.p.h.

Schoenfeldt Firecracker, Tony LeVier

Marcoux-Bromberg, Earl Ortman

Ike. (Jim Borton collection)

Mr. Mulligan. (Jim Borton collection)

No name in the fraternity of American air racing is more revered than that of Benny Howard, father of the immortal Howard DGAs. *Top,* it was as an airmail pilot in 1929 that he hit on the idea of building himself a racing plane. He then teamed up with the brilliant Gordon Israel. (Jim Borton collection). *Bottom,* in 1936, Howard's wife Mike begged to copilot *Mr. Mulligan* in the Bendix. As Israel had predicted, she could be no help in an emergency; the plane crashed and both nearly died. (Jim Borton collection)

1930 Crowds

In front of the hangars in 1939. (Bill Sweet collection)

Running to the scene of the William Warrick and Paul Bloom crash during the sportsman pilot race in 1932. (Jim Borton collection)

Female pilots. (Jim Borton collection)

1948
National
AIR RACES
Official Program & Log
7
50¢
22ND ANNUAL WORLD'S
PREMIER AIR CLASSIC
Cleveland · Sept. 4·5·6

★ DAILY PROGRAM of EVENTS ★

The Management reserves the right to make necessary changes in events.
Listen for Announcements.

SATURDAY—September 4

Announcers:
JACK STORY, Chief
HASKELL A. DEATON
TED WINTERS
BILL SWEET

Qualifying Trials Sponsored by
The Industrial Rayon Corporation

Exclusive Radio and Broadcasting Rights
Columbia Broadcasting System

Television—WEWS

Downtown Press Headquarters: Carter Hotel
Firestone Tire & Rubber Company

LONGINES—Official Watch

☆   ☆   ☆   ☆

BENDIX TROPHY RACE—Transcontinental Speed Dash—Long Beach, California, to Cleveland, Ohio.
Planes will arrive at approximately 2:00 P. M.

"R" Division	"J" Division
Winner................................	Winner................................
Second................................	Second................................
Third.................................	Third.................................

11:30 A. M. GOODYEAR TROPHY RACE—1st heat —2 mile course—8 laps.

11:50 A. M. KIM SCRIBNER — National Glider Aerobatics Champion. EXHIBITION—Civil Air Patrol.

12:10 P. M. WOODY EDMONDSON — National Aerobatics Champion—The Standard Oil Company of Ohio.

12:20 P. M. THRASHER TWIN ERCOUPE EXHIBITION—Nationwide Food Service Inc.

12:30 P. M. GOODYEAR TROPHY RACE—2nd heat—2 mile course—8 laps.

12:50 P. M. SOHIO BAND—The Standard Oil Company of Ohio.

1:00 P. M. OFFICIAL INAUGURAL CEREMONY—F. C. Crawford. Aerial Salute to Star Spangled Banner—Parachute Jump by Dave Binns.

1:15 P. M. BEVO HOWARD—Aerobatics—flying a Buecker-Jungmeister—The Ohio Oil Co.

1:25 P. M. GOODYEAR TROPHY RACE — 3rd heat —2 mile course—8 laps.

1:45 P. M. SOHIO BAND—Demonstration of Fulton Airphibian. ARRIVAL BENDIX FLYERS.

2:00 P. M. U. S. AIR FORCE—Flight Demonstrations.

2:30 P. M. DEMONSTRATION BY 155th FIGHTER SQUADRON — Tennessee Air Guard—The American Steel & Wire Co., Sub. U. S. Steel Corporation.

2:50 P. M. BETTY SKELTON—Women's National Aerobatics Champion—The Steel Improvement & Forge Co.

3:00 P. M. ROYAL CANADIAN AIR FORCE — "Vampire" Jet Duo.

3:10 P. M. INTERMISSION — SOHIO BAND — The Standard Oil Company of Ohio.

3:30 P. M. TINNERMAN INTERNATIONAL TROPHY RACE—105 miles—7 laps— 15 mile course.

Winner................................

Second................................

Third.................................

4:00 P. M. MARCEL DORET—International Aerobatics Champion. FRED NICOLE—French Aerobatic Star.

4:20 P. M. DEMONSTRATION OF NAVY AND MARINE FLYING MIGHT

4:50 P. M. PRESENTATION—Bendix Trophy Race Winners.

4:55 P. M. PRESENTATION—Tinnerman Trophy Race Winners.

5:00 P. M. JIMMY GRANERE — Comedy Aerobatics.

5:10 P. M. GOODYEAR TROPHY RACE — 4th heat—2 mile course—8 laps.

5:30 P. M. DELAYED PARACHUTE JUMP — Jack Huber.

5:35 P. M. SOHIO BAND. GRAND PRIZE DRAWING.

AVIATION BALL — Carter Hotel

Be sure to see the U. S. A. F. B-36 on exhibition daily — South Ext. Runway 36 L

The Tinnerman Trophy was presented after World War II to winners of an annual 105-mile closed course race for P-63 airplanes. Bruce Raymond and his *Galloping Ghost* won in 1946. (Frederick C. Crawford Auto-Aviation Museum)

As his ground crew removes his parachute after his 1946 Thompson win, Tex Johnston finally has time to kiss his wife. (Frederick C. Crawford Auto-Aviation Museum)

DAILY PROGRAM of EVENTS

★ ★

The Management reserves the right to make necessary changes in events.

Listen for Announcements.

SUNDAY—September 5

Announcers:
JACK STORY, Chief
HASKELL A. DEATON
TED WINTERS
BILL SWEET

Qualifying Trials Sponsored by
The Industrial Rayon Corporation.

Exclusive Radio and Broadcasting Rights
Columbia Broadcasting System

Television—WEWS

Downtown Press Headquarters: Carter Hotel
Firestone Tire & Rubber Company

LONGINES—Official Watch

☆   ☆   ☆   ☆

ALLISON TROPHY EVENT will be flown by U. S. Air Force Jets from Indianapolis to Cleveland and will start from there at approximately 2:30 P. M. finishing here about 35 minutes later.

Winner..

Second..

Third..

11:30 A.M. KIM SCRIBNER — National Glider Aerobatics Champion.
EXHIBITION—Civil Air Patrol.

11:50 A.M. SOHIO BAND—The Standard Oil Company of Ohio.

12:00 Noon BETTY SKELTON—Women's National Aerobatics Champion—The Steel Improvement & Forge Co.

12:10 P.M. GOODYEAR TROPHY RACE — 1st heat semi-finals—2 mile course—10 laps.

12:30 P.M. THRASHER TWIN ERCOUPE EXHIBITION — Nationwide Food Service, Inc.

12:40 P.M. BEVO HOWARD — Aerobatics—flying a Buecker-Jungmeister — The Ohio Oil Company.

12:50 P.M. SOHIO BAND — Demonstration of Fulton Airphibian.

1:00 P.M. OFFICIAL INAUGURAL CEREMONY—Aerial Salute to Star Spangled Banner—Parachute Jump by Dave Binns.

1:15 P.M. ROYAL CANADIAN AIR FORCE—"Vampire" Jet Duo.

1:25 P.M. JIMMY GRANERE — Comedy Aerobatics.

1:35 P.M. DEMONSTRATION OF NAVY AND MARINE FLYING MIGHT.

2:05 P.M. WOODY EDMONDSON — National Aerobatics Champion—The Standard Oil Company of Ohio.

2:15 P.M. KENDALL TROPHY RACE for women pilots only—75 miles—5 laps— 15 mile course.

Winner..

Second..

Third..

2:45 P.M. INTERMISSION — SOHIO BAND — The Standard Oil Company of Ohio.

3:00 P.M. PRESENTATION — Kendall Trophy Race Winners.

3:05 P.M. ARRIVAL AND PRESENTATION — Allison Trophy Event Winners.

3:10 P.M. MARCEL DORET—International Aerobatics Champion.
FRED NICOLE—French Aerobatic Star.

3:30 P.M. SOHIO HANDICAP TROPHY RACE —105 miles—7 laps—15 mile course.

Winner..

Second..

Third..

4:00 P.M. U. S. AIR FORCE—Flight Demonstrations.

4:30 P.M. DEMONSTRATION BY 155th FIGHTER SQUADRON — Tennessee Air Guard—The American Steel & Wire Co., Sub. U. S. Steel Corporation.

4:50 P.M. PRESENTATION — Sohio Handicap Trophy Race Winners.

5:00 P.M. GOODYEAR TROPHY RACE — 2nd heat semi-finals—2 mile course—10 laps.

5:20 P.M. DAVE BINNS—Comedy.

5:30 P.M. DELAYED PARACHUTE JUMP— Jack Huber.

5:35 P.M. SOHIO BAND.
GRAND PRIZE DRAWING.

NATIONAL FLYING FARMERS DAY—See page 51 for details of awards.

In the traumatic 1947 Thompson, Ron G. Puckett was one of three to pull off the course with engine trouble. (Dudley Brumbach and Bud Yassanye collection)

Anson Johnson won the 1948 Thompson. (Frederick C. Crawford Auto-Aviation Museum)

"Fish" Salmon with his happy family after winning the Goodyear Race in 1948. (Frederick C. Crawford Auto- Aviation Museum)

DAILY PROGRAM of EVENTS

The Management reserves the right to make necessary changes in events.

Listen for Announcements.

MONDAY—September 6

Announcers:
JACK STORY, Chief
HASKELL A. DEATON
TED WINTERS
BILL SWEET

Qualifying Trials Sponsored by
The Industrial Rayon Corporation

Exclusive Radio and Broadcasting Rights
Columbia Broadcasting System

Television—WEWS

Downtown Press Headquarters: Carter Hotel
Firestone Tire & Rubber Company

LONGINES—Official Watch

11:30 A.M. KIM SCRIBNER — National Glider Aerobatics Champion.
EXHIBITION—Civil Air Patrol.

11:50 A.M. SOHIO BAND—The Standard Oil Company of Ohio.

12:00 Noon WOODY EDMONDSON — National Aerobatics Champion—The Standard Oil Company of Ohio.

12:10 P.M. THRASHER TWIN ERCOUPE EXHIBITION—Nationwide Food Service, Inc.

12:20 P.M. SOHIO BAND AND ANNOUNCEMENTS.

12:30 P.M. GOODYEAR TROPHY RACE — Consolation Race—2 mile course—8 laps.

12:50 P.M. PRESENTATION—Goodyear Consolation Race Winner.
SOHIO BAND.

1:00 P.M. OFFICIAL INAUGURAL CEREMONY—Aerial Salute to Star Spangled Banner—Parachute Jump by Dave Binns.
PRESENTATION—Saturday and Sunday Trophy Race Winners.

1:20 P.M. BEVO HOWARD — Aerobatics — flying a Buecker-Jungmeister—The Ohio Oil Company.

1:30 P.M. U. S. AIR FORCE—Flight Demonstrations.

2:00 P.M. DEMONSTRATION BY 155th FIGHTER SQUADRON — Tennessee Air Guard—The American Steel & Wire Co., Sub. U. S. Steel Corporation.

2:20 P.M. BETTY SKELTON — Women's National Aerobatics Champion—The Steel Improvement & Forge Co.

2:30 P.M. GOODYEAR TROPHY RACE—Final Race—2 mile course—12 laps.

Winner ....

Second ....

Third ....

3:00 P.M. DEMONSTRATION OF NAVY AND MARINE FLYING MIGHT.

3:30 P.M. INTERMISSION — SOHIO BAND — The Standard Oil Company of Ohio.

3:40 P.M. DEMONSTRATION OF FULTON AIRPHIBIAN.

3:45 P.M. PRESENTATION—Goodyear Trophy Race Winners and Plaque Awards.

3:55 P.M. THOMPSON TROPHY RACE — 300 miles—20 laps—15 mile course.

Winner ....

Second ....

Third ....

4:50 P.M. PRESENTATION — Thompson Trophy Race Winners.

4:55 P.M. ROYAL CANADIAN AIR FORCE — "Vampire" Jet Duo.

5:05 P.M. MARCEL DORET—International Aerobatics Champion.
FRED NICOLE—French Aerobatic Star.

5:25 P.M. JIMMY GRANERE—Comedy Aerobatics.

5:35 P.M. DELAYED PARACHUTE JUMP— Jack Huber.

5:40 P.M. SOHIO BAND.
GRAND PRIZE DRAWING.

WOMEN PARTICIPANTS' BRUNCH—Carter Hotel

James H. G. MacArthur, Royal Canadian Air Force flight lieutenant, was the only Canadian ever to fly the Thompson races. His Spitfire qualified in 1949. (Dudley Brumbach and Bud Yassanye collection)

Steve C. Beville in a qualifying run for the 1949 Thompson Trophy Race. (Dudley Brumbach and Bud Yassanye collection)

1949 Bendix transcontinental record-holder was Joe Debona. (Dudley Brumbach and Bud Yassanye collection)

The military at the postwar air races: General Hoyt Vandenberg and General Jimmy Doolittle discuss relative odds of pilots and planes in 1949; a demonstration of rescue and evacuation helicopters; a fly-by of heavy bombers in formation. (Frederick C. Crawford Auto-Aviation Museum, Dudley Brumbach and Bud Yassanye collection, Crawford Museum)

Famous racing pilot Bill Falck with his Formula One speed plane *Rivets*. At the 1977 Cleveland Air Show, Bill suddenly veered into Lake Erie and the plane disappeared in the water. (Bill Sweet collection)

Steve Wittman, always the man to beat throughout the golden age of air racing, shows off his latest creation in 1975. (photo by Bob Hull)

Betty Skelton was one of the most popular aerobatic stars of the late 1940s. Slow-flying stunting aircraft a few feet off the ground have only seconds to respond to engine failure or other constantly occurring problems. (Jim Borton collection, Bill Sweet collection)

Aerobatic star of the more recent National Air Shows, Harold Krier. (Jim Borton and Bill Sweet collections)

Marlyn Rich originated a dazzling trapeze spectacle suspended from a hovering helicopter at the postwar National Air Races. Each performance she tried to better her record of somersaults while 75,000 people counted out loud. (Bill Sweet collection)

Dave Binns always portrayed the character "T. Collins Hennesy, inebriate extraordinary." (Bill Sweet collection)

Riding a bicycle thousands of feet in the air while suspended from a low horsepower, vintage model airplane. (Bill Sweet collection)

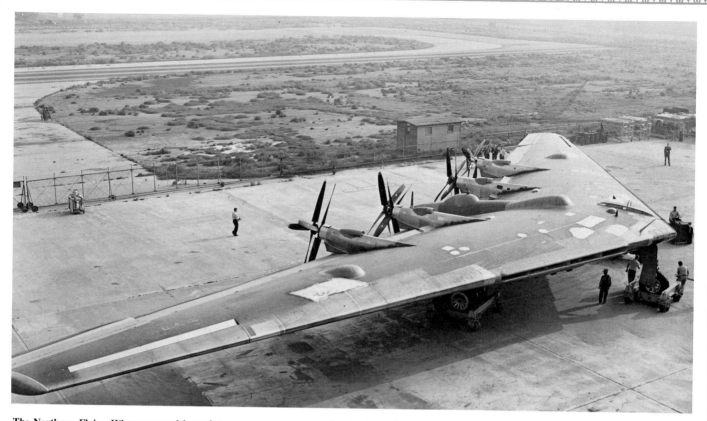

The Northrop Flying Wing appeared imposing on paper, awesome in the air, but failed to become the plane of the future. (Bill Sweet collection)

This incredible German Fokker airplane visited American air shows in 1934. Crew members could ride inside the wing, change sparkplugs and oil, and overhaul an engine in midflight. (Bill Sweet collection)

A 1910 Lincoln-Beechy pusher plane at the National Air Shows. (Bill Sweet collection)

The only Ford Trimotor built with pontoons. (Bill Sweet collection)

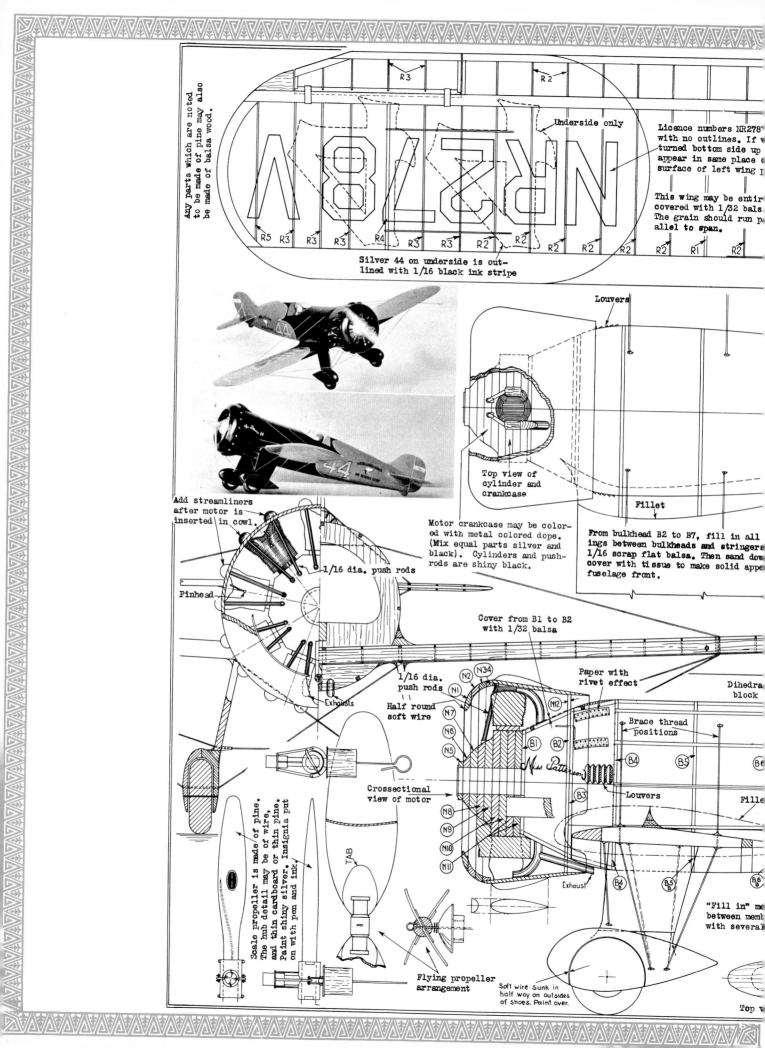

Any parts which are noted to be made of pine may also be made of balsa wood.

NR278V

Underside only

R3   R2

Licence numbers NR278... with no outlines. If ... turned bottom side up ... appear in same place ... surface of left wing ...

This wing may be entir... covered with 1/32 bals... The grain should run p... allel to span.

R5 R3 R3 R3 R4 R3 R3 R2 R2 R2 R2 R2 R2 R1 R2

Silver 44 on underside is outlined with 1/16 black ink stripe

Louvers

Top view of cylinder and crankcase

Fillet

Motor crankcase may be colored with metal colored dope.
(Mix equal parts silver and
black). Cylinders and push-
rods are shiny black.

From bulkhead B2 to B7, fill in all
ings between bulkheads and stringers
1/16 scrap flat balsa. Then sand dow...
cover with tissue to make solid appe...
fuselage front.

Add streamliners
after motor is
inserted in cowl.

1/16 dia. push rods

Pinhead

Exhausts

Cover from B1 to B2
with 1/32 balsa

Paper with
rivet effect

Dihedra...
block

1/16 dia.
push rods

N34
N2
N1
N7
N6
N5

Half round
soft wire

N12
B1 B2

Miss Patterson

Brace thread
positions

B4   B5   B6

Crossectional
view of motor

N8
N9
N10
N11

B3

Louvers

Fille...

TAB

Scale propeller is made of pine.
The hub detail may be of wire,
and thin cardboard or thin pine.
Paint shiny silver. Insignia put
on with pen and ink.

Exhaust

B4
B

B5
B

B6

"Fill in" me...
between memb...
with several

Flying propeller
arrangement

Soft wire Sunk in
half way on outsides
of shoes. Paint over.

Top v...

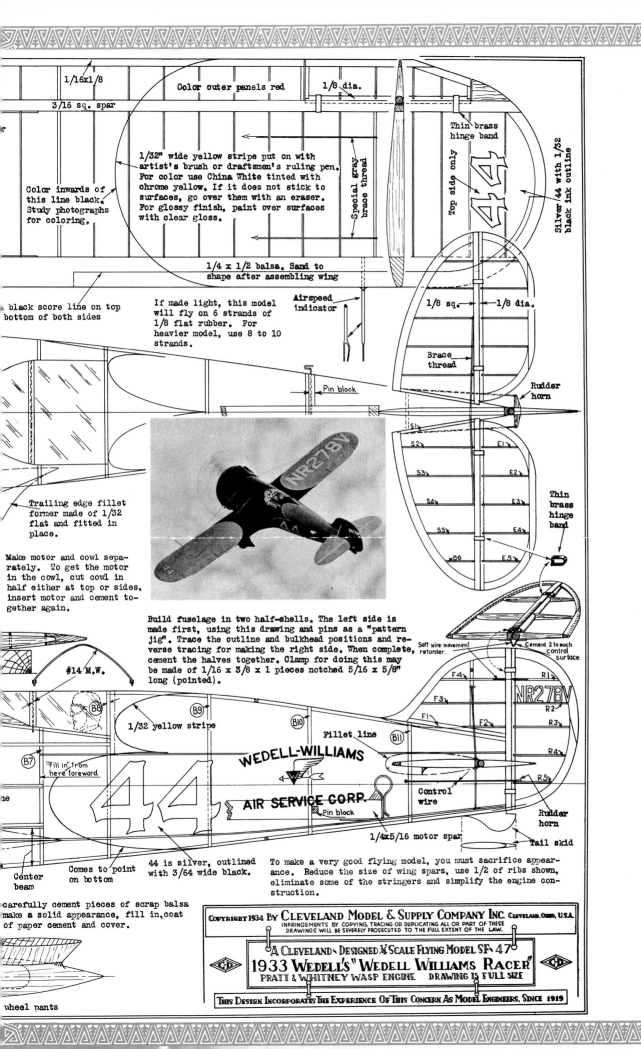

1/16x1/8

3/16 sq. spar

Color outer panels red

1/8 dia.

Thin brass hinge band

Silver 44 with 1/32 black ink outline

1/32" wide yellow stripe put on with artist's brush or draftsmen's ruling pen. For color use China White tinted with chrome yellow. If it does not stick to surfaces, go over them with an eraser. For glossy finish, paint over surfaces with clear gloss.

Special gray brace thread

Top side only

Color inwards of this line black. Study photographs for coloring.

1/4 x 1/2 balsa. Sand to shape after assembling wing

A black score line on top bottom of both sides

If made light, this model will fly on 6 strands of 1/8 flat rubber. For heavier model, use 8 to 10 strands.

Airspeed indicator

1/8 sq. — 1/8 dia.

Brace thread

Pin block

Rudder horn

S1
S2
S3
S4
S5
S6

E1
E2
E3
E4
E5

Thin brass hinge band

Trailing edge fillet former made of 1/32 flat and fitted in place.

Make motor and cowl separately. To get the motor in the cowl, cut cowl in half either at top or sides, insert motor and cement together again.

Build fuselage in two half-shells. The left side is made first, using this drawing and pins as a "pattern jig". Trace the outline and bulkhead positions and reverse tracing for making the right side. When complete, cement the halves together. Clamp for doing this may be made of 1/16 x 3/8 x 1 pieces notched 5/16 x 5/8" long (pointed).

Soft wire movement retarder.

Cement 2 to each control surface.

#14 M.W.

1/32 yellow stripe

B8
B9
B10
B11
B7

F4
F3
F1
F2

R1
R2
R3
R4
R5

NR278V

Fillet line

"Fill in" from here foreward

WEDELL-WILLIAMS

44

AIR SERVICE CORP.

Pin block

Control wire

Rudder horn

Tail skid

Center beam

Comes to point on bottom

44 is silver, outlined with 3/64 wide black.

1/4x5/16 motor spar

To make a very good flying model, you must sacrifice appearance. Reduce the size of wing spars, use 1/2 of ribs shown, eliminate some of the stringers and simplify the engine construction.

carefully cement pieces of scrap balsa make a solid appearance, fill in, coat of paper cement and cover.

wheel pants

A CLEVELAND DESIGNED ¼ SCALE FLYING MODEL SF-47
1933 WEDELL'S "WEDELL WILLIAMS RACER"
PRATT & WHITNEY WASP ENGINE   DRAWING IS FULL SIZE

THIS DESIGN INCORPORATES THE EXPERIENCE OF THIS CONCERN AS MODEL ENGINEERS, SINCE 1919

References

Very special thanks are expressed to the staffs of the *Cleveland Plain Dealer,* the *Cleveland Press,* and the former *Cleveland News* for their incredible success in preserving a living history of the Cleveland National Air Races. Appreciation is also expressed to the following specific writers and sources.

Akron Sunday Times. "Take to the Air, Girls!": 2 August 1932.
Bohrer, Walter, "A Deadhead Sees the Races." *Western Flying Magazine:* October 1935.
Caldwell, Cy. "Review of the National Air Races." *Aero Digest:* 1939.
Christy, Joe. "The Shady Lady of the Skies." *Argosy:* December 1961.
Coggswell, John F. "Expect the Unexpected from Doolittle." *Boston Post:* 24 May 1942.
Experimental Aircraft Association. *The Golden Age of Air Racing: Pre-1940.* 1963.
Glover, Charles. "Turner, De Seversky Say Air Force Weak." *Dayton Daily News:* 1953.
Harmon, Walter F. "Was the Gee Bee Plane Unsafe?" *Springfield Republican:* 3 March 1975.
Janes, Ted. "Best Damn Pilot the U.S. Ever Had!" *Men Magazine:* September 1960.
Kling, Rudy. "What a Racing Pilot Thinks About." *The Sportsman Pilot:* October 1936.
Lawyers Title News, California Edition. "The Sky's No Limit."
Matthews, Birch J. "The Bridesmaid: the Earl Ortman Story." *American Aviation Historical Society Journal:* 1962.
Porter, Philip W. "Pylon Events Should Cease." *Cleveland Plain Dealer:* 7 September 1949.
Roarch, Robert W. "2,000 Mill Around Scene at Crash." *Cleveland Plain Dealer:* 6 September 1949.
Schreiner, H. L. "Fabulous Flyer." *American Aviation Historical Society Journal:* Fall 1972.
———— "Wings for Youth." *American Aviation Historical Society Journal:* Spring 1972.
Shenkel, William T. "Municipal Airport Is Realization of Shorty Fulton's Dreams." *Akron Times Press:* 7 August 1933.
Shepard, Joseph K. "Fabulous Flyer." *Indianapolis Star Magazine.*
Turner, Colonel Roscoe. "Air Racing Was Like This." *Pegasus Magazine:* October 1956.
Tracy, Charles. "Odom Plans to Win Two Big Events in Air Races." *Cleveland Press:* 24 August 1949.
White, Clarice R. "Miss Earhart Honored Guest at Reception." *Cleveland Plain Dealer:* 1 September 1932.

Index

Page numbers in italics indicate photographs.

As a boy, author ROBERT HULL watched the National Air Race pilots do their pylon flips forty feet over the apple trees of the Cleveland countryside. For eighteen years, he wrote and edited industrial journals and newspapers, and has received thirteen awards from the All-Ohio Conference of Business Communicators and their Cleveland affiliate. He has written *The Search for Adele Parker,* about the mischievous lady who replaced Annie Oakley in the Buffalo Bill Wild West Show, and *The Wizard of the Winds,* a biography of Ward Van Orman, world champion balloon racing pilot. Presently devoting himself full time to writing, Mr. Hull is a member of the American Aviation Historical Society, the American Air Racing Society, and the Aviation and Space Writers Association. He lives with his wife Jessie, a published writer specializing in children's stories and light verse, and teen-agers Rob and Lisa in Bay Village, Ohio.